NO STONES IN HEAVEN

ALSO BY ARLENE SWIFT JONES

MEMOIR:

God, Put Out One of My Eyes

POETRY:

Deenewood, A Sequence

Pomegranate Wine

NO STONES IN HEAVEN

a novel by

Arlene Swift Jones

NO STONES IN HEAVEN

Copyright © 2014 by Arlene Swift Jones.

Special First Edition, 100 copies

All rights reserved. No part of this book may be used or reproduced in any manner whatsoever without written permission except in the case of brief quotations embodied in critical articles and reviews.

Cover photo by Arlene Swift Jones in 1951, in Storekvina, Norway of Bjarne Røysland (Victor Swift's first cousin) standing on the spot where Grandfather Swift was born.

Farm Photo, page 308: Harold Benzig
Author Photo, page 309: Paul Cryan

Book and cover design by The Troy Book Makers

Printed in the United States of America

The Troy Book Makers • Troy, New York • thetroybookmakers.com

To order additional copies of this title, contact your favorite local bookstore or visit www.tbmbooks.com

ISBN: 978-1-61468-211-0

HISTORICAL NOTE

As in all stories of immigrants, this book carries with it an older story that began somewhere else.

In Norway, a ship's carpenter named Lars Larsen and three other Norwegians were captured at sea during the Napoleonic Wars and imprisoned together by the British. For seven years, from 1807 to 1814, they survived in a makeshift hell: a fleet of decommissioned ships at anchor that served as a floating prison—each derelict hull filled with ten times as many men as had sailed her, rotting in a marsh near Chatham Harbor, a British naval base on the Thames.

They were spiritually rescued by William Allen and Stephen Grellet, renowned Quakers who frequently visited the prison hulks where the Norwegians were incarcerated. The four men held the first meeting of Friends in Larsen's house in Stavanger, Norway, in 1816, two years after they returned home to a country sagging with poverty, backwardness, and oppression. Within ten years, these former prisoners, now Quakers, would lead the earliest organized Norwegian emigration to the United States. In 1825, fifty-three Norwegians, most of them Quakers and Quaker sympathizers, sailed for America on the Restaurationen, a ship commissioned and built by Lars Larsen.

In August, 1846, Tollak Torgrimsen from Røyseland, a valley up in the hills from Flekkefjord, was among the Quakers to assemble in Stavanger. His oldest daughter, Anna Tonetta Tollaksdatter, fourteen, accompanied him. On June 5, 1853, when Anna Tonnetta was twenty-one years old, she exchanged marriage vows with Karl Jonsen fra Eikhom at the yearly meeting in Stavanger. Karl was the third son of a "bonde," or small farmer and landowner, whose land was farmed by two older sons. He would come to Røyseland. As husband to the oldest child, he would someday be in charge, taking on the responsibilities of Tollak Torgrimsen and sixteen generations of Torgrimsens before him stretching back to the fifteen hundreds in Røyseland.

In ten years' time, seven children were born to Anna Tonetta and Karl Andreas Jonsen at Røyseland, and the eldest was, like Anna Tonetta, a girl. Her name was Anna Kristina, and she was born in 1854. She was my great grandmother. She was the first of Tollak's family to leave for America.

The establishment of a Norwegian Quaker meetinghouse and boarding school called Stavanger, in Legrand, Iowa, is documented. The immigrant population moved rapidly into the Midwest, attracted by the "American Dream," which in this case was the rich, black soil rolling in endless virgin acres. Several generations later, the dream ended: corporations gradually consumed the family farm. But the long roots of origin and birth touch all immigrants. The stories of the children of Kristina and Salve and their children are based on personal knowledge. We remember who they are.

NO STONES IN HEAVEN

CHAPTER ONE

Kristina Karlsdatter Røyseland stood in the Stavanger kitchen of her employer, Endre Dahl, mixing bread dough. On the scrubbed wooden table lay a small salmon she had just bought in the harbor market. She would poach it for the noon dinner with Dahl and his guest, Ashbjorn Kloster, the Stavanger Quaker temperance leader. Behind her was a woodburning stove, broad backed and big enough to cook for dozens. Iron pots hung above the stove, seasoned black and smooth; copper pans shone above a wooden worktable. The kitchen was large and plain, but warm and inviting.

Upon seeing the salmon, Dahl's kindly eyes crinkled with a smile. His appearance in the kitchen was unusual, so Kristina was curious. "Temperance in food, too," Friend Dahl said to her, seeing the lunch she was preparing was not simple. "I came to say that thou hast a visitor."

Kristina hesitated then washed off her hands at the sink and untied her apron.

"I think thee knows this young man," Friend Dahl added. "He waits in the parlor."

Kristina blushed and smoothed her thick tawny hair. She followed Endre Dahl. He was the same height as Kristina and wore a dark suit with a midthigh jacket and a fully buttoned vest over his white shirt. His gray hair was full, his face as angular as his body. At the parlor door, he stepped aside, motioning for her to enter first. Kristina saw Salve Knudsen standing in the room, cap in his hand. Endre Dahl followed, bowed slightly, and said to Kristina, "Here is someone who wants very much to see you. Please sit, both of you." He then excused himself.

Salve Knudsen remained standing. He fingered his cap as he shifted his weight. Kristina looked into his eyes, but his gaze was too intense, too intimate for her to look long. She looked around the room at its severely plain furnishings. At a time when fashion was ornate, in Dahl's Quaker home there were no paintings, no carved rosewood or inlaid woods, no tapestried upholsteries, blown and cut glasses, bronzes, ornate serving dishes of silver, all normal in such a house in Stavanger in 1878. Why, at this moment, did she see the absence of things she'd never had or wanted? Kristina looked at the squarish oak furniture and felt comforted: it corresponded to the lack of ornamentation on her dress. She tried to think of everything else but the man standing in front of her.

She looked beyond Salve Knudsen into the street, watching how the cobblestones led on and on, from one to another; she saw the small white-clapboard houses of Røyseland.

At age twenty-five, she was the eldest of ten children: her youngest sister, Sarah, was only two. Of her six brothers, the eldest two, Johannes and Tollak, their pale cheeks gaunt under steely blue eyes seething with discontent, were regularly imprisoned for holding to their Quaker beliefs. In two more years, Staale would join them, and then Karl, and Peder. Finally Tore. Unless, she thought, they would follow Salve. She knew he had come to say good-bye.

Military service was a major issue, not only for Quakers. The *Morgenbladet* reported, "In earlier times many a young bonde maimed himself to escape military service; in these more civilized times, he emigrates." The Quakers' pacifism was treated as general refusal—they were imprisoned along with others. Even the new Dissenter Law did not exempt them from military service.

The *budstikke* in itself was nothing—a hollow wooden cylinder of worm-eaten oak, about twelve inches long and two inches in diameter. Carved into the top was a worn resemblance of a crown, branded with the royal cypher. A spike at the bottom was stabbed into the door of the summoned man, an authority to which all men must bow. It had summoned Quaker men to a prison sentence for holding unlawful religious meetings. It had summoned another man after the burial of his son for a fine of ten specie dollars. It had summoned one to a fine for being married unlawfully. It would fine another to pay for burying his children in unconsecrated ground, when it would not allow him to bury them otherwise. Unless, of course, they were baptized, and they, as Quakers, rejected baptism. The innocence of birth needed no purification.

In Norway, the budstikke would, in addition to Quaker marriage and burial practices, summon them for refusal to tithe, for refusal to bear arms. It would lawfully seize their property, confine them to prisons, seize their children and forcibly baptize them, and then charge sums for having done so. The budstikke would seize fuel wood, stoves, furniture, cows, goats, sheep—anything removable and salable, even farms, for refusal to pay what the Quakers called church taxes. Tithing, the church called it.

Kristina had promised herself when she left home for Stavanger that she would never marry. But she looked at this man in front of her, fumbling with his cap, unable to say what she wanted most to hear. Salve cleared his throat and began, "Kristina Karlsdatter, thou knowest what I shall tell thee."

Did she know? Her heart beat loudly; her thoughts flew back and forth from Røyseland to Stavanger, from Grandfather Tollak to the man in front of her. A flame burned inside of her like a small red coal: she saw her mother, Anna Tonetta, big with pregnancy time after time, with another child to care for, to weave for, to ask the grain patches to be kinder, to beg of the budstikke that it come less often. Her father, Karl, had bought more land, but there were more children. She thought of her promise to herself to return to Røyseland to care for her parents and Tollak. She'd thought, *Women would be better off not to marry*. Except that childless women were an oddity, persons without place or even gender, even though laws keeping unmarried women in the status of minors had been struck down. But all that was before she met Salve Knudsen.

Like other Quakers of his age, Salve Knudsen had been imprisoned five times for refusal to serve in the military, kept for much of it in solitary, subsisting only on bread and water. His brother, Christian, had died of cholera in prison. A sister had died of whooping cough at age seven. Salve had sat up with her, holding the small bones that reminded him of a bird's wing they were so frail, her skin light as feathers. He'd held her when she died, when her breath just slipped away from her, and her arms had dropped away from his neck, like dead twigs blown down by the wind.

His mother had cut a white paper into a snowflake and placed it over her face in the coffin; his father nailed the coffin lid shut, and then they'd carried her to the boat. Salve had wanted to lift up the top and breathe his life into her lungs instead of covering her with unconsecrated earth. He couldn't forget leaving her like that. It was that burial and Christian's that made the Knudsen family *fra Lyngdal* plan their emigration to America. By custom, Salve, the eldest son, age twenty-three, would be first.

Tomorrow, he would leave on the *Emigranten*. Now, he stood before a woman he hoped would one day be his bride, wearing a dark, heavy-vested suit, with narrow, high lapels on a high-buttoned vest, a collarless linen shirt. A red-blond beard deepened the blue of his eyes, and he held a navy sailor's cap in his hands.

He shifted his feet, paused, and cleared his throat again. "I am going to *Amerika*. I have little hope of asking for thee here, in Norway, so I have not asked thy father. He will think it a poor bargain, to wait for a man who will disappear into the wilds of Amerika. So I ask thee nothing." Even though Salve's family had long planned for him to emigrate, he had been in no hurry, until he met Kristina Karlsdatter. In Norway, he could offer her nothing but hard work, children, and poverty. In America, he would become rich.

Hearing these words, Kristina looked him full in the face. Her eyes met his. He reached for her arms with both of his, leaning forward, and then withdrew, straightened himself up again, adding, "But I tell thee that I shall return for thee, and then I shall ask, and it may be that thou wilt not be free. But I will return."

"Salve Knudsen," Kristina said, her eyes crystal with tears, her mouth trembling. "I will wait for thee." She stood and went to him, touching his hands that still held his cap. He smiled. His hands brushed her shoulders so lightly that she wasn't sure he had touched her. Then he left, before either had said another word.

In the harbor of Stavanger in 1878, many of the Norwegian ships at anchor had been sailing the seas since the turn of the century, some sloop-rigged like the now-legendary *Restaurationen*, some double-masted brigs like the *Emigranten* and the *Norden*, both of which could still be found harbored there in winter, before the emigrant season began in late spring and early summer. An expert crew compensated for a ship's age, crewmen who had been at sea since they were eleven-year-old cabin boys. Old ships were anchored next to bigger and faster sailing ships that, even as early as 1860, had reached North America in thirty-nine days, in a good wind and fair sailing.

Most of these vessels, old and new, had been built in small shipyards in and around Stavanger, or farther north from Bergen to Trondhjeim. The industry employed thousands: men who lumbered and men who transported the tall ship's masts and lumber from mountain and coastal forests; ships' architects and designers, builders, carpenters, sailmakers: all understood the stress of the sea at its worst. Ships were schools for prospective managers of fleets and for sailors: skippers rose from their ranks.

Thirty-eight years earlier, in 1841, only one Norwegian ship had regularly carried emigrants and a cargo of ore to New York. Nine years later, there were twenty-nine. They wintered in the harbors of their home port, many in Stavanger. In winter, many skippers or their agents traveled to coastal and mountain villages recruiting passengers. "Soul-buying," the newspapers called it, reporting that some skippers accepted promissory notes for passage, or accepted as payment what people expected to get for property they would sell at auction in the spring. Priests and magistrates denounced the skippers for encouraging movements of citizens, even though the law that read, "It is forbidden to remove from the King's realms and dominions" had been removed from the legal code in 1840. But the king's laws were left to magistrates to enforce, and magistrates knew how far it was from Sweden to Stavanger.

In 1849, British Parliament acts had opened colonial traffic to foreign ships. Norwegian ships could then transport emigrants to Canada and return with timber for England; from England, they could transport miscellaneous cargo to the Baltic or to Norway.

For the next fifteen years, nine-tenths of the Norwegian emigrants traveled on Norwegian sailing ships bound for Quebec, the heyday of Norway's sailing vessels: her shipping industry surpassed that of nearly all larger seafaring countries. Her ships carried salmon and cod to Europe, whale oil, timber, hides, and granite from Stone Age sites to world markets. They returned with wheat for those who could afford it. They brought coffee and sugar, furniture and textiles to satisfy the tastes of the wealthier population. In 1878, the busy harbor did not indicate an imminent crisis.

But steamships had already replaced most of the merchant fleets in other seafaring countries. Side by side with the sailing ships, the steamships looked like huge dismantled hulks, stripped of their masts, rigging gone, their long prows blunted. The tall-masted ships sat proudly at anchor, counting the days before they were scuttled. Scuttled, too, would be a way of life in existence since Vikings skimmed the seas in their swift, shallow ships—all lost to the Industrial Revolution, of which the great emigration was a part. It was a mass movement.

Norway had few people to spare in the late eighteen hundreds, yet three-quarters of a million people left the country over the course of fifty years. What had begun as a family exodus was now a migration of unmarried youth, not primarily *bonder* but tradesmen, shipbuilders and carpenters, joiners—all those once employed in the industry of sailing ships. Seamen, too, were among the new emigrants, passengers for the first and usually last time in their lives.

Unlike the days when emigration was forbidden, gone were the admonishing priests waving letters from "Amerika" that described disease and death on the frontier, and *bonder* with wives and their many children clutching their own success-story letters. No one warned the Norsemen of fearful monsters in the sea anymore: the unknown was known. Emigration caused a stir only among officials who tried to keep some tally of the floodtide departing. Money flowed back to Norway from new American relatives; photographs arrived of well-dressed, contented landowners, former cotters.

Clergymen were among the emigrants, their black-frocked figures seen waving to colleagues on departing ships.

On June 10, 1878, Salve Knudsen brought his oxblood-painted dome-topped chest to the harbor of Stavanger to load on the brig, *Emigranten*, en route to America via Quebec, from which he would travel by waterways to Chicago, and from there by train. This path to the American Midwestern farmlands had become a thoroughfare for Norwegian emigrants. Salve Knudsen was part of the second major wave of emigration from Norway.

Kristina Karlsdatter clutched her merino shawl about her, her gray-green eyes looking like the color of the harbor on the chilly June day. She watched Salve Knudsen board the ship and the brig pull anchor. Slowly, the ship eased out of its berth and began to move, more cumbersome than graceful, more like an ark than a sailing ship. Slowly it caught the wind, rocking slightly as it did so. Then it went underway, more smoothly, and then surely. Kristina waited among the onlookers standing on the dock, some in tears, some with smiles, some with thoughtful but grave faces like her own. Almost all were friends and relatives of passengers. One by one, they turned and went their way.

Kristina waited until the ship was as small as a gull's wing on the horizon. It had rained for a moment, and then suddenly, the sunshine played upon the fjord, at first in streaks, and then in a great sweep. Kristina saw a rainbow span the fjord, and then emerge from the white sails on the ship taking Salve Knudsen to America. She knew that she would wait for the man who had just embarked, and she was certain that he would return. She had no idea how many years it would be. She glanced at the cathedral, remembering the story of how her mother had sat there so many hours alone, ridiculed by the clergy for her Quaker beliefs. Its shadow reinforced her resolve, her faith, and her patience. She needed patience now.

Kristina retraced her steps through narrow streets rising up from the harbor, her laced boots clicking on the cobblestones. She looked down at her dress, holding up her skirts slightly, and she rubbed the black wool between her fingers. She'd bought the wool at the market in Stavanger and made the dress as her mother had taught her, with a white lace collar, and buttons like tiny mouse eyes. Still holding up her skirts, she turned at Klostergate to number 32, a large ochre-painted clapboard house. Her thoughts, like drifts of clouds over the Stavangerfjord, mixed last week's event with remembrances from her childhood.

She was happy at Endre Dahl's house, almost guiltily so. She'd learned to cook food she had first seen in the Stavanger market when she was fifteen: salmon, sea trout, and halibut instead of herring and dried cod, whale meat, which tasted like beef, though she had eaten beef with repugnance, because it had meant the slaughter of a cow or a calf. She sent almost all of her income to Røyseland but still felt that she lived better than she ought. Endre Dahl's large house was redeemed by his generous sharing; she thought about the scarcity of everything at Røyseland, except for hard work. Still, she missed its simplicity, its clean poverty.

She entered the house, thinking of how Salve's cornflower-blue eyes would suddenly light up with laughter when his face was still sober, that he could laugh just with his eyes, silently—a Quaker laugh, she thought. She thought of his sun-bronzed face framed by bushy yellow hair and how it reddened in the sunlight, of his tall frame and broad shoulders, and of how lean he was—too lean, she thought. She wondered if his eyes at this very moment looked over the slate-blue water toward America, or if they looked back toward the shores he had just left. Kristina entered the kitchen, with its wooden tables and checkered rolling pin, and sat in a wooden chair at the table, taking up her mending. Her hands were never idle.

Now that Salve Knudsen was gone from Norway, life would not be very different for Kristina Karlsdatter. Although she had seen him infrequently, he had still been a presence: the air they breathed had been from the same shores, the same land had connected them, over *berg* and *dal*, transmitting their thoughts of each other, even though the thoughts of the known limits of their future together in Norway were sober. Because of those limits, he was gone, and she returned to the dark halls of 32 Klostergate thinking of former promises to herself, changed so surely by Salve Knudsen. Her promises were now to him. He was the remembered sun in the sky during a Norwegian winter.

This promise did not escape Endre Dahl, nor Salve's parents and her own. Kristina wrote to Røyseland as plainly as the Quakers dressed. "I have promised to wait for Salve Knudsen to return from Amerika. He will not ask thee, Father, if we may marry, until he returns. But I have promised. I am well. Yours, with God, Kristina."

Once he had settled, Salve Knudsen wrote to Kristina from Iowa, from a place with a strange name: Winnishiek. "An Indian name," Salve Knudsen had written. "I work for a Norwegian farmer from Haugesund. I earn two dollars and a half a day, along with room and board. Government land costs $1.25 an acre, land already homesteaded costs up to $10. I will return a landowner, and as you know, I want to buy near a Norwegian Quaker meeting at a place called Legrand. All are Norwegian, many from Stavanger Meeting.

"Kristina, the land is like the sea, vast and endless, and when the wind blows, tall grasses dip and bow like waves." He described that he saw no classes, that tradesmen and farmers, whether they were landless new immigrants or owners of a hundred or more acres, were all the same, even lawyers and people in towns. He'd never seen anything like it in Norway; no man was servant to another, no occupation too lowly for any man to do. He saw a German doctor care for his own horse, next to a former cotter from Gubrandsdal, who had a horse as well. But Kristina, he wrote, the priests from Norway have arrived as well, yet they were not in any authority over him or anyone—they could be friends, and most of them were against alcohol, not like the Germans and the Irish. He told how he ate Norwegian food, but everyone ate pork. "Kristina, everyone works so hard, but they laugh and tell stories and are happy. They know each will have a large *gaard*, and no one will take it away. As for me, know that I will build thee a house on my land before I return. Kristina, when I think of thee, I work twice as hard."

Many brides-to-be waited in Stavanger, in coastal villages, and in the mountains for the return of sweethearts. Wives and children waited for passage money; brothers, sisters, and parents waited, for news, for fare, for land to be bought, for a house to be built, for the return of the new immigrant. No Norwegian family was exempt from waiting for news from America. Men who left as *arbeidsfolk* or as *husmaender* returned, remade, and their remaking was visible in the tilt of their jaws, the cut and fabric of their clothes, the money in their pockets.

All Norway knew of Trygve Olafsen, the poor husmaend's son, rejected by a rich bonde as his daughter's suitor. So, like others in difficulties, or those free enough to look for adventure, Trgyve left for America, to return a rich man after many years, finding the once-rich farmer mired in debts, his estate nearly bankrupt. Trygve saved the gaard and married the farmer's daughter. She had waited faithfully for him: everyone in Middle America was Trygve.

Salve Knudsen wrote every month, of the labor he did, the land he'd found at Stavanger, Iowa. For the last four years, he wrote from Legrand, "With a bank loan, I have bought a piece of land here where there is a Quaker meeting called Stavanger. One of the founders, Anna Ravnaas, now Olesen, is from Stavanger. She remembers attending your mother's wedding so long ago, at Stavanger yearly meeting. You will be at home here, Kristina. I hope to return in the winter of 1885."

In the fall of 1884, he wrote, "I have booked passage on the *Enigheden* to arrive in February. Kristina, I cannot believe that I will behold thee soon. My heart must wait; the months till then will be longer than the seven years."

The *Stavangeravis* reported that the *Enigheden* was due into the port of Stavanger on February 12, 1885. On that raw February day, Kristina Karlsdatter waited at Dahl's house until he reported news that a ship thought to be the *Enigheden* was sighted. Although no rain or snow fell, the wind gusted with force, not dangerous to sailing ships, but bitter for citizens waiting in the harbor. Kristina Karlsdatter was among them.

She thought of all the ships that had left Stavanger, the many returned, the many that didn't, of how many women had waited and still waited for ships that never came. She thought of husbands never returning, sons, brothers gone to sea graves. She thought of

Lars Larson, who long ago had been a prisoner of war with her grandfather. They had been visited by Swedish Quakers during their confinement, and both men became Quakers. Kristina's grandfather had chosen to stay in Norway rather than emigrate, but Lars Larsen had been seduced by America's promise of religious freedom and rich land. Larsen's ship had sailed from this same port sixty years ago, a tiny ship fit only for coastal shipping. And yet, the ship had made it, and in some way, that little ship's success was why she was standing in that same harbor, waiting for a man who had gone to America because of Lars Larsen. And she would be next to go. She believed that emigrating was God's plan for her, and so it was also her own.

The *Enigheden* loomed larger and larger, coming into harbor under partial sail, in February's noon light. Sailors leaped to furl the many sails as the ship berthed, hands on deck and on the quay working in perfect unison. As the gangplank settled into place, both passengers and spectators tensed; relatives or friends searched faces they hoped to recognize. Family members who stayed behind wondered what manner of man would return to them, and in the answer, they would learn more of America than they would from any *Amerika bok*.

For returning passengers, the Old Country would never be the same. They were now Americans who longed for the Old Country; but in that Old Country, they would find themselves restless, wanting to return to America. Home eluded them.

Kristina saw Salve Knudsen striding off the ship. He looked like a man who, by comparison, had been a boy before. She did not greet him but hid among the crowd before returning to the house of Endre Dahl, her face slightly red. There were Quaker customs she could not break, to greet even her betrothed in such a public place. She would wait for Salve Knudsen at Friend Dahl's house.

The afternoon passed with no word from Salve Knudsen. Each hour passed, until the early darkness and a fog covered the city softly and thickly, and still no word from Salve Knudsen. Each hour was like the years that Kristina Karlsdatter had waited, counted out day by day, week by week. Her agitated face didn't go unnoticed by Friend Dahl.

"Kristina Karlsdatter, thou must have patience," he said kindly, noticing her agitation. She believed that Salve Knudsen had changed his mind, or that he had forgotten her, that he had found someone else in Iowa, or that, somehow, he had seen her and had decided that she was now too old for a new life in America. She was already thirty-two, too old to marry, anyway.

"Thou must wait upon the Lord." She looked at Friend Dahl's graying hair and the white bushy sideburns which framed his face, his blue eyes. "Thy Salve has gone to his home and to Karl Jonsen, to ask for thee. Abide, child." She flushed and set about her duties with more energy.

At five o'clock, a knock resounded on the heavy oak door. "Lie down, heart," Kristina whispered as Salve Knudsen entered the door she held open.

"I came," he said. "I said I would." He extended his hands, his arms, this husky gold-haired man, whose confidence shone around him, and as quietly as she could, thinking he could hear the beating of her heart, she went to his arms then withdrew to arm's length, her hands clasping his.

"I am here," she said. She could not say more. Any hesitation she may have had was gone in an instant. She would go anywhere with this man—all that she had ever known, she would leave, for him. *With* him…

"I was worried. You didn't come." She felt awkward with words, blurting out things she didn't mean. She saw that his clothes were changed, his haircut. She would not say she knew how many hours had passed since his ship had docked.

Salve lifted her face with his hand and looked into it. At the same time, his right hand thrust in his jacket pocket. He brought out a small box with the name of a Stavanger jeweler.

"You didn't think I'd come without this, did you?" he asked, releasing her to open the box. She held up a simple gold band.

Kristina Karlsdatter and Salve Knudsen married on February 28, 1885, at Røyseland. Kristina wore a black, stiff, two-piece silk dress that buttoned in the front. The blouse had pleats on each front panel. The skirt was flared at the hemline with pleats in back giving a practical fullness. A small white collar and white cuffs were its only decoration. Quietly tailored and beautifully sewn, if not very bridal, it would have multiple uses. Kristina's hair was pulled back in a large yellow knot; Salve's was cropped close to his head, but his beard was wide and free. In his American ready-made suit, he was already different from the rest.

Kristina's grandfather Tollak spoke—he was now seventy-eight years old. "More than thirty years ago, my daughter, Anna Tonetta, and Karl Jansen took their vows in Stavanger, contrary to the law of this country. Now their firstborn, Anna Kristina, and Salve Knudsen take vows still in disobedience to this country's laws. And then they will leave us."

Tollak's hair was white and bushy; he was energetic and unwithered with age. He would live fourteen more years and die quietly in his sleep, but as he spoke of his first granddaughter's departure to Amerika, his voice trembled slightly. In Amerika, he said, his great-grandchildren would not defy the law to marry, nor would their sons go to prison for refusal to bear arms; he hoped their daughter and new son would keep faith and remember Røyseland and those who remained there.

"Let us believe that, being free from disobedience, they will not forsake struggle nor forget what it is to suffer for conscience's sake." His eyes washed suddenly with tears, for Tollak was remembering the last visit of Knud Slogvig, who had emigrated to America with Lars Larsen when Anna Tonetta was a small child. Knud's stories of their prosperity had tempted Tollak, and he had questioned his decision not to emigrate year after year when times had been bad. He remembered Knud's description of Amerika. "It is a paradise, Tollak. The land is black and fertile. There are no stones in heaven." Knud motioned to Tollak's land, hard with rocks, as if he wanted to free Tollak from the bruises the stones would offer his family. The richness of Amerika seemed to appear before Knud's eyes like a rich man's table. But Tollak had fixed upon remaining in his land of stones, his Røyseland.

That he had stayed, he was glad. Røyseland—their birthplace and burial grounds—was filled with voices of his grandchildren. But the departure of Kristina was the beginning. Would Røyseland remain an empty shell, he and his wife, Sidsel, and his son-in-law, Karl, and his daughter, Anna Tonetta, staying here alone to die? "If I have been a hard taskmaster, well then, the times required it," he said. Would better times reduce their vigilance, destroy their faith?

Tollak paused and looked at Anna Tonetta and then at Karl Andreas, both silent. "So be it," he said. "Go with God. And now, let them proceed with their vows." So his first grandchild, Kristina Karlsdatter, and Salve Knudsen pledged to each other, "In the presence of the Lord, and before this assembly…to be husband and wife until the separation by death."

They ate the food of the country, herring, cheese, dried lamb, with the family of Salve Knudsen. Kristina's younger sisters, Sarah, aged nine, and Anna, thirteen, replenished the plates of food, casting worried looks at Kristina. They saw their older sister twice a year. They'd been to her room in Dahl's house to stay with her, they knew what she looked at when she got up in the morning, the clothes she put on, the food she cooked, the people she saw, the streets she walked in. Their other sister, Severine, now twenty-five, was married and had moved away; Staale, twenty-two, was a schoolteacher in Kvinesdal.

As the time of departure neared, voices grew louder, as if to postpone leave-taking. Anna Tonetta occupied her hands with Kristina's dome-topped trunk, adding a leather-covered Bible and the Quaker marriage certificate to its contents of bed linens, a waffled rolling pin, down comforters. Kristina's mother was in her early fifties and had borne ten children, all of whom—except Kristina—lived within fifty miles. Her iron-gray hair was still full, braided and wrapped around her head, her features still handsome, her figure strong and lean. Karl approached her to take the trunk so he could mount it on the carriole. He placed his hands on her shoulders as she bent over the trunk, pulling her up to face him. He saw tears she tried to hold back; he could not stop his own. He motioned to Staale to help him with the trunk.

Kristina approached. Her hands didn't know where to be or what to do, and words wouldn't come. She lingered with her mother, remembering her visits to Røyseland twice a year, and how in Stavanger she remembered daily, Røyseland's simple, scrubbed interior, where sunlight played with the shadows and glowed into baskets of wool, inviting comfort with rosy softness, how her handsome, now-aging mother presided over it, her hair now the color of the wool she spun and wove. Her face was the inventory of her life: someone who would never ask for less to do or less to care for.

Kristina was stung by the awareness that she was leaving Røyseland, perhaps forever. She would bear her children away from home, without kin, without the familiar rooms, without all the things that were testimonies to Anna Tonetta's nurture made into love like the chain of her wool: out of it, she fashioned warmth and protection and belief. Kristina did not know the color of the air that would greet her in the morning light, the feel of spring, how it breathed and in what place. She did not know what daily horizon would greet her eyes, what trees, if there were trees, or stones, if there were *royse* that now, at Røyseland, seemed like jewels. Kristina knew nothing of what was ahead of her, nor would her mother ever know into what air her daughter would disappear.

These thoughts of mother and daughter circled between them, thoughts as present as the presence of God in silent meeting, now expressed in an equally silent departure. Embraces and words were brief and unlingering, followed by hands pressed between father and daughter, sisters and brothers. Tollak's firm hands closed over Kristina's strong and calloused ones. "Go with God, my daughter," said Anna Tonetta. Her unsteady hands grasped Kristina's lost ones.

Kristina placed her left foot on the pedal to hoist herself up on the seat of the carriole. She felt Salve's weight added. He took the reins. *Whither thou goest I will go*, she repeated to herself, remembering the biblical passage from Ruth, staring back at *Mor* and *Far* and *Bestefar* Tollak, the blur of his white beard. She could see Anna Tonetta standing motionless and all the members of Røyseland and first day meeting through brimming eyes. Her throat knotted. Fare thee well!

Go with God! they said.

The realization that *she* was now *they* came quietly, almost as the sun's warmth may be so briefly interrupted by a wisp of cloud that the lack of warmth is unnoticeable to anyone not watching that wisp. The chill cannot be traced but comes as a disturbance from an unknown source.

Then they were gone—mother, grandfather, sisters, brothers, uncles—all. Kristina was aware that she was seated next to a near stranger and that she was leaving everything and everyone she had ever known—her home and her country, its pathways, its shores and valleys—that she was going to an unknown country with a man named Salve Knudsen formerly *fra Lyngdal* and now *fra Amerika*.

Bog! Hjelpe meg!

CHAPTER TWO

Kristina stood on the rear deck of the small coastal steamer looking down at the white wake of the water frothing in the blue sea. She raised her eyes almost reluctantly, wanting to see—but *not* wanting to see—the harbor of Flekkefjord, the white, red, and ochre houses rising above it, and then, beyond the rooftops, the hills. She memorized the sight of the valley behind: its exact width, the stream running through. In the far horizon, she saw the low mountains against the sky and, beyond that, where she could not see, lay Røyseland.

Salve stood, silent, beside her, watching her. He placed his right hand over her left, a big firm hand; she felt its farmer's coarseness. "Thou will return, I promise. With thy children." He squeezed her hand. She did not look at him but gazed again at the white wake below.

"The water, it is white with spray, like the falls at Rafoss," she said, and her own eyes were misted finely—like the falls, she thought—a mist she tried to not let collect into a little rivulet of tears. She kept looking at the white foam, standing next to a man for whom she had abandoned everything known to her.

Both of them were awkward virgins in their thirties, although many Norwegian girls in Iowa had hoped to make Salve otherwise. Kristina had had no such temptations or opportunities, living in the house of a Quaker. The very idea of sex except within marriage was unthinkable to her. At this moment, it was almost unthinkable anyway. She had no desire for it; she feared it and felt totally insecure about her own body, unknown to her, unseen by anyone since she'd been a girl at home. Her body was something to be hidden, every centimeter of it, her legs and feet encased in dark stockings, boots over the ankles, and to make doubly certain her extremities would not show, dark skirts covered them a second time, a third time, with overgarments. Only her face, part of her neck, and her hands had ever been visible, and now…On the small overnight steamer, passengers must share sleeping quarters, so she would be safe for one day more.

Four days later, Kristina stood on the deck of a Norwegian sailing ship, America-bound, on the arm of her husband, looking into his clear blue eyes fixed firmly on the horizon. It was already the New World for them, discovered in a sparse bedroom of Endre Dahl's house. In these short days, her body had become real to her; she was conscious now, of how it moved, of the breaths she took, thinking of how her breasts swelled each time, conscious of her legs, her back, how they combined together to let her walk, how they fitted together with Salve's own. That he, too, had body parts different from hers, but his had been made for hers. She thought of this new knowledge, smiled at Salve, and then looked down into the busy harbor.

She'd been in Stavanger over ten years and had watched many come and go, mostly all sailing ships, mostly Norwegian. Now, many of them loading cargo and passengers were European, and they provided food, the baskets and hampers of smoked and dried fish, meat, and fladbrod. But more dome-topped trunks were being loaded than ever, most belonging to young men leaving the country whose shipping industry had abandoned them. There were fewer farmers among them, and fewer families.

Kristina watched the faces of the new emigrants: both anticipatory and uncertain, faces looking back to the solid streets of the harbor as they carried bundles and duffels up the many gangplanks. Returning immigrants were more confident, some even seeming boastful, as though they had nothing new to learn: their bodies seemed to say they were already American.

She looked at Salve's face—his was among those returning, his face confident and calm, whereas she felt her own tension rising. Without him, her insecurity would be visible in the way she would cling to the rail, probably clutching it as though it were Stavanger itself. She pressed Salve's arm.

Both were unaware that they were part of the third largest wave of Norwegian emigration—from 1879 until the mid-1890s—precipitated by Norway's lagging behind in the quick sweep of industrialization across Europe. They were on one of the remaining Norwegian sailing ships, which provided them with food in an attempt to compete with steamers.

Who could ever have thought that anything could threaten the security of Norway's shipping industry, her ships with the tall masts from Norway's great forests? Who could ever match the skill of the craftsmen who knew the strengths and weaknesses of the wood in their hands, how to lay stress, where? Who could compete with the training of her sailors who began their long apprenticeships at age eleven, who knew every line and sail and every temperament of every rigging? Skippers and crewmen scoffed at steamships. But now, one by one, the ships were sailing a last voyage; they were accumulating in shipyards, unwanted, riding high in the water with empty hulls. The sounds of hammer and saw were no longer heard, nor the sight of ribs crisscrossed, men's backs bent over in rows, shaping, bending, adhering wood to wood in graceful yet solid forms of sloops, yawls, schooners. By the time the Norwegian industry looked up from its labors, they saw nothing but steamships, and they themselves had built none.

But America was becoming a nation: explored, occupied, populated, cultivated, and exploited. Railroad companies had Norwegian American representatives in state immigration offices who met the ships in New York, who watched their former countrymen disembark, observed their walk, their clothing, to determine what their trades were, and from among them, which ones to recruit. They knew that farmers were most reliable, the poorest of them and most isolated recognized by their homespun. Some agents called them pieces of Norwegian beef in *wadmal*, reeking of *gammelost* or *spekemat*, or aged cheese, smoked fish, and lack of soap. Maybe they were joining a brother, or a friend, an acquaintance as a hired hand, until such time as America tested his true worth. If he never gained paradise, it was because he didn't seize it, and a better man would. The railroad employers looked for the best backs to make or break; some they would break. Some immigrants, innocent and trusting, found themselves indentured, when they didn't even know the word. They found out.

"Salve…" Kristina said as their ship pulled its anchor. She wanted to know everything at once: the land, the people, the climate, where to buy things she needed. Her life had existed between Røyseland and Stavanger. Beyond that, she could not imagine. "Salve," she repeated, her eyes shining, the orange flecks like sparks in the green-gray horizon of her eyes, and soon the sea as well. "I wanted to say to that I have waited for this day for many years, and I thought to be afraid. But thou knowest, I know, we have become one. And, I say then, I will go with thee, whither thou goest." She dropped her eyes, amazed at what she had confessed. Love had given her a tongue to speak!

"Kristina," Salve said, words rising like lumps in his throat, "*Kristina Min*, I, too, waited for thee." He looked abruptly away and straightened shoulders he'd bent over her. "Kristina, thou dost not mind, traveling on a sailing ship? Next time you come back, there won't be any sailing ships."

"But why should I mind?"

"It is longer and not so comfortable. And we will land in Quebec. From there we must go by waterways to Chicago, then by train."

"Is it so long, then?" Kristina had no idea how long or how far it was. She thought they would be extending their wedding trip together. She did not know that she had had the only holiday of her life there in Stavanger, in the house of Endre Dahl. Four days!

Now she shared cabin space with six other women, shared communal *lyse* and their telltale red marks on the skin: the itching and the shame were unseen, but only those women unused to them were ashamed. They doused themselves with powders from the captain's store. The only thought that made it bearable was the journey's end. The space was too small, the air fetid, all but one of her cabinmates were used to lyse—she did not even want to change her clothes. On decks the weather was too cold, uninhabitable, except for sailors. And Salve—Kristina saw him gripping the rails, watching the waves, waiting to step on shore with his bride, dreaming of sons, of planting, of harvesting, of more and more land. She knew his thoughts, because his eyes would get that faraway look, his mouth would turn upward very slightly into a slight and amused smile, and his chin stuck out just enough to show his determination.

At Quebec, trunks were transferred to inland waterways; Kristina heard languages she could not understand. In Chicago, boarding a train, she felt as strewn about as her belongings. Trunks were somewhere in the baggage department, Salve assured her. She clutched a leather bag from Endre Dahl whose top opened and snapped shut like great fish jaws, and a woven wool bag from Anna Tonetta, filled with knitted sweaters. In the train, Kristina twitched her body slightly, as if she were thinking of fleas and lyse and her constant effort to get rid of them, feeling herself permanently scarred. So relieved that this would be the last stage of their journey, she didn't even ask how long they would be on the train.

On crawled the train across a land without hills, with no mountains to climb, no fjords to go around. The sameness lengthened into a great emptiness so vast that Kristina could not believe that such a bigness existed. "Isn't it wonderful, Kristina," Salve said at intervals, a man returning. She was still leaving home. "Kristina, look," and Salve pointed to the horizon, his eyes a bright, hard blue, "as far as the eye can see, such rich, black land!" He took both of her hands in his and looked at her, seated across from him. "Kristina, now I have only 120 acres. But we will buy more and then a little more. And our sons..." and he leaned forward to touch her shoulders, but he looked through her and still saw endless planted fields, waving with grain. Kristina withdrew her hands from his, embarrassed at his public show of affection.

She looked around at her fellow passengers, but no one was watching her. "Salve, is it all so...so flat?" It seemed as though she was seeing Røyseland for the first time, seeing its hills and valleys on the far edge of the distant flatness, like a mirage. Such flatness couldn't last forever! All the way from Chicago, the horizon was a large unending ache of unfamiliarity, as though the hills had been cut off with a great knife like mounds of butter, and squashed into the valleys to fill them up. The horizon extended itself farther and farther, beyond reach, beyond even where her eyes could rest themselves.

There was no end.

So there was no beginning. It was she who would have to make one, and she didn't feel big enough to be a beginning. She felt strangled by a landscape that allowed her no shadows to show that she existed, no unknown corners of herself in which to hide, to think, to be.

Another low cluster of buildings: the train crawled to them and stopped. Another few passengers were ready to get off, worried that they were at the right place, that they had all of their belongings. They checked suitcases, bundles, satchels over and over to make certain nothing was forgotten. A woman descended with her three unruly children; Kristina had observed her green velvet dress with its big sleeves and a soiled spot on her breast. A child had stuck out his tongue at her, and she had responded with a flat, hard slap on his face. Where was this woman going with three children, in a space empty of everything but a few houses? Did she have somewhere a house, beds, a husband, cooking pots, a rolling pin, blankets? Even with those, could she *live* in such a place?

Then Kristina dozed and was awakened by Salve. "We are coming into the station, Kristina." He rose and pointed to a graveled square around a flat, rectangular building, its roof extended far beyond the exterior walls. She asked why, and Salve answered, "Snow." She didn't understand.

Salve started to collect their belongings, and Kristina saw his lean, muscular body and the set of his jaw, a man about to unfurl the eighth wonder of the world to the eyes of his bride. He had waited seven years for this moment. He was an American, a landowner. Soon she would see.

"We are here, Kristina. We are here!" he said as the train came to its customary jolt, as Salve guided her forward with his loaded arms. She descended the metal stairs onto a square of gravel, her thoughts interrupted by voices in Norwegian, greeting Salve Knudsen.

"*Wilkommen, Kristina Karlsdatter, kone Salve Knudsen.*"

It was Ole Kvinlaug, once of Kvinesdal Meeting, who now shook hands warmly, both of his on each of theirs. Ole and Salve loaded their trunks from the baggage car onto Ole's wagon drawn by two horses, big, heavy horses, she noted, not like the little Norwegian ponies. And then they were off to the four-room clapboard house belonging to Salve, which sat on his farm of 120 acres.

The horses snorted in the chill air. The snow had melted, but the landscape had not taken on the hope of spring. Grasses and stalks of the last season lay lifeless and withered. If you had asked Salve what he saw on this day when he brought his bride from Norway to his farm in America, he would say that he already saw shoots of yellow-green wheat coming through the half-frozen earth, and he would say that he saw new white lambs in his green pastures. He would think that his Kristina, too, would soon round and ripen. Kristina saw an emptiness, merciless in its glare, interrupted only by occasional, lonely farm buildings.

They rode the four miles till they came to Salve's white house with the single red barn. The horses drew to a stop in front of the house. Salve sprang off the carriage, and the springs quivered for a moment under the loss of his weight.

"Come, Kristina. You are home," he said, extending his hand to her, helping her down.

"It is, it is..." Kristina said, but words wouldn't come. What she wanted to say, she didn't want to say: *Is this my space, inside these narrow walls, for the rest of my life?* The emptiness engulfed her before she even entered.

Inside she found a place clean and scrubbed, like Norway, a safe place. She entered and saw a kitchen and a living room. Then she walked from one to the other—a bedroom and another room, mostly empty. Salve had made some of the furniture, a bed like her own at home, where she would put her sheep's wool mattress. He'd made straight chairs, a table. His own oxblood dome chest stood in the living room. A bench, upholstered with faux leather, stuffed, arrested her eyes. "A sofa," Salve said. He'd been waiting to see her surprise.

Kristina walked to the sofa, touched it lightly with her index finger, then crossed the living room back to where Salve stood near the kitchen, and put her hands on his for a moment. She entered the kitchen with its woodstove, kitchen pots—some from Norway—a table and chairs.

"I have brought you some bread," Ole said. "And some fennelor. And some of last year's potatoes. They are beginning to sprout. You will have your own in a few months—little ones, at least."

Kristina looked startled, wondering at Ole's remark as she looked into his face. He began to smile and looked at Salve, smiling broader. Salve looked back at her until she, too, was smiling, her sadness broken as they all laughed.

"Potatoes, I said," emphasized Ole. "Only potatoes."

"You will have coffee?" Kristina offered.

"Do you have coffee?" Ole asked, almost taking a chair.

"We are Norwegian, aren't we?" She smiled. "Salve, in my trunk, the one from Stavanger."

"I, too, have coffee, Kristina Min," and Salve went to the cupboard in the kitchen, opened the door, and brought out a package of coffee beans and a small coffee mill.

The sun gathered into a ball of redness on the flat Iowa prairie, now farmed and fenced and wrested away from its buffalo and Indians, while Salve and his bride and Ole Kvinlaug, all once from Norway, ate bread and fennelor and drank coffee. The light faded, lingering as it flattened and spread on the wide horizon. Ole said his good-byes as Salve lighted a kerosene lamp, and Ole's shadow preceded him all the way to his waiting carriage. For the first time since she laid her eyes on the glaring Midwestern landscape, Kristina saw the comfort of shadows, flickering. The yellow light danced and lingered in the beard of Salve Knudsen, reddening it. It shone in his eyes. This man was now a part of her and she of him. They were far away from home: she would have to make a new one.

Tomorrow, she would begin. Tonight, they would rest. She opened her trunk from Røyseland to find blankets and bed linens. Before her eyes focused on the contents, Kristina's nose brought Røyseland before her: fladbrod baking, the odor of the washed wool, the wildflowers that grew, even the sounds of the waterfall at Rafoss. Then, in the trunk's darkness she felt something hard, something her fingers searched, something as familiar to her hands as her mother's face.

It was the brass candlestick, and a candle wrapped carefully and tied to it with a strand of wool. Kristina held it to her face, breathing in the touch of her mother's hand, which had placed it there. Wordlessly she held it up to Salve, who couldn't know its meaning for her. And then she lighted it, diminishing the flame of the kerosene lamp so that the light from Røyseland illuminated the house on the prairie.

CHAPTER THREE

The American Quakers outdid their English forebears. Where the Quakers were plain, those in America were plainer, in manner of living, in housing, and in dress, so that when Kristina Karlsdatter walked into the Iowa Stavanger Meetinghouse for the first time, the differences were evident. A low, rectangular building had a board platform extending halfway around the outside. There were sex-separated entrances and seatings, so that Kristina parted with Salve on the platform. The seats were benches, plain and straight, that faced a raised platform with two rows of seats for the Elders. The women wore scuttle-shaped bonnets tied under the chin; some men had adopted the high broad-brimmed hats of the English Quakers, but most wore what they had always worn—a Norwegian sailor-type cap with a small visor.

Clothing of these Norwegian immigrants was either Norwegian homespun, or American machine-made; Kristina would learn that they were mail order. Both kinds were lumpy and ill cut. Kristina wondered if her fine seams would be held in question. She wondered why these rich American farmers wore clothes so poor and plain. Altogether the colors were of such a sameness that everywhere she looked, from clothes to the gray walls of the meetinghouse to the flatness and colorlessness of the sleeping prairie, there was a uniformity.

Initially, most Norwegian immigrants took their father's given name as a surname, with the usual addition of *son* or *sen* but, because there were so many Oles and Lars and Knuds, they took place names from Norway: Kjormoe, Huseboe, Vinje, Gimre. One family adopted West for a surname, because they went west; three brothers at the new Stavanger Meeting had three different surnames. *Datter* was abandoned for women; usage became the same as for men: their maiden names ended with *son* or *sen*. Kristina was known as Kristina Karlsen. Salve used his father's name of Knudsen.

Ole faced this congregation from the seats of the appointed Elders in front, holding his hands palm forward to quiet the hum of voices. His eyes were hardly visible under the brim of his hat, but they were known to all as kindly and gentle eyes that could turn to a steel flintiness in seconds.

"What wouldst thou?" he said, holding up both hands to subdue the excitement. "If thee wouldst have God enter this meeting, forbear!" His voice boomed the last word. "Now," he continued in the stilled room, "let us wait upon the Lord." And he sat down.

Perhaps most of the congregation on this morning hoped that the silence wouldn't last forever. The children hoped that the meeting would not be more than an hour, that someone would speak so that their squirming might be less noticeable. The benches were hard and straight, and there was nothing to look at. How many times had they counted floor boards or window panes? Children would have stared only once at the Elders, who made short work of staring children.

Whoever had a concern might speak and eventually be appointed ministers to represent their meeting at yearly meetings, even meetings abroad. For Catholics, or Episcopalians, the sight of this gathering would be strange: more than one hundred persons, one-third of them children, sitting in a barren room in total silence, heads bowed, while an imagined clock would tick on and on, like a photograph of an event rather than the event itself. Visible to many present would be another figure in the room, standing off to the side or in front of the Elders, facing the congregation, almost transparent, holding a hand up the way Thor Anbjornsen did, to achieve silence. So invited and waited for, He would surely come. That is why this group waited so earnestly for His presence.

Elder Ole Sawyer stood up to his bent-over five and a half feet, his ever-present Norwegian cap looking more lived-in than ever. "God has favored us," he said. "We are growing. Those of us who lacked bread and freedom in Norway are with us now, but we must not forget those who remain. We thank God now, for our school, our harvest. And I, too, am ripening." His voice rasped and quavered, competing with the noise of faint stirring of small feet as he sat down.

Did he hear a muffled voice stifling a laugh?

Thirty-five soundless minutes passed before a gray figure in a scuttle-shaped bonnet stood, whom some called a sweet singer, and others called the devil's ranter. Women and men alike stood in awe of her oratory and of the face that burned under her bonnet. Today the finger would point at one of them: God would reveal, through Ina, the tune one had hummed, the seller of the horse with undisclosed heaves, or the woman who gossiped.

No man present wanted his wife so noticed as Ina Tobiasdatter Christiansen. Short messages of thankfulness, of appreciation for safe arrival and prosperity in the New Land, were always appropriate from a pious and submissive woman, even though Quaker women had long been ministers. But jealousy, along with fear, plucked quietly and unseen, ugly and yellow. Her voice began its quavering way, which would reach a high monotone. Exhorting, blaspheming, pleading, her voice shrilled and drilled.

Ina's feet bled in the Exodus from Egypt: she was Moses delivering the Commandments, her eyes of fire. She was John the Baptist baptizing the Lord Christ, mixing her own words with Scripture. "Remember those who brought the seed of Abraham to the New World. Tear out vanity, tear out all temptations that lead down, down to the yawning gates.

"The love for Christ has departed from the people, and the Grand Enemy has made inroads among us and has scattered the flock. Among you is a sinner. Oh, return to the Spirit, ye who have partaken of the fleshpots of the earth, who have sung His praises with sounding brass and clanging cymbals and strings of the devil's instruments."

Her eyes fixed on a new immigrant arrival as she sat down.

Thore Syvertsen, seated next to Salve, fainted. Salve supported his leaning body. His fists clenched, his face white, he whispered to Salve that the hand of God had singled him out to chastise him through Ina; he had brought with him from Norway the "strings of the devil," a country fiddle, because it had belonged to his late father. His whisper was so hoarse that it carried and reverberated in the stillness of the meetinghouse.

"Who dares say there has not been a prophet among you!" Ina's voice rang out.

Kristina glanced at the frozen faces in the congregation. She saw members entranced by Ina and children strangely soothed by the drone of her voice. She had wondered if persons listened to what Ina said, or if her voice alone was her instrument. Kristina looked back at Ina's face, pale, raptured. In that moment, Kristina wondered if Ina had been sent as a warning to this flat prairie, filled with once-devout Norwegian Quakers now becoming too rich. *Easier for a camel to pass through a needle's eye than for a rich man to gain heaven.*

The sun had alighted on the bonnet of Ina Tobiasdatter, making her stand out from all others. This sign was not lost on those who feared her, nor those who were still in some trance from her words. Under the hat of Thor Anbjornsen, however, his blue eyes had turned steely gray. He stood and shook hands with Christian Gimre, and Ole Sawyer signaled the end of meeting while Ina was still speaking.

When the congregation exited the meetinghouse to the wide porches, it was as noisy with voices as it had been silent at meeting. Friendships were deepened, quarrels often mended. Children were released from parental control, but in or near the meetinghouse, where laughing and playing were severely forbidden.

Ina Tobiasdatter Christiansen stood apart. Few wanted to be scorched by her piercing eyes, many were in too much awe of her to talk about canning and children and gardens. She lived too far away from Kristina to exchange visits, even if Kristina had wished, nor did Ina's husband have a carriage. Meeting was the only time Kristina saw her, and then they spoke politely. Ina accepted her isolation as a price to pay for being called. No one would challenge that she wasn't, and although Kristina had first been both angered and instructed by her cousin, she was uncertain whether or not Ina's voice was from God or the devil.

Tonnes and Gonne Medhus stood up and shook hands, but simultaneously a woman stood up, saying, "I want you to recognize my right to continue."

Kristina looked around the room and noticed that few persons seemed to be surprised at the subsequent events.

"Thou has closed it whilst God was speaking to me! Thou has closed it against the voice of Him who would speak now, to you, through me."

This woman looked like the others in her prairie-colored clothes, but her face was set and hard. A determined face, Kristina thought, who did not understand what was happening, or know the speaker. At no meeting she had ever attended had the right to speak been so rudely interrupted.

Men and women got up from their places, ignoring the speaker as they passed through their sex-separated doors to the platform porch where a buzz of conversation began, none of which concerned itself with Serena Roinestad. Kristina hesitated, wanting to remain and speak with her, but other women urged her outside.

"You are Kristina, Salve's wife. Welcome," said one. "I am Ingeborg Heggem." "I am Thorina Meltvedt." One after another, they came to speak with her, then a tall and smiling man with a wide-brimmed hat, the man who had welcomed her in meeting. "I am Sigbjorn Rosdale, and my wife, Malinda. Welcome, Kristina. Will you and Salve partake with us?"

"Yes," Salve answered, standing next to her. "Kristina will enjoy that."

Horses with carriages waited, tied to a railing, while worshippers lingered, standing next to the waiting horses, chatting. They were lively and gregarious and worldly seeming to Kristina. Was there nothing on the minds of these Norwegians that they could have a meeting for worship with nothing but silence? There were no boys going to prison, no cows seized, no crop failures. And who was it who wouldn't allow a member to speak? Who are these Quaker Norwegians? Kristina wondered.

Salve helped her into the carriage, and they drove off to the house of the Rosdales, although more churchgoers walked than rode, their workhorses too large for carriages. Many insisted that horses, too, be given a day of rest. Salve had a light horse in addition to his team of Belgians, the heavy cold-bloods of Europe. He, too, believed that his horses should have a day of rest, but he did not want Kristina to walk to meeting. Now he talked and snapped the reins, "You see, Kristina Min, you will be happy here. There are more Norwegians here than you saw in a year at Røyseland," he said as they drove off to the house of the Rosdales.

"But who is Serena? Why wouldn't they let her speak?"

"Kristina, there are some disagreements here about the way to run meetings, about the way to pay for the meetinghouse."

"Pay for what? There is little to pay, Salve."

"Pay for the building itself, the wood in winter. And there is talk of a school," Salve answered.

"But Quakers always share as needed, and they don't need much, Salve."

"Truly, Kristina, I haven't been totally aware of what has been going on. I don't like quarrels. I've waited for you to spend more time at meeting. There is talk of assessing members."

"You mean, like the Lutheran church, like the church we fought against for so long? *Ja*?" Kristina asked in amazement, inhaling her breath.

"It's only talk, Kristina. But they are all good people."

She wondered if Salve really knew. It was true that she would see more Norwegians here than her parents saw in an entire year at Røyseland. But there, and in Stavanger Meeting, they shared grievances—seizures, fines, and imprisonments, and sharing made them easier and bolstered lagging faith. What happens to faith confronted with plenty?

There were twelve people at the Rosdales' table, including six Rosdale children, from six to eighteen, Ole Sawyer, clerk of the monthly meeting, and his wife, Hellen, and Anna Ravnaas. She and Soren Oleson, her husband, founded this New Stavanger Meeting—they were the first Quakers in Iowa, and because of them this group sat here today. Anna had sold her farm after Soren's death and moved to Paullina, Iowa, where land was cheaper. There she established the Mapleside Quaker Meeting near West Branch, but she visited Stavanger regularly.

Kristina watched these people, seeing how comfortable they felt with each other, which made her feel the more ill at ease. Norwegian carved wooden spoons, a small painted chest, a miniature hand-carved *snekke* complete with oars, made an unknown house more familiar, but she had only to glance out the window to know that she was in a strange country.

"All was quiet today before the storm, Salve Knudsen," Ole said, his steely eyes piercing the gaze of anyone who met them with his own. He wore a hat with a narrow brim, a combination between the sailors' and the Quakers' hats, a hat that looked as though it hadn't been removed in years. Kristina found herself wondering if he slept with it. His clothes were undistinguishable from his own antiquity—every wrinkle had earned its place. "And what says your new bride?"

"She does not know there is dissension, Ole. She has just arrived."

"Kristina Karlsdatter, your grandfather Tollak would wish to have you back at Røyseland, if you disappoint him here," Ole continued, addressing her. Kristina did not know of what she was being accused before she had committed the sin. But as Ole continued, she soon understood. "You are not for the new ways, are you?" He had met Tollak once, he said, and Anna here, attended the meeting when her mother took vows. "Dost thou know of it, Kristina?"

"It was before I was born," Kristina answered, nervous to be so directly addressed and wondering about the new ways.

"Thou sayest so?" Old Ole's steely eyes mocked her as she realized the stupidity of her remark.

The group shifted uncomfortably until Malinda said, "Kristina, everyone has heard of Tollak Røyseland. I am proud to know his granddaughter." Kristina smiled at her and relaxed.

Anna Ravnaas said that she remembered Anna Tonetta well, that she was a true daughter of Israel, and remembered her bridegroom, Karl, that Kristina's mother was her age, asking how Anna Tonetta fared to see her daughter depart. She reached across the long oval table and patted Kristina on the forearm, saying, "You haven't come to the end of the world, you know, child."

"You will find out, Kristina, that we are becoming evangelists, here, some of us," Ole continued. His face softened as he continued to explain that the conflict was old, and it was between Quakers who were content to sit in complete silence if need be, as of old, rather than to have speakers exhort the members to search for sin in their hearts, dragging it out for all to see, ranting about the devil.

Silent grace brought them back to the quiet presence of God in the house, and then Malinda passed boiled beef and potatoes, roasted pork, applesauce made from apples kept in the fruit cave. There was wheat bread, but also fladbrod and *lefse*. Ole talked while they ate.

Kristina wasn't certain that she wanted to know all that he said, how dissension rankled the community. Already she could tell that these Quakers were not like those in Norway, that maybe it was the flatness that changed them in some way and would change her, that in its sameness, each person had to try to be different. Maybe it was the lack of anything to fight for, or against. "We're building a new continent," she'd heard Salve say, over and over. But this house was different, too, far more substantial than any farmer would have in Norway. Even a clock in a wooden box, a larger table than she had ever seen except at Endre Dahl's house, with a center pedestal instead of four legs.

The quarrels of the Quakers had arrived long ago in Norway, but they had passed through and gone on as the tremor of a passing storm ebbs and dies. Kristina sat there chewing beef, thinking of Reier Reierson, merchant from Stavanger, who often interpreted for visiting English Quakers, how he'd written a refutation of some English paper—she was only sixteen or seventeen when it happened—and presented it at yearly meeting in Stavanger. The meeting rejected it and its premise. After that, Reier Reiersen had emigrated with his widowed sister, whose skipper husband had gone down with his ship. She had a daughter. Where had they gone? Had she asked, Anna Ravnaas would have told her that Reiersen was one of the signers of a letter recommending her, Anna, to American Friends, written in 1856, as was Endre Dahl and Asbjorn Kloster. Anna would also have told her, had she asked, that this

Reier Reiersen and his sister and her daughter had come to this very community, but that he had never attended the Quaker church. His sister and her daughter were Lutherans.

The dozens of things Kristina wanted to know she didn't ask. But she didn't have to. Malinda said she would come to see her this week, to see what she needed, to tell her how to find it. Kristina was comforted.

Malinda was as good as her word. She came to Kristina's house midweek, driving a single horse and carriage, bringing fladbrod, last year's potatoes, carrots, and apples from her root cellar. More important, she brought news.

Malinda was a plump, cheerful, and vigorous woman. She tied her horse to the hitching post in front of the house, talking while she gathered up her basket. Kristina noticed that a small button was off of her shirtwaist and saw herself to be judgmental.

"Now let's see what you need, Kristina, wife of Salve. We are glad you've come. That man has been inseparable from this farm ever since he came here, looking at it for years before he could buy it, and then building this house." She nodded toward it as they entered together. "Nice job he did, too. And this furniture." Her eyes swept the room. "But now he'll be a little more sociable." She put her hand on Kristina's arm, saying, "He's a good man, Kristina Karlsdatter," looking into her eyes as though to find whether or not Kristina was worthy. And then she patted Kristina's arm. "Now, what can I do for you?" she asked, and Kristina knew that she had somehow passed the test. She was happy to be called *Karlsdatter*.

They took places at the kitchen table, and Kristina poured coffee, saying, "You can tell me about Serena Roinestad."

"But how did I know you'd ask me that?" She paused. "I did know, because it is obvious that there is a problem at meeting. Those of us here have got a bit used to it. But for someone who knows nothing about it..."

"Salve told me nothing. Until today. Even then, he didn't tell me very much."

"That's because he doesn't really know very much. He hasn't been involved. He's been totally dedicated to"—Malinda looked around the kitchen and glanced into the living room—"to building a home for you and bringing you here."

"Then what is it?"

"Kristina Karlsdatter, it is simple. The meeting is divided between those who want to keep the old ways and those who want the new." She explained that some wanted a paid minister, assessments, that some even wanted to sing hymns and to stop the queries. Those who kept to old ways got very wrought when Serena spoke, and that was why Ole didn't want her to, because she stirred up people to high emotions, called herself the voice of God Himself, and God could speak *at any time*. Tonnes didn't want them to hear a voice that challenged every shadow on the prairie as the devil. "It is easy for the devil to travel here, Kristina. But not to hide."

Kristina had been so fearful that Malinda had come to persuade her to go along with the newer ways that she laughed in relief.

"Kristina, do you think it humorous?" Malinda placed her hands on her hips as she looked at Kristina, her face curious.

"Malinda, oh no, I am only relieved. I thought that you, maybe that you..." She couldn't finish.

"That I agreed with Serena?" Malinda said, laughing. "No wonder you laughed. I will tell you what is most important that you know here, Kristina," Malinda continued, scrutinizing Kristina. "You need to know what things grow well here." She explained how the seasons were different from Norway, that the soil was different, how she would give Kristina seed potatoes, cuttings from berries, seeds of vegetables, that seeds could be started now, in cold frames that Salve must build. How Kristina would be doing more outside work than she did in Stavanger.

"Did Endre Dahl have a gardener?" she asked Kristina. "I wish you could have brought some fresh cod. I miss it. Herring, too, But you'll find at the Legrand store, dried cod in boxes, and *lutefisk*. And hardtack." She told how the store even had pure washed Norwegian wool, but she thought maybe Salve would get some sheep, although they ate the grass too close for cattle. "The winters are bitter, Kristina." She said they were nothing like Norway, that boots, sheepskins were needed for bitter cold, and wind lasted for days, that going to meeting was impossible.

Malinda described things Kristina needed to know and perhaps would not have thought to ask: that a cave—their *stabbur*—had to be dug in the ground to keep things from freezing, that it kept potatoes and carrots, turnips, cabbage all winter and would keep milk, cheese, dried meats in summer—even fresh meat for a while.

Kristina found herself talking to her mother, in between the words and sentences of Malinda. *Mor, it is all right. I will be happy. Mor, listen to me. Thank you for the lysestake...*Tears came often and quickly to her.

Malinda saw, and placed her arms on Kristina's shoulders. "Kristina, you will be homesick, but you'll soon not have enough time. Maybe you can get your parents to come here, and—"

"No, Malinda, Grandfather Tollak is too old. He's seventy-seven. Mother wouldn't leave him."

"Well, you'll go back someday, with a fine brood of children. When is your first?" Malinda smiled at her. "It's always like this at first, but you'll be all right. Everybody helps. And we have Bertha Norland, the midwife from Roldal, land of trolls. She's a spinster, short and warty, like a troll herself. But she's good."

"But—but," Kristina sputtered.

"Kristina, you're pregnant," Malinda announced, simply.

And Kristina's face changed from tears to bewilderment to joy. "But why do you think...Malinda, am I truly?"

The two women embraced each other. "I am so ashamed of myself, Malinda, for not knowing, for these tears," which Kristina dried on her apron.

"Never be ashamed of tears, Kristina, they keep you pure. Remember them. And now I must go. *Uff ta!*" she exclaimed. "It's late."

In October, at the meeting for worship, Ole Sawyer, clerk of meeting, called the small Stavanger meetinghouse on the central Iowa prairie to order. A celebratory mood was in the crisp air, the sky above was as blue as the summer sea in the Stavangerfjord. Brilliant oranges and reds of maple and oak, tawny golden yellows of poplars put alight by the hand of God—a blaze of fire before the death of summer, God's nature gaudy compared to the black and gray uniforms that filed into the gray meetinghouse.

Besides summer's richness, the Stavanger School had opened its doors for the first season. Indebtedness was minimal because of volunteer work; the total cost had been $2,741.25. The first floor had a large assembly room, small classrooms, a small parlor, and a central hall leading to the upstairs dormitories. The basement contained the kitchen and dining room. Coal-burning stoves provided heat, and the students were required to carry the kindling and the coal, and to tend the fires.

Twenty-four boarders and twenty-two day students were enrolled. Room and board for an eight-week term was twelve dollars, tuition was three dollars for primary, four for advanced. Students were to speak English familiar: to use *thou* and *thee*. There was no uniform since clothes worn for common, as everyday clothes were called, were uniform enough. There were to be no musical instruments, no books other than those chosen by the school. No one had a musical instrument anyway; few had books other than the Bible and *Farmers' Almanac*. The school day would begin with recitation of memorized Bible verses. New immigrants were allowed to audit English classes.

So the prairie had now established a boarding school, farmers had built more farm buildings, acquired more land, more animals, and the Quaker community around Legrand, Iowa, was growing.

CHAPTER FOUR

On December 30, 1885, the temperature outside was zero degrees, and the sun reflected blinding prisms of light on eight inches of snow when Salve Knudsen harnessed his red mare, Solveig and hitched her to his cutter. The harness was stiff in his hands from the cold, and he had warmed the bit less than he ought, but the cutter was light and would glide across the snow.

The landscape lay white and still like some great Arctic wasteland, except for the occasional and comforting outline of a barn or the smoke curling out of a house's chimney. When the snow was deep, communication between the houses was by foot. Sometimes there was none for days at a time, except for those Norwegians who had remembered how to make and use skis. Such deep snow didn't usually happen by December 30; then there was less than six inches, but the cold itself was huge and white, and the slightest sound crackled in its brittle air. Salve set off at a trot, restraining the mare, tensed by his abruptness. Her warm breath and his etched little white puffs in the sharp blue of the sky. Feeling the warmth of the sheepskin at his feet, Salve pulled it up over his lap. Had it not been in the cutter already, he would have forgotten it.

He was on his way to fetch the midwife, Bertha Norland, who lived eight miles away, an unmarried woman who had her own farm and farmhouse. There were always new immigrants to work others' land until they moved on to buy their own farms, and such independence gave Bertha Norland the freedom *not* to be referred to as a spinster. "Long in the tooth" was used to describe her behind her back; married women could be any age without appellation.

Salve's first stop was at the Rosdales to tell Malinda that Kristina's labor had begun. Malinda had heard the clip-clop of the mare's hooves on the frozen ground, the squeak of the snow under the light runners—she had been expecting this visit. She already knew that

Salve would look a little frenzied and need her reassurance that women gave birth in all parts of the world without problems. Brisk Bertha would have no patience with his worries.

"Hallo!" she hailed him, opening her kitchen door to the waft of icy air.

"Malinda, I'm going for Bertha. Kristina is alone."

"Sigbjorn will take me right away." She waved him on.

Kristina's first pains had begun at daybreak; now it was already nine o'clock. Salve fed the livestock while she had made breakfast: coffee, bread, cheese, fried eggs, and porridge, which only he had eaten. "Thou art not well?" he asked her.

"We'll be well enough before the day is over."

Salve had looked at her quizzically, until he had understood the "we" not to mean him. In minutes, he was off, excited, worried, hating to leave her, waving to Kristina.

She had woven blankets, hemmed cotton flannel sheets, made little vests of wool and of cotton. Salve had made a cradle. Important to Kristina was the fact that they had had their first harvest together, and she had learned about new fruits and vegetables, grains, meats and how to preserve them, thanks to Malinda. Salve had dug the cave for the vegetables they had grown. The barn had four cows, three horses, and a dozen lambs, not to mention the chickens, a few ducks to eat over the winter, and pork, already butchered and made into sausages, hams, lard. Malinda had taught Kristina how to preserve meat they had never had in Norway.

"Where did you learn all this?" she once asked Malinda, who'd answered, "From the German community at Dillon, and some from the Indians who taught the first settlers, they say. The Indians taught us how to make fennelor," and she'd laughed, referring to the dried lamb that Norwegians had made for generations.

While waiting for Malinda and for Bertha, Kristina laid out blankets and the winding sheets that swaddled newborns. Occasionally, she leaned over to grasp a kitchen chair. Most of the time, she sat next to a kitchen window opaque with frost, etched with geometric stars and snowflake crystals, brilliant in the sun. Kristina had never seen its like before, but she had never experienced such cold either. She couldn't see outside or the approach of the Rosdale carriage, the dark horses moving in the blinding whiteness, the sharp black shadows of the wheels turning on the snow—Sigbjorn thought it too early for sleighs—but she could hear the crunching and the squeak made by the wheels.

"You're right on time, before the big snows," Malinda called, ushering herself into the house with a slice of chill air. "Now, to bed with you. How far apart are your pains? If Bertha doesn't make it, goodness knows we can manage." She added under her breath, "We women have to be brave. Men worry more about their mares, except for Salve."

Why couldn't she be more like Malinda, cheery and uncomplicated? Kristina wondered. She couldn't tell how frightened she was, but with Malinda here, her fears and worries vanished. Malinda's presence was like that. So Kristina smiled and said to herself, which really was to her mother, *Mor, it is all right. You know, because you've been through this so many times.* She had got into the habit, in the many hours she was alone on the farm, of addressing her mother in her thoughts. So alone she had never thought to be, within walls, which were the only protection between herself and the great emptiness. But now there would be someone to share the walls.

Bertha Norland arrived, brisk and businesslike. She regarded the stage of Kristina's labor, timed the contractions, pressed on Kristina's belly, checked her vaginally.

"Uff-ta!" she said. "A long ways to go." Bertha's presence made Kristina long for her mother. She would have liked a gentle presence, instead of this squat, wart-faced woman with bristles on her chin, her eyes bright and blinking and yellowish, like a toad's eyes caught unawares. Bertha ordered Malinda around, to bring hot water, to bring wet warm cloths, over and over, so they would always be warm and waiting, to bring coffee for herself. She scolded her patient. "Now be patient. Don't grimace so. This won't hurt you."

Karl Salvesen's cries broke the brittle silence of the noon hour and caused three women to laugh and a man's face to light with thankfulness. Even unsmiling Bertha laughed to hold such a strong child in her hands, slippery and squirming. "Hungry, he is. Well, he'll soon take it out of you, Kristina Karlsdatter. He's just like his father," Bertha said as she roughly passed this child to his mother.

Washed and swaddled, the baby lay in Kristina's arms. "Come in," Bertha commanded Salve. "See your son."

"Karl Salvesen Røyseland," Kristina said, looking up at Salve. "Is the name all right?"

Salve knelt by the side of the bed, his big hands awkwardly attempting to touch his son, his eyes wet and his voice husky. "Ja, Ja, Kristina Min! After your father and—and Røyseland."

"Touch him, Salve, he is yours." Salve laid one calloused finger on the infant's cheek.

"Kristina, let us take Røyseland for our American name, from here on, in his honor. But let's call it Roseland. And do we need Salvesen?"

"But he *is* Salve's son!"

"He is, without saying. But we are Americans. We don't need so many names in America." He smiled and stroked Kristina's forehead. "It isn't so important who your father is and where you come from; it's what you do, Kristina Min."

But it is important, Kristina was thinking. *It is important who Karl is, and Knud, and Tollak and Anna Tonetta.* She blinked back tears, her joy mixed with sorrow. One tear falls for each one of them, she thought, and one for Røyseland. Kristina didn't know how different was the meaning of Roseland, as though one could turn black into white by naming.

"Kristina Min," Salve added, still kneeling, "We may need a bigger house."

Kristina touched the head of her husband and new father: *Mor, he is the rain to me and the sun in the sky. Mor, now I understand your many children.*

Bertha Norland observed this scene as though she herself had made this child, as though, perhaps, she lay as Kristina lay, encircled by the arms of a man whose son she had just borne. And then her face hardened, and she turned away. But no one noticed Bertha; even Malinda, who usually saw everything, was also too occupied and happy with the success of Kristina's first delivery. Weren't midwives destined to be forgotten if the birthing were a success? But Bertha didn't like to be forgotten.

* * *

On November 20, 1887, Kristina and Salve Roseland, along with their two sons, Karl, aged two, and Knud, six months, drove the eight miles to Marshalltown to Apgar Photography Studio for a family portrait. Kristina and Salve both wore their dark wedding clothes, and the small boys wore the clothes of infants: long white linen dresses with tiny collars. They were photographed in the studio, a study in black and white, next to a faux-marble fireplace with a flower-embossed facade and marble vases on the mantelpiece. Salve was sitting in a throne-sized chair holding Karl, the five bone buttons of his wedding suit buttoned, his vest hidden behind the white linen dress of Karl, seated in his father's lap. Kristina was standing, holding six-month old Knud. She hadn't wanted to be photographed next to such fanciful objects, but it hadn't seemed important to Salve and the Apgar Studio didn't understand why she had protested, or why it was that Quakers didn't admire such things. Kristina hadn't wanted to cause a disturbance, but she was troubled by Salve seated in a pompous chair with leather arms, decorated with purple ropes of twisted fringe. Salve's beard was wider and freer than it was in his wedding photo, and his broad face and steadfast eyes and heavy sun-browned face and windburned hands said to all the world: I am Salve Roseland, farmer and landowner, and I am an American, husband of Kristina and father of two sons. Here they are. Here we are.

Kristina sent the finished photograph to Anna Tonetta with a letter that said: "Mor, here we are with our two sons, Karl and Knud, named after father and Salve's father. We are well, and we are content.

"America is different from what I heard about Amerika. Few in our world wear fancy dress, but we are plainer than most and are seeming shadows when we appear in the town of Marshall, where others may wear silk and wools with checks or plaids, and we, mostly black wool or gray cotton. We keep our faith but are not as strict as at Røyseland. There are others here who now have paid ministers, yet call themselves Quakers, but the Stavanger Meeting has separated us from them. Some of them have taken to wearing clothes of some color; others want to hymn in meeting but can't get permission. There are some ranters like the American woman you told me about at the meeting when you and father were married. We read Scriptures at home each morning and keep silent prayer, too. Here we are, Mother Anna Tonetta—Salve and I, and Karl and Knud, Salvesens."

She wrote the letter by the light of a candle in the brass candleholder her mother had placed in her trunk. Every day her hands touched, lifted, and dusted the candleholder. She argued with herself about polishing it with wood ashes, believing that cleanliness was godliness, wanting her house to sparkle and invite God's presence. But she knew that her mother's fingerprints were on it, that she could touch where her mother's hands had touched. Even if it blackened, she would not polish it.

As she wrote, she thought about the candleholder and then about herself, wanting to tell her mother of the comfort she had, of her fear that such comfort would seem ungodly. She wanted to tell of the desire she felt for her husband. *Mor, is it sinful to experience such pleasure in it? Is physical love supposed to be for women a duty only?* She wanted to ask if Anna Tonetta had enjoyed sex, but she couldn't even finish the thought: there was no one to ask, not even Malinda. She wanted to tell her mother how Salve worked with a furor, both enchanted and unbelieving at what the soil produced, that Salve thought of nothing but a bigger barn and the fine house he was building, that Lars Bryngelsen, the carpenter from Stavanger, worked for him building and building. Houses for corn, hay, cattle. *Houses, Mor, for pigs*! But that the winters were bitter, and that all animals needed shelter, and they themselves would even have a furnace in the cellar that would heat the house above it.

She got up from the table where the candle flickered and went to listen at the children's door. Salve was checking the livestock before going to bed. Hearing the boys' even breathing, she returned to the letter that formed in her mind and not on the page. She pulled her merino shawl more tightly around her as she felt the evening's chill when the fire went low, thinking of what she wanted to write but couldn't, wondering if her mother could read the sadness in her face in the photograph, because, when it was taken she had been thinking of her mother and father and Tollak and Røyseland, land of stones: *We fought them for our bread, as you still do. And we fought to keep the budstikke away, we learned to bear prison.* Now, she was in America, wife of Salve Knudsen. That this photograph was taken so that Anna Tonetta and Karl and Tollak might share in her sons so faraway. And that if her face was sad, she was, anyway, content with her new life. That not even the sound of a pebble grated on the plowshares, that the land was flat enough to be pulled by horses. *Mor*, she wrote, *I am often lonely for Røyseland*, but Kristina meant that she was lonely for its simple poverty.

When Salve returned from the barn, Kristina folded the short letter, which had taken so long to write, and placed it in an envelope with the photos. The day that Kristina's letter was taken to the Legrand post office by Salve, who had to buy a new saw blade at the general store, Ina Tobiasdatter, daughter of Anna Tonetta's brother, Tobias, embarked from Stavanger, Norway, to America, by way of New York.

Quaker tailors in England in the late sixteen hundreds burned their silks and ribbons, Quaker merchants ceased to sell rings and toys, Quaker families gave away veneered and garnished furniture and replaced them with decent plain ones of solid wood; fancy paneling, twisted banisters were replaced with plain woodwork painted a plain gray color. There were not, even for the earliest Quakers, any gravestones, no flower gardens, no musical notes either from human voices or from instruments, no theater, dancing, or reading of fiction. Such things, the Quakers believed, heightened the imagination, and thus enticed men and women to the excesses of the flesh, and the flesh was evil.

In the Stavanger, Iowa, community there were no veneered tables to get rid of, but all aspects of the families' lives, from dress to household furnishings, gardens, private business affairs to community affairs, were answerable each month to the queries at monthly meeting.

At the queries, Ole Tostenson was reprimanded for whistling a tune while working in his field—he had been overheard by Thore Medhus who was on his way to Legrand. Marthe Ingebritson reprimanded her six-year-old son for using the word "darn" to a frog that didn't want to be caught. That same son reported that his friend, Frichjof, had said "gee" at the same time. Helga Botnen was spoken to for having a coverlet on her bed that had the outline of flowers in needlepoint. Gardens should not be for show, although roses were allowed. Lars Stangeland would allow his wife to have only white roses and not red ones. "The color of the devil," he said, one day in meeting.

"Lars, wouldst thou eat only green apples?" Salve Roseland asked him. No one dared laugh.

The monthly meeting was concerned about the origin of some of these wrongdoings: Where had Ole heard the tune he whistled? Who had used the swear word used by Martha's son?

In a farming community in Iowa in the late eighteen hundreds, it wasn't difficult to be free of corruption, isolated and homogenous as it was, since corruption must come from without. Meekness of spirit helped to keep it out: rebellious natures meant trouble.

When she arrived in America, Kristina's cousin, Ina Tobiasdatter, was twenty-three years old, her scuttle-shaped bonnet discouraged glances and encouraged meekness, but underneath it was a perfect oval face with chiseled nose and full lips, dark brows over blue eyes, yellow hair. But beauty itself was suspect. *Handsome is as handsome does* was the rule. If one looked underneath her bonnet into the eyes of Ina Tobiasdatter, they returned one's gaze as serenely as they ought. Kristina saw Røyseland in Ina's face. Ina was to stay with Kristina and Salve to help with the household as long as Ina needed to, which meant until she married.

"How art thou?" was Ina's greeting as she descended Salve's carriage, which brought her from the Legrand train depot to Salve's house. She untied her bonnet strings and removed her hat where they stood, in the kitchen.

"Please sit while I make coffee," Kristina offered, and Ina sat on a wooden chair, watching Kristina's preparations as Kristina's questions poured out. "And Røyseland? Mor? Far? Thy father, Tobias? And Bestefar Tollak?" She put the coffee on to boil and sliced bread, unrolled the water-sprinkled lefse, spreading it with butter and a generous sprinkling of sugar.

"They are well. Tollak is hearty, but he is old." Yes, nearly eighty, Kristina knew.

"And my little sisters, Anna and Sarah?"

Ina Tobiasdatter sat on the straight chair, smoothing her gray skirts. She was not someone Kristina knew well, but she was in America and in Kristina's home, and she was Kristina's cousin, one of many who would be offered a home in exchange for house help. Ina was quick to examine Kristina's circumstances.

Her blue eyes traveled around the kitchen, the cabinets for dishes and pots, the pullout flour bin, sugar bin, the small pantry off the kitchen. She could see into the living room in this small house, and her eyes came to rest upon the horsehair sofa. If Kristina had been regarding her carefully, she would have seen her lips tighten.

"Anna and Sarah want to come to America. They all do. All Norwegians want to come. The priests are again interfering. Even though the Church now sends ministers, they try not to grant permission to emigrate. So people go anyway. Tollak is saddened by it, feeling left. 'I have nothing to go for,' he says, 'and everything to stay for,' he says. 'Røyseland,' he says." As Ina related these things, Kristina looked away.

Salve noticed. He had been sitting aside, listening. He joined the conversation, "You must see our sons. You will, tomorrow, when they wake. Then you will see the land, the cattle, Kristina's stabbur." And he winked at Kristina. "It even has grass growing on the roof, just like in Norway," referring to their vegetable cave.

"And how fares the New Stavanger Meeting?" Ina asked, directing her question to Salve.

"It goes well, but there are some differences of opinion about how to conduct the meetings for worship. Stavanger Meeting has chosen to remain conservative and broke off from the Legrand monthly meeting. Some still aren't satisfied," Salve said, wanting always to pacify rather than agitate.

"We don't have problems of our young men going to jail, Ina. Nobody seizes our cows or pigs. There is no budstikke, and so we find smaller problems to disagree upon," Kristina said, pouring the coffee from the blue enamel pot it was boiled in, into the white, utilitarian cups.

"Oh, but we did have Quakers in jail once, Ina." Salve told how, in Marshalltown, Sigbjorn Rosdale and Christian Tjossem and Ole Olsen went to apply for their naturalization papers and were put in jail because they wouldn't take off their hats. They wouldn't eat the supper brought to them, because they said they hadn't earned it, and they said they had to go home and feed their hogs and milk the cows. Salve chuckled and leaned back in his chair, adding that the judge found out they were Quakers, so he apologized and let them go. "So you see, Ina, we too have been jailed here." Salve's eyes twinkled with pleasure at the benignity of their sufferings in America.

"Salve, we have forgotten how to suffer," Kristina said, looking at her husband with her steady orange-flecked eyes. "Sometime we will need to know."

Salve was startled by Kristina's remark. She had laid the table in the kitchen and poured the coffee. Each pulled a chair up to it, heads bowed in silent grace.

When Salve and Kristina raised their heads and their eyes after silent prayers, Ina still sat there with her head bowed, so they had to honor her and bow theirs again. Ina remained still and silent with bowed head while the coffee cooled. Still she sat. Finally, she raised her head, eyes still closed, and said in a voice unlike her speaking voice, a voice that Salve, especially, would learn to dread, "God, let not the seeds of damnation fall upon this house, let us walk humbly and cast out the devil, and let sin fall behind our steps. Amen."

Both Salve and Kristina were startled to hear "devil and damnation" spoken in their house. Just as they didn't need baptism to cleanse them of their sins, they didn't need cleansing from what they didn't have. Where God was, there was peace. But Ina was a guest, a cousin, and would remain with them for some time. For now, they would say nothing. After Ina's words, Salve forgot Kristina's.

Ina responded more to ministers like Sybil Jones than to the older Quakers' quiet and unflinchable faith, who knew *peace that passeth understanding*. In Norway, they had needed courage to withstand hardships, inflicted by church and state. In America, the devil had retreated; Ina was born to seek him out, and she would devote her life to it.

Ina Tobiasdatter remained with them for a year. She was industrious, clean, and neat, responding quickly to what needed to be done without asking. But there were other things.

"Kristina, when I mended Knud's shirt, a piece of tatting was torn, so I removed it. He does not need decoration. Only the devil does."

"Ina, he is only a child."

"And wine is only wine, at the beginning. Lace is an early step along the way," Ina answered.

"On the way to what, Ina?"

"The road to hell is paved with vanity. Kristina, don't you know the devil loves your perfect handiwork. You call it housekeeping." Ina looked hard at Kristina, with intense, penetrating eyes.

Ina's beauty was subtracted by the coldness of it, Kristina thought. She was beginning to fear her.

But Ina continued. "Kristina, your perfection should be spent on your soul and Salve's, not on your house."

Kristina never told these things to Salve, that her own piety was daily held to up to examination by Ina Tobiasdatter. Ina's presence became the eye of God, or the devil, who observed Kristina's daily activities, condemning a tuck, a vain stitch.

At Røyseland, Kristina had placed butter in wooden carved molds copied from a mountain flower. Tollak himself had carved the mold and presented it to her before she left. Now the only decoration left in the butter was the mark of the butter paddle as she made the final gestures on its finished mound. In such little ways, she won Ina's approval, and she now wanted Ina's approval. Kristina put away a silver spoon with a twisted handle and a gold-washed spangle hanging from it, a gift from Endre Dahl.

Who could have known, Salve thought, *that there is poison somewhere in the heart of this clear-eyed girl!*

A year later, Ina married Sundoff Christiansen. Salve was relieved but troubled for Sundoff, who was too new an arrival to know a great deal about Ina. But Sundoff needed a wife, and he was as handsome as Ina. He was not a man of determination, but Ina had enough for them both. Kristina, too, was relieved by Ina's departure, but Ina's conscience remained with her.

It wasn't only Salve's household that suffered from Ina's presence—the Meeting, too, felt her stings, both in worship and in the monthly meetings for business when the queries were answered. To some members, Ina would drive the moneylenders from the temple: She was God's instrument, and who could ignore God's voice? For many, Ina Tobiasdatter destroyed the quietness and communion of Quaker worship. Lines were drawn, but they were not clear-cut: Quaker practice was threatened by frontier evangelical reform, but no one could determine exactly where and how Quaker silence and patience mixed with brimstone. The question, which troubled thoughtful members of Stavanger Meeting, was *who* designated Ina—God, or herself. But Ina Tobiasdatter was the granddaughter of Tollak, like Kristina, his flesh and his nurture. So they tried to be patient.

A year and a half after Ina's departure, Kristina and Salve's first daughter, Marna, was born; two years after that, another son, Johann. Then two more daughters two years apart, named Inger and Klara—six children in less than ten years of marriage. All of them were delivered by Bertha Norland, who remained two to three days after each delivery to help with the new child. Kristina found, increasingly, that Bertha's presence was the worst part of her delivery and confinement.

Each time Kristina lay in childbirth, Bertha's toad eyes fixed on her, amber and unblinking, as though waiting for a spider to hatch, or for a fly whose iridescent wings would be snatched out of midair. "Harder," Bertha would say, "push harder," slapping Kristina's swollen abdomen, kneading it so that it hurt. *She is from Roldal where they believe in trolls*, Kristina thought. Bertha talked less and less to her and more and more to Salve. From her bed, Kristina would hear them in the evening, talking about crops, about planting only in the waxing moon, Bertha would say. And Salve would agree. They spoke of breeding cattle, too. Men's things, not women's.

The children didn't like her either. "Fetch this," Bertha would say. "Get that." The Norwegian girl house helpers dreaded her arrival. Kristina never discussed Bertha with Salve. Ina's year in the Roseland household made Kristina discuss household problems less and less. Ina had became a thorn, but she was Kristina's thorn. And she needed Bertha.

By the time the fourth child was born, the house was finished and a second barn built, big enough for ten horses, a dozen milk cows, and hay to feed them all winter. Salve bought more land until he had a section of rich Iowa farmland, six hundred acres, a mile square. He had built a large hog house and a poultry house.

The new house had a cement-floored basement for vegetables and fruits, although Kristina still preferred the cave. She hadn't argued with Salve about the expansions—they needed more space, but she was too busy with pregnancies and babies and the household to occupy herself about the farm buildings and land. But the scale of it all sat like a lump of dough in her stomach, which would neither rise nor digest. *How much is enough?* she asked herself.

CHAPTER FIVE

"Kristina Min, are you all right?" Salve asked his wife as he lay next to her, aware of her night restlessness. He placed his hand on her breasts, respectful of her belly, big with her seventh child. "Are you both all right?" he asked again as he lightly placed his hand on the about-to-be-born mound of child. Kristina squeezed his hand.

It was early March 1897, the time of predawn, when Kristina was wakeful with thoughts and the discomfort of full term. The snow was still deep, but by now it was tattered by winds, gutted by freezing and thawing, blackened here and there in spots where the sun had melted through. Such sporadic melting was the only sign of spring; at this time of year, a blizzard could come as easily as rain. This past winter, snow had drifted to heights of ten feet and they had been snowed in, without outside contact for several weeks at a time. Karl and Knud had remained at the Stavanger boarding school. Kristina had worried that the school might run out of coal, that epidemics of whooping cough or scarlet fever might invade the school. During the winter, four of her children had had serious cases of measles, and there had been nothing to do for them but cool them with cold cloths, yet not let them chill in unheated bedrooms. Marna, aged seven, had helped with Johann, who had been sickest. His temperature had reached a danger point, and Kristina watched, helplessly, his flushed cheeks and burning eyes. His forehead scorched the back of her hand. Waiting and hoping and praying were all that could be done, but he, and they, had got well. Only little Klara had not come down with measles. Would she still?

Kristina felt her seventh child move vigorously, knowing that her sleeplessness preceded her labor. She didn't hear a sound from the children, but she was aware of the cold's utter silence as it curled around the corners of the down quilt trying to enter. The most intense cold seemed always a prelude to morning. Or perhaps she merely felt it more severely when she was most awake. She heard Salve's regular breathing—he had promptly gone back to sleep. He sleeps as undisturbed as a well baby, Kristina thought, and the children, too, in this big house with its oak woodwork and oak floors, the oak horsehair sofa. She noted the faint smell of varnish made pungent by the cold winter air, the oak smell changed to varnish long ago. *But now and then, the wood tries to keep its own smell,* she thought, *in the kitchen woodbox, the wood smell wins, keeping true to itself.* She noted the whiff of kerosene from the extinguished lamps, the candle wax from the boys' rooms, which lingered long after she had tucked them in. But the odor of sleep predominated: Salve's slightly acrid, the boys' more like month-old puppies, the girls' like lambs, although Kristina knew it was from the lambswool coverlets over them. If she were to walk blindfolded into the bedrooms, even if the children had switched rooms, she knew that her nose would tell her who was there. Little Klara still had a sweet baby smell, like a kitten; soon hers would change, with a newborn baby smell in the house again. Little Klara would be relegated to a new role—the next-to-youngest child. She wondered how the child would adjust, spoiled as she was by herself and all the others, because she was the youngest.

She twitched her nose, as memory brought the odors of Røyseland to her: barley used in fladbrod, the lye smell of lutefisk, codfish balls in a white sauce, the earthy smell of potatoes before they are cooked, with a bit of clinging earth, cheese and milk odors on wooden tables that remained traceable in the scrubbed wood, wood ashes on the hearth's fire. In America, their odors were different. The house was different, their food was different: they ate meat rather than fish. Now she noted the predominant taint of varnish, but dominant over all was the smell of bitter cold.

Mor, I have water in the kitchen. Not like the spray from the falls at Rafoss, filled with pine and rocks and the sea air, but water that I pump right into the kitchen from a well under the house. Mor, I always talk to you with words I never write. Somehow I am thinking about potatoes, how Ole said when I arrived that there would soon be little ones, meaning potatoes, and I thought he meant children. That was fourteen years and six children ago. Soon there will be seven. Potatoes are shriveled now. Not like me.

In the cave are pails and pails of milk that Siri skims for the cream and churns into butter in a big round barrel churn. I make more cheese than we can eat: curd cheese, caraway cheese, foods, as you taught me. The milk we don't use is fed back to the calves—the poor cheated creatures suck on the fingers of the boys held in a pail of skimmed milk until they learn to drink. They bawl endlessly in the barn, missing something large and comforting although they don't know what it is. Mor, the barn is a man's world, full of horse sweat and leather, cows' milky ever-present odor, birth smells, rich hay, even the wastes of the cattle and horses, which smell like nutty walnuts. Salve's barn is not like the stable where Christ was born as Røyseland is, with its few goats, a cow or two, and the sheep, each with a name. Each one seemed so trusting, so innocent, looking to me for comfort.

Salve would call me foolish if he knew what I was telling you, because animals don't have souls. But they were my flock. Here the cattle, the sheep don't have names. The horses do, but they are too big to be trusted, and the cattle are too despairing and too busy reducing their mountains of hay. They behave as though they aren't going to get enough—they grasp hay, tossing their heads, and then they chew and chew and chew. Then Salve and the boys feed more hay which they chew and chew. It never stops.

Mor, I am foolish. I have my own flock now, who look to me, trust me, need me. Six, and within days, another. My house is like Salve's barn, always a new life. I am forty-three years old, and I have been gone from Røyseland for fourteen years that have fallen through my fingers like sand. Sometimes it seems as though I have been away forever. I see your face, and Far's, and Tollak's. I wish I could run my hands over his face, but he would feel my tears. You would understand them, Mor. I want to touch the lines on your face, which I know so well—they will have deepened. One by one, your children have deserted you, and your brothers' and sisters' children, from the valleys and the fjords and the hamlets, from Kvinesdal to Stavanger to America. I hear Tollak saying, "How much goods does a man need? How much is more?"

Mor, I have thoughts black as the forests in Norway that lie deepest in the mountains where the trolls live, that we never believed in. Bertha says they are evil spirits from the devil. You would sometimes think Ina

Tobiasdatter grew up with trolls and believes in them. Some people have never escaped them, even here in America. Bertha hasn't, but she comes from Roldal. That is why people listen to Ina, Mor, because so many of them here at the Stavanger Meeting came together from the dark mountain forests of Roldal, where the demons could always hide. Here they can only hide in their hearts, and Ina has come to show us our hearts. Strange that Ina and Bertha hate each other when, in some ways, they are so alike. But Bertha is unmarried and feels it—no man could look at her. Mor, you will say that I have learned to judge, when you always taught me "Judge not, that ye be not judged."

My mind wanders, Mor. My thoughts are dark. I am afraid, and I don't know why. I think because I have too much, because I haven't earned it. Everything is too easy. Salve is kind and loving. He, too, thinks he has too much. But he keeps on trying to get more, and he keeps on getting more. He buys more land and then needs more horses to work it. And machinery, Mor. Papa would be amazed to see the machinery that tills and plows and sows and cuts, all work Papa does by hand, or with one pony. It seems Salve will never stop, he keeps on working harder, getting more and more. He says that I must keep him pure, that too much happiness tempts the devil. Mor, we never spoke of the devil at Røyseland. Ina has brought him, and Bertha carries him about with her on her warts and the hairs growing out of her chin, all the way from Roldal. But when I touch Salve, I forget the devil and Ina and Bertha.

Kristina reached over and put her hand on Salve's shoulder—he was on his side facing her. She touched his face, and he didn't stir. She felt a throb of desire. *Mor,* she continued, *I am full term, and I still desire him. Because of it I have done nothing but bear children and feed and clothe them, but I feel their souls lack nourishment from me. I haven't suffered one whit here for my faith that you and Father and Tollak fought so hard to believe in. I feel that He has forsaken me, or I Him, and I don't know where to find him. I have, Mor, because I can't accept what I can't have. I want Salve, but I also want the simpleness, the pure poverty of Røyseland. Mor, Hjelpe meg!*

Kristina cried out in the beginning light of dawn. She awakened, wondering at her dream, because in it she saw her mother's face.

She had looked into her mother's eyes!

A sound of little feet shifted her thoughts, a sound no more than a whisper rustling along the cold oak floor. It was little Klara, whimpering in the night, perhaps dreaming as she often did. Kristina reached down from her high bed and lifted up the two-year-old who cried, "Mor, Mor," through her tears, her cheeks red and wet, her small body heaving with sobs. She put her arms around her mother's neck, a soft curling form with icy feet.

"*Lille* Klara, sleep. Go back to sleep." Klara snuggled between father and mother, content and warm, while Kristina thought of the miracle just occurred: how an answer had come to her in her need, how she had been called back to the prairie in America by the needs of her children who would become what she would make of them. That is the message Kristina Karlsdatter Roseland received. God was speaking to her, through her mother, through her child: *A little child shall lead them.* At peace, she went back to sleep facing Salve, touching his shoulder, Klara curled between them.

Morning came cold and clear. Some of the snow would melt by the time noon arrived, Salve thought as he rose and glanced out the window, then looked upon Kristina and little Klara snuggled next to her. His clothes were on the straight-backed chair next to his side of the bed, and he tried to put them on without awakening either, the one-piece long underwear. A "union suit," they called it in America. Then a blue cotton flannel shirt and gray heavy cotton cord trousers. High-topped shoes over his woolen socks, a black woolen vest over his shirt.

"Salve, you are already dressed. See who is here!"

Salve sat down on the bedside and placed his arms around his wife. "Yes, I see. Stay in bed, Kristina, I feel you should stay here, in bed, just for a while. While I warm the house. You haven't slept well."

"I dreamed a bit, Salve, that's all. And then Klara came, crying. She was so cold."

They both looked at the sleeping child, who was often fretful. "She is so, so peaceful, and cozy, Salve. She won't be happy to have a new baby around, will she?"

Klara was spoiled by her older brothers and sisters. At age two, she had already learned the advantages of being little. Whether she was temperamental or spoiled, Kristina didn't know, but she was more fretful than her other children had been, her hair darker, straighter than the bushy red heads of hair her sons had. Only Marna had hair texture resembling Klara's, except that it was blonder. Klara's eyes were gray, blue, sometimes greenish, with dark brows slashed straight above them.

"No, but I will," Salve answered. "Are you all right?" He meant did she think it would be today.

Kristina shook her head negatively, but she wasn't really sure. She didn't want Bertha around until it was absolutely necessary.

At breakfast, Salve said, "Let us bow our heads in silent grace." Feeling the onset of labor, Kristina looked at the eight people seated around the breakfast table, counting Siri, the house helper and Nils Tollefsen, who had arrived in September and would stay until he had money to be independent. Kristina saw that Siri couldn't cook and wash for them alone, even for a few days, though Knud and Karl were remaining at the boarding school except for weekends, if the roads were passable enough through the snow to come home. Siri was only eighteen, and Klara was already whimpering with neglect; it would be worse when she would have to take second place to a baby. So it would be Bertha again who stayed. Kristina sighed, impatient to finish breakfast. Breakfast was not a meal they lingered over—there was too much work to be done, inside and outside. There was little or no conversation over the substantial food the family consumed: meat, cheese, cooked porridge, breads, coffee.

No one was allowed to leave the table until all were finished, but Kristina caught Salve's eye as he leaned back in his chair, finishing his coffee—*it is time*, her eyes said. *Time for Bertha.*

Siri was attentive to Klara, picking the crumbs from her apron before she was allowed to leave the table. Marna was waiting for Inger to finish when Salve stood, the signal that the meal was over, finished or not. "Johann," he said, "you stay with Nils this morning and help him with the chores. Marna, you help Siri, and watch Klara.

I am going to get Bertha."

"Mor, may I help?" Marna asked Kristina.

Kristina put her hands on each side of Marna's perfect oval face, holding it close to her own and replied, "Marna, do you remember when Klara came? When Inger came?"

"I remember Klara, Mor, and you were in bed for days, you were so sick. Will you be sick again?"

"No, Marna, I wasn't sick. I was only tired."

"Then you'll be tired again?"

"Yes, a little bit, Marna. Do you want a brother or a sister?"

"A sister, Mor, then I can teach her things. The boys are always outside. I can teach her to sew, and knit, all the things you've taught me." Kristina looked at Marna with pride; she was a serious child, accomplished for her years. It was hard to be the first daughter in a large farm family.

Salve arrived with Bertha within an hour. She was dressed in a black wool skirt and black jacket with full sleeves, a white blouse underneath it, a black silk bow tied around the collar. Bertha had deviated from the code of Quaker dress, but who ever really said that she was a Quaker? Her thin graying hair was pulled in a tight knot on top of her head, *like a knob handle she could be picked up by*, Kristina thought as Bertha whisked into the room. She wore her warts with aplomb, as though they were beauty marks. But Kristina was happy to see Bertha, perhaps for the first time. Her pains seemed the same, but she was tired, more than she remembered even before delivery.

"Uff-ta! Another child. When will you ever learn? Aren't there enough in this family? What room do I have this time? I have to go and change. Has your water broken?" Bertha didn't even look at her as she spoke.

"The guest room at the top of the stairs, Bertha. The same room you've always had. Yes, the water broke when Salve went to get you."

Bertha returned to Kristina's bedroom in her gray cotton dress with pinstripes and a bib apron that amply covered her dress. She tucked a white towel of Kristina's into her waistline, and set out to regard the stage of Kristina's labor.

"I guess I'll be here for a while. You could have waited awhile, you know. I don't think you're close yet," Bertha commented, while she examined the linens and infant blankets laid out by Kristina. "You've had an easy time, generally, haven't you, Kristina?" Bertha said, as she leaned over to regard her charge. "Maybe your luck won't hold this time. Who knows?"

"Why do you say that?" Kristina's throat tightened.

A large squat woman looked upon another woman in a position where she would never be: bearing the child of a man she loved and who loved her. Bertha's ears were still hearing Salve's praise of Kristina during the carriage ride. "I waited for her, and she for me, for seven years, Bertha. Imagine that! And I wouldn't trade her for all the golden wheat and corn that are in my barns. She is my gold. Deliver her of this child, and I swear it will be the last." She remembered his voice going husky, as she heard the clop of the horses hooves on the crusty frozen roads, and she remembered his face filling with emotion, his eyes swimming.

Love? Love is like that? she had asked herself, and she didn't know if she hated Kristina or Salve more at that moment. Now, as she bent over Kristina, she knew.

"The head isn't positioned right," Bertha said in measured words. "We can do nothing but wait."

Bertha's words came to Kristina like a sentence. Six deliveries without any real problems, and now this.

"You're not so young anymore, Kristina Karlsdatter. This sometimes happens in older women."

Kristina heard it again—the sting in Bertha's words. Condemnation.

Bertha's eyes narrowed as she looked at Kristina. Why, she wondered, should it all be Kristina's, and not hers: children, Salve, love. She had never known a man, nor had any man ever looked at her. When he did, like Salve, he told her about another woman, one he loved. Who lay here now.

And so the day began. And wore on slowly. Noon arrived. Kristina heard the Quaker silence of grace at the noon meal, and then the clatter of knives and forks on plates with their now-distant familiarity, Bertha's voice commanding obedience from Marna, who disliked Bertha as well, Kristina knew. Salve was silent. Afternoon drained thinly into evening and the supper sounds came to her. Although she heard these sounds three times a day, it seemed as though she was hearing them for the first time, as though she had never seen where little Klara sat next to Siri and Marna, Salve at the head, then Johann and Marna, Nils and Bertha on the other side, Inger next to Bertha. *Bertha in my place*, Kristina thought.

Had she known Bertha's thoughts, Kristina would have sent her away.

Bertha knew that eventually the child would turn and be born. She knew also that it could and would be born without her help, but that Kristina would be so badly torn that infection would be certain, if she did nothing. That she did not have to lift her finger against Kristina, Bertha knew; it was the trolls' doing that she would die. Or God's.

Kristina asked for Malinda. Salve went to get her, against Bertha's wishes.

"She can do nothing," Bertha said.

Kristina bit into the rough cloth Bertha Norland gave her to keep her voice from crying out, but her voice seemed separate from her. Each thrust of pain was one more she thought she could not bear. And the day stretched on and on, into night. When Malinda arrived, she sat with Kristina, gripping her hands, looking across at the narrow, cold eyes of Bertha. Malinda did not like her but had no reason to distrust her.

The children went to bed, wordless and frightened. Malinda comforted them. Salve came in Kristina's room and wiped the perspiration from her face with his blue handkerchief. Kristina didn't want him to see her, worn from labor, sweat drenched.

"The position is wrong," Bertha told Salve. "I can't do anything to change it. We will have to wait."

"Salve, please go out. Salve, this is not a place for you," Kristina pleaded. "I'll be all right. Pray for me."

Salve prayed endlessly and endlessly, "I will lift up mine eyes unto the hills from whence cometh thy help. I will lift up mine eyes,

I will lift up mine eyes…" kneeling in front of the horsehair sofa, his head bowed on his hands. Salve knew that his beloved Kristina was telling him that there was no way to interfere with God's will, that one should pray for the grace to accept whatever came. He didn't hear a slight form kneel beside him until he heard Marna's voice saying, "I will lift up mine eyes and please make Mor well."

By the pale light of dawn, the child was born. Bertha said, "A son," and raised him up by his feet until he cried. The yellow shadows of the kerosene lamp cast his shadow upon the wall—a small round head with legs held by the squat figure of Bertha, *the troll herself,* Kristina thought, *from Roldal.*

His cry was weak, as weak as Kristina was. She was badly torn, exhausted, both Bertha and Kristina knew. Malinda went into the living room where Salve sat. "You have a son," she said, but there was no joy in her voice.

Salve entered where Kristina lay, his face taut and white. "We will call him Staale, after your brother, Kristina Min. He is a fine boy." His hands reached for Kristina without touching her, his caresses showing in the way his fingers curled by his side, aching to touch, not daring to, fearful of inflicting more wounds upon her body, his voice husky, his eyes wet.

Did Salve know that Staale would not live? Should I speak of it? Kristina thought. *The Lord giveth and the Lord taketh away. Amen.*

And Staale died in Kristina's arms the next day, too injured and too weakened to live. The following day, he was taken to the meetinghouse in a white coffin, dressed in a white linen dress, followed by all of Salve's and Kristina's children, except Klara and Inger. The Meeting would sit in silence, and Nicholas Larssen would speak of the necessity for readiness, and acceptance of the will of God. Readiness for death was life's main mission, and readiness was submission. There would be no tears, and grief would not be spoken of.

To Kristina, lying at home, Bertha remaining with her, that coffin was proof that she had replaced God with the world's goods: for houses, for a horsehair sofa, for barns and more cattle. And she was not allowed to cry.

"Well, that was your last child," Bertha said. "Klara should have been your last."

Kristina couldn't even protest. Bertha was right, troll that she was. But to what extent she was one, Kristina would never know. Nor would Salve—Bertha counted on Salve's trusting nature to believe the best of people until the worst was proved. But Salve was the reason for her pain, wasn't he?

Kristina's fever began on the third day. It began stubbornly, earnestly. She felt the little flames begin at her feet, slowly moving upward through her ankles, the calves of her legs, arriving at her knees. "Bertha, Bertha, some cool packs. I have the fever," she called, meaning the dread fever of childbirth, so feared by women and caused by the lack of the simplest sanitary precautions—postpartum fever.

Bertha sat in a chair by Kristina's bed, knitting. The rain had finally come, washing away the snow. Kristina could hear it falling and falling, slowly, steadily on the roof. She found it comforting. Rain was a promise of spring, of new shoots in the bare fields, of green grass on the cave roof.

Bertha still sat and knitted. "Yes, Kristina, you have the fever. It is the devil's curse!" And she leaned over her patient, eye to eye. "You know that, don't you!"

Kristina saw a hard cold eye impaling her own, and she was strangely frightened. "Bertha, please some cool cloths." Bertha was efficient but her hands lacked love, her touch was harsh, her ministrations not cooling to Kristina's burning fever.

"Bertha, you are from Roldal..." Kristina said.

What more could Bertha say, when her words burned Kristina with their truth?

Kristina lay and looked around her bedroom, feeling a stranger to it. In this room she had borne her six children, but she had conceived them, too, in this house, lying in Salve's arms. What was first four walls became the circle of her world, the fruits of her love. The light was wan on this rainy day. Salve's reddish dome-top chest was blackened by its shadows; her mother's brass candleholder sat on a shadowy oak chest of drawers. She felt strangely peaceful. She lay and contemplated the flames, how they hesitated and then moved up her thighs, moved to her buttocks.

By the fourth day, Kristina felt the flames arrive at her breasts, swollen and burning with unconsumed milk. Then her arms seemed like flames themselves, engulfing her burning face. The house was silent. She didn't hear the clatter of knives and forks, didn't hear Salve say at the table, "We will now give silent thanks to the Lord…"

The children, one by one, came to look at their mother; Kristina saw that they saw her as some fearful thing, their eyes round with wonder, their faces stern and grave and tearless. She held out her hand, but only Marna touched it and placed it on her cheek. Kristina felt her hand wet with Marna's tears. Knud and Karl, too, Kristina saw, were home from school. Why?

Salve sat by her side, his cool hands pressing the flames. *Can he see them flickering?* Kristina wondered. *He must watch out so they don't catch onto his clothes, reach for his red hair and thick beard, and burn his coarse, capable hands.*

"Kristina," he said.

I can't hear what he said. Am I Kristina Karlsdatter Røyseland, no, Kristina Karlson Roseland, wife of Salve, gone to America? Am I the mother of six, no, seven children? Where is Tollak? Anna Tonetta? Karl Jonsen? Who—oh where am I? If I could lie down in the cool waters of the streams at Røyseland which would take me down, down into the Flekkefjord, past Rafoss and its cool spray, on down into the cool sea, where the flames would sizzle and go out. Here there is no sea, only endless stretches of black earth, no stones. No stones. No sea. The flames flare up in my yellow hair.

"Kristina, Kristina," a distant voice. "Kristina Min…Kristina!"

Salve's voice!

Large cool hands tightened around her head, her shoulders, her waist, her body, trying in a human gesture to catch what was fleeing. Salve Roseland flung his body over Kristina Karlsdatter, to catch the thread of breath that remained. But it was already too late.

CHAPTER SIX

On March 3, 1897, Salve hitched up his mare to drive to the Rosdale farm to fetch Malinda. He didn't want Bertha's brusque, unloving hands to wash and dress Kristina for the last time.

Salve didn't want to arrive. He wanted somehow to be suspended between departure and arrival, somewhere in no place at all to remind him of where he was and what he was doing, undertaking so strange and impossible an errand from which he would stir to find that he was merely delivering some *kringla* to Malinda sent by Kristina. Or lefse. Or plums in August, or *kranzenkake* for Christmas. But Salve realized that his hands were bringing nothing to Malinda's house but the burden of his grief, which stretched out ahead of him like the barren March road, with half-frozen, half-thawed, rotted snow in patches, like scars from severe pox. His mare trotted on then raised her head to sniff and snort into the air, perhaps at the strong odor of a skunk whose sudden sharpness was an assault on the senses. But the mare didn't hesitate.

Salve had left Bertha presumably in charge of a household he had normally taken for granted: Kristina had been there. He hadn't even comforted his children. They had been left on their own to deal with the tearing loss of their mother's death—his own was so deep that he simply could not face theirs. He felt guilty because of it, but he had had no choice. Now, as he neared the Malinda's farm, he wished the mare would stumble, throw a shoe, develop an acute attack of heaves, do anything to prevent his arrival, so that he would not have to say words he'd never said before. But Malinda's house loomed in front of him. There was no stopping the mare, who trotted right up to the door, quite unaware of her master's state of mind. There she stopped without signal.

Even as he arrived, Malinda appeared at her front door, and he didn't have to speak the words—they were written on his face. In haste,

Malinda snatched a shawl and a bonnet, untying her apron at the same time she tied bonnet strings. She ran toward Salve and put her weight on the mounting stirrup as the carriage swayed toward her.

Salve turned the mare around, while Malinda placed her hand on his forearm in the way of comfort, to let this man know that she understood the burden of his grief. Salve knew that, dear as Malinda was, it was he who returned to a house of mourning and a house of motherless children, whose faces already haunted him as they clung to each other. He hadn't even explained to them what had happened, but he knew that they knew. Death has a way of informing a household that it has come.

Karl and Knud, aged ten and twelve, had gone to the barn, a source of their play and of their work, helping to bring hay to the cows, oats to the horses and sheep. If anyone looked for them, Karl would have been found with his face buried in the neck of one of the gentle work mares, Knud holding a calf tightly to his face, so that his tears disappeared into the thick hair of the calf. The calf butted its head against Knud, treating any creature as a potential mother with a food supply.

Malinda pulled her shawl around her, up to her neck, feeling the chill of March in the open carriage. Salve had not bothered with the usual lap robe; nothing could warm the chill in his heart, and his body didn't matter. But he noted Malinda's chill, and looking at her for the first time, silhouetted against the fence rows along the snow-patched road, he said, "Malinda, if only Kristina hadn't had a seventh child! How could I have known? Six children is enough. And now, they are motherless. And I..." He surveyed the horizon on either side, fields that stretched on seemingly forever. He shook his head as though confessing his sins of possession, wondering what his land meant to him now, now that he'd lost the reason for wanting it.

Malinda had known him when he first came to Legrand. When he first bought the farm he lived on, everything was for Kristina. And then, Kristina's arrival. Malinda liked Kristina immediately...The children began arriving. A new house was built. More land bought, Salve working like a madman, and now that he had everything, he'd lost the reason for having it.

Malinda knew without doubt that Salve must now examine his life to find reasons for her death. Both Malinda and Salve realized that Kristina would expect him to. Malinda wondered if finding reason and acceptance were the same thing. Was the land itself responsible, which offered up to its servants such riches that they had never before seen or believed possible? Was the black soil, then, merely a form of the devil himself? *Had God tested him*, Salve wondered, *and had he failed?*

Malinda knew that she must speak carefully to him. "Salve, you must grieve," she began. "And I must grieve, and so must your children. When the wounds of her loss begin to heal a bit, you must remember the gladness she brought to you. She will never be gone from your life, and your children are her over again, you and she as one, united in life. Remember that. Don't look for causes—there are none. Nor are there any answers right now. God works in mysterious ways, Salve. Try to remember that." She touched his bare hands, which were fixed on the reins. They were cold, their callouses deep.

Salve looked at her briefly then turned his face to his house, now nearly in front of them. There were tears in his eyes, and Malinda saw that he was wondering how he was going to have the courage to enter.

Malinda stepped down from the carriage and entered the house, while Salve unhitched the mare and took her to the barn. Marna, nearly nine, white-faced and silent, greeted her. She was comforting Inger, five, and Johann, six, who were aware of disaster but not of its source. Klara, two and a half, was fretting for lack of attention. Malinda draped her shawl over the coatrack in the front hall as she reached for Marna, throwing her arms around the silent girl. No one spoke until Bertha entered from the kitchen, her manner unchanged from her customary briskness.

"I'm glad to see you here, Malinda. You can decide what dress to use." And she strode off, washbasin in her hands, toward the room where Malinda knew that Kristina lay. Malinda hesitated before following, looking at the children, wondering where she was most needed.

"Marna, where is Siri? And the boys?"

"Siri's in the kitchen, I think. And Karl and Knud, I think they're in the barn." Malinda knew that Marna would try to care for the younger children, to keep them out of the path of Bertha for as long as she remained. Marna was a nine-year-old child, tall and thin for her age, suddenly thrust into a role that would change little for the rest of her life: household cares, children, comfort-giving. Her eyes were gray, her hair smooth and ash blond. Her face was Kristina's, sober and trusting, her cheekbones sharply outlined. Her nose, however, seemed to come from somewhere else: it was neither as broad as Salve's, nor straight like Kristina's, having a slight aquilinity like that of Tollak Røyseland, three generations back. Malinda had never noticed before what Kristina had always told her, that Tollak was present in Marna's nose. Like a flash, it came to Malinda that she had seen Marna's face on a photograph of Tollak in an oval frame—the face of Marna.

Malinda squeezed both of Marna's shoulders gently. Then she glanced toward the kitchen but walked toward the room where Bertha had gone, leaving Marna to turn away and lead the small children to the kitchen. She opened the door slowly, not wanting to enter any more than Salve did. Bertha was bent over the still form of Kristina, washing her draped body. It didn't seem to Malinda that she washed a patient differently alive or dead—it was her usual brusque and indifferent way. Bertha didn't turn her head as she continued with her task, saying, "Too many children. Who needs so many children? And what now are they to do, motherless?"

Didn't Bertha care at all? Malinda looked at Kristina's body, not wanting to believe that Kristina no longer inhabited it, that it had become a heap of flesh. There was still color in her cheeks. Would the red of her fever ever go away, or was it imprinted on her forever? Her body was still limp—Malinda could tell by the way Bertha picked up the arms. "I'm leaving her hair for you to do. Find a dress, will you?"

Malinda went upstairs to the closet in Salve and Kristina's bedroom, to look for Kristina's wedding dress of dark silk. Kristina had let out the seams twice since childbearing. The closet was orderly and smelled of cedar and lavender. On the bureau baby clothes were laid out, some newly made, a lace collar on a long white dress. Kristina must have considered it for the child's burial, rejecting it for another. Malinda's eyes blurred, and she fumbled with her hands on the clothes. She located the dress, took it off the hanger, placed it over her arm, and descended the stairs. She had helped to prepare a body for burial before, but it had been an eighty-year-old member of Stavanger Meeting, childless and ill.

She hesitated on the open oak stairway, holding the dress in both arms. Salve entered the hallway at that very moment, through the kitchen. Seeing her, his hands made a forward gesture, but when he saw what she carried, he turned abruptly and went into the parlor, opposite from the room where Kristina lay. All farmhouses had a downstairs bedroom used as a guest bedroom, a room in times of illness, a room where the dead of the family would lie before burial. Into this room Malinda hurried.

"It took you a while. Here now, get me some more warm water," Bertha said, nodding to the wash basin. "Not that it makes any difference what temperature the water is, but my hands get cold." Malinda left without comment, draping the dress on a straight chair.

When Malinda returned with the water, Bertha washed Kristina's face, roughly, drying it superficially. "Now, help me get her dressed." Bertha stood, hands on her hips, surveying the pile of clothes. Malinda thought she was too cheerful.

Undergarments first, stockings, petticoats—each item took considerable effort on the part of the two women to raise and manipulate limbs, torso, her head that rolled backward. Kristina's body was an object, and Malinda held back from treating it so. But Bertha didn't seem to notice at all. "Nice seams she sewed, aren't they? She learned good needlework in Stavanger. Uff-ta, pity to bury this dress, isn't it?" Bertha didn't look up as she spoke; her hands worked quickly, lifting, manipulating. Buttons closed. "Now, Malinda, you comb her hair."

Malinda had never held Kristina's hair in her hands; it seemed alive. So thick, it sprang back in her hands, like dark corn silk, yet her face was so still. Malinda's tears fell rapidly on the floor, on Kristina's hair. "Sentimental woman," Bertha exclaimed. "Like Kristina."

Malinda finished and knocked on the door of the parlor where Salve sat alone.

"Ja?" Salve answered.

"I want to know if I can help with your plans. The household, I mean. The children." She spoke outside the door.

"Come in. Come in. I hadn't thought…"

"May I suggest something?" Malinda said. Salve motioned for her to come in. "You need someone besides Siri. Of course, I can take the younger children for a while, if you want."

"Malinda, I haven't thought about tomorrow. I can't leave yesterday." He dropped his head in his hands, then leaned forward suddenly, searching Malinda's face with his own. "Tell me, was Kristina happy, Malinda? Do you know? Did she talk to you about it? I mean, she was so alone here in—in America. I'm just beginning to see that."

"She had her family. She had you. We were friends, good friends." Malinda was hesitant.

"But did she talk to you about Norway? About being away from Røyseland? Malinda, please tell me."

"She missed her parents, I know, and she missed Røyseland. We all miss Norway, don't we?" Malinda knew what Salve was asking, and she knew how desperately Kristina missed Anna Tonetta and her father, Karl, her aged grandfather, Tollak, how she had quietly expressed to Malinda the feeling that the godliness was slipping out the lives of the Norwegians once they became established in America. Even Salve, in his running after the goods of the world from the black rich land and losing the reasons for which they came. Kristina hadn't said it like that, but she was so lacking in guile that her face was easily read. Malinda felt it, too, the gradual lessening of godliness, pettinesses creeping in. Hardship and sacrifice made sterner people. She used to tell Kristina that an easier life was not sinful, but she, too, had misgivings. Now she watched Salve struggle with his own doubts. How did you offer, in place of stones, a whole continent of flat black earth and expect no greed, no overzealousness for the wealth one never had for generations? These were the America promises, weren't they? Riches?

"Salve," Malinda said, coming to him, placing her hand on his shoulder in the parlor. The oak horsehair-stuffed sofa seemed heavier than usual and more durable than the man now diminished by its brooding permanence. "I remember one thing that Kristina said to me. I was talking about Sarah's arrival, and I asked Kristina if she didn't wish sometimes she could go to Røyseland. She said, "I belong here. When I met Salve Knudsen, I said to myself, '*Whither thou goest, I will go.*' And I am here."

Salve glanced quickly at Malinda. A smile swept his face and then quickly passed. Only a few days ago, Malinda had stood in the same place, bringing news of the birth of a son. The light was dim now, fading to dusk. Malinda's face held the light, not a beautiful face: too angular, eyes almost too wide, a pointed chin that should have belonged to a smaller face. But it was a face made more beautiful by deep gentleness and love.

"Salve, Siri can't manage your household. Ask Bertha to stay. I'm sure she will, that she is probably planning to, but only if you ask her." Malinda said that while Bertha could wound with her blunt tongue, she was also prickly and stood upon ceremony. She would let it be known that staying was a favor, even if she wanted to.

"Is there no one else?"

"She is competent, and she knows your house and children."

"Must I do it today?" Salve asked. Malinda had to turn away her face from his so that he wouldn't see the tears that arrived suddenly again.

"No, in a few days' time. When you feel up to it. But..." Malinda hesitated, stepping back a step from Salve, who had raised his head and was looking at her. "There is something else you must do, today. The children need to know you haven't forgotten them, that *you* are here." The implication of the children's loss was lost on his own.

How long had he been sitting here, examining every stage of his life together with Kristina? He had brought her to America only fourteen years ago, away from everything she'd ever known, from her mother, and father, from Røyseland to America. She hadn't had enough contact with the New World to even learn its language. Even their meeting was in Norwegian, or worse, in a language that Americanized Norwegian, or Norwegianized American English. In this new, small Quaker community, they were nothing but a small island in a big sea, and the sea was powerful and would consume the island. Why hadn't he seen that before? He'd already seen other children of older immigrants speaking the American language, ashamed of parents who hadn't learned it, ashamed of grandparents in awkward black clothes, queer bonnets, and broad-brimmed hats, relics from a former place and time. Malinda was right, it was time he thought of his and Kristina's children.

"Malinda," he said, standing and placing his hands on her shoulders, "You and Bertha, you have finished, ja?" He couldn't say what task he was referring to, but Malinda understood and nodded. "Then call the children, and we will go in."

Minutes later, five children stood with him, staring at the body of their mother, dressed in the dress they knew she wore for special occasions. Inger ran to her, crying *Mor!* but Marna grabbed her before she reached the bed. Inger cried out again, and Marna held her by both arms. Johann clung to Marna, and even though Salve had his hands on the shoulders of Karl and Knud, one on each side, each one seemed alone in grief and disbelief. Malinda had left Klara with Bertha. Marna's eyes seemed distant; she looked beyond and not at the body of her mother, her face white and taut.

"Let us pray together," Salve said, bowing his head. "The Lord giveth and the Lord taketh away." He could say no more.

The next day, Kristina was buried, in the same bleakness of weather as her arrival in Legrand. Winter hadn't let go, and spring hadn't come. The black and gray clothes were more at home in such seasons, dark and indistinguishable from the weather. After the short service in the meetinghouse, the congregation followed the coffin to the cemetery behind it and watched the lowering of the coffin into the ground. There were no family plots, and Kristina's body occupied the space next in line because burials took place in order of their occurrence, row after row, grave after grave. Each Friend passed by, picking up a handful of dirt to throw on the coffin. Each pressed Salve's hand and looked with pity, or did not look, at the silent children.

Last, Sigbjorn and Malinda Rosdale, who remained standing with Salve and his family. Then Ole Sawyer stepped up in his ancient hat and stood with them. Another figure, in gray clothes and a gray poke bonnet, approached Salve. Seeing that it was Ina Christiansen, Malinda tensed, and she reached out toward her involuntarily. Ina's eyes swept over the scene, the open grave at the end of the row, the silent children. She reached to touch Marna's cheek, then went to Salve, first looking down into the grave and then into his face.

"I have a message for thee," she said, her eyes fixed on his face. "Thou must answer to this!" And her eyes looked toward the grave for a brief moment.

Salve whitened, turned, and led the way to his family carriage, followed first by Marna and the two youngest, then by Karl and Knud. They hadn't heard Ina's words; nor, he hoped, had Malinda. And he would never tell them. She was the angel of death.

* * *

"Bertha Norland," Salve Roseland said to her three days later, after breakfast. "I would speak with you, in the parlor." Salve had hardly spoken with his children during this time. Meals were silent grief, instead of grace. Inger and Johann quarreled, while Marna tried to pacify them. Klara fussed and was held by Bertha. Karl and Knud were still out of school, and this morning, like most of the mornings, they went to the barn hastily and silently.

"Papa, we'll watch the heifer," Karl said, referring to the next one due to calve. Marna helped Siri clear up the breakfast plates, giving one at a time to Inger to carry. Bertha got up with Klara in her arms and followed Salve.

"Please sit down," Salve said in the parlor, while he abstractedly decided whether to sit or stand, but Bertha was already seated on the sofa, her warty face held to the smooth rosy skin of Klara, whose arms were around her neck. A few strands of gray hair escaped her tight topknot. "As you see, I am in need of a housekeeper. I thank you for staying on, and I must ask you if you would consider staying for a while longer. Until I can find someone more permanent."

"I will stay," Bertha answered without hesitation. Her eyes glinted to small points as she added, "The children are too weepy. They need some discipline, you realize."

"Bertha, it is only days since their mother died. They miss her. She was—"

Bertha interrupted him. "It has gone on long enough, this crying in their rooms, in the barn, wherever they are, refusing to work. It is unseemly." Klara had put her head against Bertha's big breasts, sucking her thumb. As she spoke she stroked Klara's hair.

"Klara is too young to understand," Salve commented, watching her, realizing the redundancy of his remark. "If you would stay, I would be pleased."

"Ja, I will stay." Bertha looked so pleased with herself, so confident, that Salve wondered for a moment if he had done something he would regret. He didn't like her attitude about the other children—he didn't even like her. But he had no choice, and for now, they would survive Bertha.

Even after Salve left the parlor, Bertha remained for a few minutes, confident now that she belonged there, in the parlor. She would take charge. She would become indispensable. And someday she would be more than Salve's housekeeper. Bertha had plans that had started long ago, perhaps as long ago as the birth of Marna. She wondered, *Is that why I dislike Marna?* Now, in charge, she would root out and destroy all touches of Kristina that lingered. She would replace totally the woman she destroyed—of that she needed no reminders. But Malinda sometimes made her uneasy, but there was nothing she did wrong; it was what she *failed* to do. Kristina might have died anyway, of something else, of too many children. Bertha squeezed Klara to her chest. This child would be hers, that was certain. The others? She would see.

One day, Marna found her father alone in the parlor after Sunday lunch, a habit he'd acquired after Kristina's death. He met with his conscience in the parlor, where he could expect to be alone. Marna knew that and knew also that Bertha had gone to visit Serena and Omer Vinje, who had come with her from Roldal and who farmed her land. She had driven the two-wheeled carriage and taken Klara with her.

Marna's slight and somberly dressed figure gave Salve a start. She looked so serious, so beyond her nine years. Had she become so serious since her mother died, or hadn't Salve really looked at her before? In her hands was Kristina's brass candleholder, which Marna now held up in front of Salve's eyes. "Papa, I don't like to tattle, I know you don't like tattlers, but Bertha—See Papa, Bertha has polished Mor's candleholder." And she burst into tears that gave way to heaving sobs.

Salve put his arms around her, being conscious of how rarely he had done it, even before Kristina's death, of how small her bones were, how fragile seeming. He remembered how infrequently he thought upon his children in this room, where he was trying to come to terms with himself, Kristina's death, and Ina's words.

Her light body shook in his arms, and he thought of how little she asked of him, and therefore, how little he gave. "M-M-Mor never wanted to polish it, Mor said it had her mor's fingerprints on it. Papa, is it because I took it to my room? I wasn't stealing it. I just wanted it near me, be-be-because of Mor. And Bertha knew Mor never polished it. Oh, Papa!" Marna tried to stop her sobs, but she couldn't. She stood stiff and straight, resisting her desire to thrust her whole body into the arms of her father.

As he took the candleholder in his hands, tears filled Salve's eyes. He remembered Kristina's joy and grief when she found it in her trunk, placed there secretly as it had been by Anna Tonetta's hands. That is why she had never wanted to polish it—even Marna knew things about Kristina that he didn't! The candleholder linked her hands to Røyseland, across the sea and across the vast lands of America, to Legrand, *Aiovai*, as he had first heard it.

"Marna," Salve said, putting his hands on her cheeks, wiping a tear with a red handkerchief, "we all miss Mor, don't we?" He knew that his children, except for Klara, didn't like Bertha, that Siri had asked to leave when he could find another girl. But the children couldn't leave, and he needed Bertha. Women didn't stay unmarried long when they came from Norway, and there were few spinsters. There were some widows, but either they had their own families, or they were too elderly to take on the cares of such a family as he had. He knew that his children obeyed Bertha out of severe discipline, not out of love and the natural obedience which love instills. The linen was not as white, the children's clothes were less clean and less mended, the meals not as varied nor as good. Short cuts were taken. He hadn't even known how high Kristina's standards had been until the loss of them. But the house *did* function: meals were served, children were dressed and did their chores, however mechanically they were performed.

"Marna, I will speak to Bertha about it, and ask her not to do it again."

"Oh no, Papa! She will be even meaner to me. No. please don't." Marna clutched the candleholder. Then she looked into Salve's face. "Anyway, it doesn't matter anymore. See, it doesn't have either Mor's or Anna Tonetta's fingerprints on it. It's not the same."

Salve tried to hug the stiff form. Marna bent forward to her father and put her arms around his neck, unstiffening only slightly. No one hugged her, and she didn't have a teddy bear. He stroked her hair, wondering how it was that after three generations she could most resemble her great-grandfather Tollak. "Marna, please come to me when you want to. I know it is hard for you, for all of us."

"Thank you, Papa. Now I have to go. I promised Inger and Johann to take them to the barn."

"Doesn't Siri ever take care of them?"

"Papa, she doesn't have time. And if they stay around Bertha, she scolds them. Then she spanks them and sends them upstairs. She puts them in closets with the door shut." But Marna caught herself tattling again and added, "Papa, I didn't mean to bother you by tattling on Bertha. She only likes Klara." And with that she ran out of the room as she heard a carriage outside.

As the noise of the wheels on crushed stone stopped, Bertha's voice was heard calling for Salve to unhitch the horse and help her and Klara from the carriage. She descended with the help of Salve's hand to steady her, and the carriage bounced up again as her foot touched the ground. As he prepared to lead the mare to the barn, he seized the moment to say, "Bertha, Marna has been upset because of the polishing of the lysestake." He used the Norwegian word that she used and was careful not to say who was responsible.

"I told Siri to do it, that old tarnished lysestake, thinking Marna would be pleased." Salve half believed her untruth.

"Kristina never wanted it polished, Bertha. That's why Marna is upset."

"Kristina is gone, Salve Roseland. She doesn't run this house anymore. I do. I have given up everything for this thankless job, because you asked me to. And Marna is a spiteful tattletale." And Bertha hurried into the house, taking Klara by the hand.

By late October, the air was crisp and blue with frost in the early morning, the afternoons warm and lazy, a chill setting in before dusk. Corn picking was in full swing, each ear picked by hand—aided by a half glove with a hook imbedded that would tear the ear from the tough, dry stalk—then thrown into a wagon with elevated boards stacked on the opposing side to deflect the ear. The dried leaves of cornstalks crackled and whispered as the pickers made their way between the rows. A dull thump, and then the fall of the ear could be heard throughout the land, as regular as a clock, from October until snow, usually late December.

This year, the shelves were less full, the root cellar sparsely filled. Marna, who knew all the methods and had helped during the summer, had gone to the Stavanger boarding school with Karl and Knud. Her absence was a consolation to Bertha: it seemed to her that the child had a thousand large and staring eyes, all of them Kristina's, reproaching her with their secret knowledge. Siri had found another place, and the new girl, Helga, had never known Kristina's ways to compare. That, too, was a relief to Bertha. Inger and Johann, six and seven, were easily controlled because they were both dependent upon and frightened of her. Klara was all hers.

It was eight months or more that Bertha had been running Salve's household, and Salve had not spoken to her further about staying *or* leaving. Had he looked for another housekeeper? Perhaps he didn't intend to. And if he hadn't, why hadn't he? Bertha wondered about forcing his hand by announcing that she soon had to leave, at least by Christmas.

She sat in her room after the noon meal one day in November, after the dishes were finished, for the rest that she took each day while Klara napped and Inger and Johann were with Helga. She looked into the mirror standing on her bureau and turned it so that she saw her face directly. The mirror rotated on two hinges and sat separately on its own base. She confirmed that she was not handsome, but she held her chin up and said to herself, *Handsome is as handsome does.* She wished that she didn't have so many warts on her face, that her hair wasn't graying. She wished her nose smaller, her body slimmer, more because it would be less cumbersome, rather than that she thought it unattractive.

Normally, she didn't notice her own plainness as much as she noticed others' beauty, feeling that beauty wore its own deception, whereas homeliness was closer to truth. Noticing herself now, she wondered if her lack of beauty was what caused Salve to be so uncommunicative. He spoke to her when necessity and propriety demanded, always ill at ease when he did. That it might be Salve's indifference and preoccupation didn't occur to Bertha. She wondered if he missed a woman and therefore wondered if she made him uneasy. She hungered for a love she'd never known. "My body is as empty as a grain bin or a fruit cellar in spring," she said out loud and then went on to think of the results of love she had seen, the crucifying of some women in childbed. Thoughts of Kristina passed like a small dark cloud fleeing across the sun's face. She winced.

"Crucifix of Roldal, bring Salve to me. Make him mine, if only in name." She spoke into the mirror, she walked to the window looking out on the farmyard, repeated it, and returned to look into her mirror. Maybe she should tell him that she must leave, that her own farm needed her, that Serena and Omer had bought more land and couldn't farm hers. But Salve would find a new strong and reliable immigrant to work her land, even help him to get started.

For a month already she had said to herself daily, "Yes. Today," and just as daily she'd said, "Tomorrow." But now, when the moon was waxing, she decided she must act. Tonight she would speak.

After supper, Bertha took her usual place in the parlor by the gas lamp while Helga put the children to bed. Salve entered, took his usual place in the wooden-framed chair, and began to read the Bible. Opposite, Bertha watched him, his burnished hair and thick beard reddened by the light, the other half of his face in shadow so that the same hair and beard looked nearly black. Her heart flamed up to see him there, even immersed as he was in the Bible—she read it only on Sundays. She cleared her throat, wondering if Salve would agree to look for someone else.

"Salve Knudsen," she began. He looked at her. She had tried to place herself out of the light so that her warts wouldn't be so evident. And lately, the dark hairs on her chin had grown thicker. "Salve, I want to say this to you. I have been in your household for nearly nine months. It is time I went home!"

"Yes, it has been long," Salve agreed. "I thank you for your patience." And then he seemed lost in thought. He never glanced in her direction, even after she spoke, but put his hand on his beard, thinking. He looked into the light, not at her, and said, "Bertha, I have thought about it, wondering if I should even ask you. But would you stay longer?"

"How long do you mean? I can't stay forever like this. I mean, what I mean is, as your housekeeper." Bertha dared to venture on the theme of propriety. She was, after all, a virgin lady.

"Then would you stay, as—as my wife?" Even then Salve did not look at her face.

Bertha's hand fled involuntarily to her heart. *Lie down, heart*, she said to herself. *Don't let him hear it.* "I think that would be better, than…than it is." Bertha spoke in a controlled voice.

Salve rose and touched her hand for the first time. "Well then, we must propose it to the monthly meeting." And then he turned to leave. "Good night," he said and left Bertha alone with her beating heart and heaving breasts.

She kneeled beside her chair to pray to a God she rarely addressed. Aloud, she confessed her happiness, thanking God or fate—to her they were equal—for her good fortune, confessing how she had believed more in trolls than in God, even though she'd hoped to leave them behind in the dark valleys and cheerless mountains of Roldal. She asked forgiveness of a God she didn't know, for *not* believing in Him, because she had known too many thin barley cakes, potatoes too meager, no meat except for an occasional reindeer that had smelled like a rutting goat, if the wolves had not got it first. She asked forgiveness for praying to the magic crucifix from Roldal and then thanked whichever it may have been—the crucifix or God—for granting her such happiness, promising to assume the God of Salve Roseland after she married him, instead of the church with the dragonheads outside the doors.

Bertha sank back on her knees, remembering the cross of Roldal found in the sea by sailors, the silver plaque attached to it with a command engraved on it: *Take this cross to Roldal, the darkest place on earth.* For generations afterward, the cross was known to have healed the sick and stopped the wolves from stealing the sheep and cattle. It had stopped the plague. But then, along came the man with the broad-brimmed hat, telling citizens of Roldal that the cross was evil, that if they came to Aiovai, the beautiful land, they would "hunger no more for things of the flesh nor of the spirit." Nearly the entire village vacated Roldal—she was one of them—and went to this Aiovai where they cast off trolls and the crucifix. Plenty had a way of casting off a niggardly past, but Bertha could not part with the magic crucifix, even here, even getting her heart's wish: Salve Knudsen was to be hers. But to neither the crucifix nor Salve's God would Bertha confess about Kristina, who had, after all, one child too many: *Lust killed her.* She began to believe it.

In the monthly meeting of December 1898, Salve Roseland and Bertha Norland were united in marriage. Because it was a business meeting and not a meeting for worship, none of Salve's children were present. Members shook hands afterward and wished them well. Malinda and Sigbjorn nodded formally. No one lingered.

They drove home to an unusually silent supper with the children, prepared by Marna and Helga. The only thing that signified Bertha's new status is that she moved into Salve's room and into his bed.

Bertha retired immediately after supper, changing into her nightdress, taking out the many wire hairpins from her tight knot of gray hair. Had she seen herself draped with its thin wisps she would have tried to sleep with her knot, or in a nightcap. She had longed for this moment, but she was, in fact, an old virgin filled with dread, and Salve's silence did not give her confidence. She knew that she was no temptress, nor did she know anything about a man's desire. But he would turn out the light, and he would not see her. Nor she him—she had never seen a man except in his infant form, and she didn't know how large or how hard that penis could become.

When he came, he undressed in the closet, and in his nightshirt, still in his shoes, lingered over the clothes he'd chosen for the morning as he placed them on a chair. He lifted them again, reversing the order. He moved slowly toward the bed, sat down, and bent over to remove his shoes. They thumped softly to the floor. He sighed. Quietly he raised the covers and eased himself in. He lay still. Bertha heard every creak in the house magnified by silence. He made no move toward her, so she reached over to touch the man now her husband. "Salve, my husband," she said. "I have a wedding gift for thee."

He said nothing for a moment and then, "Oh, I am sorry, Bertha. I have nothing for you." *Ingenting.* Nothing.

"I am giving you my farm. I've already changed the deed."

"Bertha, you needn't do that."

"I wanted to. This way, you'll have to be responsible for it. I have enough to do here."

And so Salve turned to her, putting his arms around her. Bertha didn't know if she should raise her gown, or let Salve, or if he would want to. She raised it. She felt his penis like a stiff rod—the suddenness of it surprised her. Before she knew what to do, before she even opened her legs or freed them from her gown, she felt Salve gripping her, breathing heavily, thrusting that erect creature toward her genitals. But before he had even penetrated her, a wetness spread on her legs, and Salve, now quiet, turned from her more in sorrow than in shame. Then he attempted sleep.

What do I need with his body? Bertha thought. *I have his name.*

CHAPTER SEVEN

Klara stood in the kitchen with the table knives in her hand, looking at Marna's hair, usually pulled back tight, now framing her face in loose waves.

"Bertha will get you for that, Marna. Do you think she won't notice?" Klara placed knives and forks on the table, looking from Inger to Marna; Marna answered Klara by blowing a piece of unruly hair away from her face. It floated back onto her forehead, and she, now fourteen years, and Inger, eleven, laughed.

"Marna, you and Inger just try to make Bertha angry. Please, please don't. Please go braid your hair," eight-year-old Klara pleaded, standing in a brown long-sleeved dress, identical to Inger's; a narrow ruffle ran awkwardly from breast line, over the shoulder and midline, down the back.

The tiny, tapestry-like pattern of their dresses resembled upholstery fabric: Bertha had bought it cheaply, as a remnant, and sewed the dresses herself. Marna had made her own: it was navy, neater, and better sewn. They all wore high-buttoned shoes with black cotton stockings. Inger's and Klara's hair, braided by Bertha, was pulled back as tightly as possible; Inger's was reddish-blonde and unruly; curly wisps kept circling her face.

Each morning as Bertha pulled it roughly, Inger stood clenching her teeth, sticking out her chin and once in a while, her tongue. "Uff-ta," Bertha said, "Trolls' hair." Inger made wry faces as Klara stood waiting her turn, giving Inger a reprimanding look. Klara had her mother's gray, orange-flecked eyes; Inger had Salve's blue ones; Klara's hair was darker than Inger's, and gently wavy. "Well-behaved," Bertha said.

"I was in a hurry," Marna said, who did her own hair. "Anyway, ironing makes me hot." She had high, pale cheekbones and thick yellow hair, parted in the middle, now framing her face in gentle waves, pulled back only slightly and tied with dark yarn. It hung down her back in a glossy tail. The loosening of it enhanced the perfect angles of her face. Her eyes flashed as she carried food from the adjoining pantry. She ran her finger along the knife blade, reached for a whetstone from the pantry, and began to sharpen it. The wooden cupboard top, except for knife marks from cutting and chopping, had been worn and rubbed to a warm patina. Klara laid the white plates on a red-checked tablecloth, setting places for everyone but Johann, now at boarding school.

Ingebjor, the present hired girl, entered, heavyset, round-faced, snub-nosed, and cheerful. She stopped to stare at Marna; reaching to her own hair, she loosened it from its knot, pulling it out over her shoulders. She looked wild—no one had ever seen her with her hair down.

"Ja, how do you think I look, Marna?" she said as she began to prepare potatoes next to the lead-lined sink. She pumped the water and washed them. "Ja, Marna, you think I look good?" The girls giggled. Ingebjor laughed as she twisted it up again into a knot.

"Here she comes," Inger said breathlessly, hearing the slight shuffling sound and the accompanying rustle of Bertha's full skirt. As she entered, she looked at each of the girls. Her looks were sermons.

"Come here, Klara." Klara meekly went to her. Bertha placed her hand on the back of Klara's head, drawing her face closer to hers, patting Klara's cheek. Klara flushed, feeling a traitor to her sisters. "What is it, then? Can't you speak?" she asked Klara, who looked helplessly at Marna. Then she saw Marna's hair. Marna made no move to pull it tighter.

"Marna, come here! Quote me the boarding school rules. Now!" She sat down in a straight chair by the table and gestured to Marna. "Here." She pointed to the space in front of her. "Stand here."

Marna stood straight and firm and looked out of the window, reciting, "No whistling, singing, laughing. No jewelry. Plain worsted material without pattern." Her eyes briefly rested on Klara's dress with its tiny design, then on Inger's, as she said, "No ruffles or trim of any kind."

"Go on," Bertha said. "Why do I ask you to repeat them?"

"Hair is to be parted in the middle and combed down smooth and plain." Marna hesitated, then continued, "Pupils are advised to check the arising of pride."

"Now don't you know what you said, Marna? Do the rules mean nothing to you?" Inger turned to leave. "Inger, you stay. Uff-ta! Go on with your work. Marna, do your hair first." Bertha turned her face from Marna, talking to herself, quoting the queries. "Do I educate children under my care, Uff-ta! in plainness of speech, deportment and apparel?" She turned to Klara, who hadn't moved. "Bring me some water."

Ingebjor and Inger put supper on. Klara heard Inger whisper, "Uff-ta," as she looked at the back of Bertha's head. Marna returned, her hair pulled back tight, her lips tight, her eyes red. Salve, stouter, with traces of gray in his red beard, entered with Karl and Knud, eighteen and sixteen, both taller than their father. A whiff of summer hay lingered in their clothes as well as an unmistakable horse smell on Knud's unwashed hands. A milkiness permeated their outer jackets. Ten cows to milk, calves to feed after the cream was separated by a hand-cranked machine. Twelve horses to feed—needed to work the land that Salve owned—and twenty brood sows, to farrow in March.

Salve looked at the faces at the table as they took places. "We will now say silent grace." All heads bowed until Salve said, "Amen." And then, "Marna, you will see me after supper." All eyes were upon her before heads bent over their food.

The knives and forks clicked on the white plates, the sweet odor of wood smoke from the stove mixed with the strong cabbage, but the coffee aroma forgave the cabbage. Conversation at family meals was limited, nearly nonexistent. The dinner table could be a courtroom: the culprit tried, sentenced, then repented and redeemed, all without a word. The children feared their father's displeasure, the few times he talked with them. They had nothing to say to Bertha, and Klara felt estranged from her brothers and sisters for loving her.

After supper, Marna stood in the parlor in Salve's presence where he sat in his wooden chair with the stuffed cushion, his face reddened by the kerosene lamp. Salve saw how grown-up Marna was, how she resembled Kristina, how little she said to him. He wished he could embrace her, but then, he never had.

"Marna, your eyes were red tonight. Have you and Bertha had another disagreement?"

Marna looked beyond him, not at him. She saw Salve's Norwegian Bible on the oak table next to the brass candlestick she had placed there for safekeeping, after Bertha had polished it when her mother died. She had stood here then, talking to her father; today she had been summoned. Marna remembered why she was here, but also the rule by which she lived—one of the queries answered at meeting: *Are tale-bearing and distraction discouraged? And when differences arise, are endeavors used speedily to end them?*

"No, Papa." She answered, gripping her hands behind her back.

"Then why the red eyes?"

"I got smoke in them, from the woodstove. I put too much wood in it, and it smothered."

Salve realized that he could not accuse her of lying, or he would be encouraging her to disobey the queries by tattling. She was also protecting Bertha, someone he knew she disliked. He realized that, at nearly fifteen, she worked most of the day—more, even, than Bertha or even the hired girl. He did not know that she crocheted in her room at night by kerosene light, that she made lace, sewed doll clothes for Klara's one doll, things that Bertha disapproved of, except that they were for Klara and were finely made. While Bertha chaffed and scolded, Marna's basic disagreement was expressed in the things her hands could do; she could do or make anything. "If it's worth doing, Marna, it's worth doing well," Kristina had told her. So her sewing and canning and cooking expressed this effort. Bertha said a crocheted collar was for vanity's sake.

More and more Marna's hands spoke for her and became her words—making beautiful things and making them in secret—she punished herself for thinking bad thoughts. *For as he thinketh in his heart, so is he* Marna knew to be true. Salve didn't know, as she stood before him, tall, slight, her face serious and sad, how she suffered the burden of her conscience: her thoughts were bad because *she* was bad, and today, she had thought very evil thoughts. Marna tried to learn not to care, like Inger, but never escaped looking for causes in herself for bad events: there was no such thing as bad luck—bad luck was one's own doing.

Marna had Malinda. Malinda came very infrequently to the Roseland house after Kristina's death, but sometimes she came just to see Marna. There was a bond between them.

"Papa, I—" Marna bit her lip, about to confess that today, when Karl brought home a fresh-killed rabbit, the little body still warm and limp, she, oh so much, wanted it to be alive again, and for a moment—only a moment—she wished it was Bertha. Instead, she asked to be excused and fled to her room. Salve knew that any moment of closeness, perhaps forgiveness, had slipped away. Marna knew that she would have to devise her own punishment.

Early the next morning, Karl and Knud were already separating the two biggest pigs to be butchered when Marna appeared, wrapped in Kristina's merino shawl, her breath making white puffs in the frosty air. The rime glittered in the morning sun but was rapidly ground into the barnyard by the movement of work shoes and pigs running helter-skelter. The pigs were already frenzied, dodging the gate that Karl carried to corner them, squealing with fright as they were herded toward the slaughtering place in the doorway of the granary. Shackled, they could only hobble. Marna leaned against the board fence, watching, her fists clenched, anticipatory, fearful for the pigs and for herself.

The shackles were connected to a lowered whiffletree, as Salve, in an oilcloth apron, approached with a sledgehammer. He didn't notice Marna, concentrating as he was upon swinging the hammer for one well-aimed blow. There was a loud crack as his hammer hit the pig's skull. As the pig fell, Karl and Knud hoisted it up into the air with pulleys until it was suspended from the whiffletree. Salve moved in with a huge knife and cut the pig's throat, severing the jugular. Blood exploded on the floor, spattering the wall opposite, the trampled frost reddened with blood. Knud held a pail under the stream of blood—Bertha wanted it for blood sausage and pancakes. The other pig screeched as Salve approached it. Marna felt sick. The second pig was hoisted in the air, throat severed. Now Salve slit open the peritoneum straight down the middle; the intestines cascaded upon the floor and the smell of hot intestines steamed in the winter air, fetid, overpowering. For several years, Karl had vomited at this moment.

Salve looked for him now, standing with his bloody knife in hand, his apron a smear of blood. Knud was attending the fire under the big copper pot where the pig would be scalded before scraping off the hair. Salve saw Marna and Karl talking and could hear their words in the sharp morning air: the pigs now were soundless.

"Marna, why are you here?" Karl asked her.

"I just came to get out of the house for a moment. It's such a beautiful morning."

"But—but why here?" Karl couldn't understand anyone being present who didn't have to be.

"I didn't watch. I just looked at the sun on the frost. It sparkles so." Marna didn't look at Karl either, who, puzzled, went back to his work. By this time, the pigs were no longer animals, they were just meat, to be eviscerated, scalded, scraped, their flesh to turn into the slabs that would be bacon, ham, sausage instead of muscle, sinew, nerve. Salve and boys would cut it into large pieces; beginning tomorrow, the rest would belong to the women.

Marna took her place alongside Bertha and Ingebjor to slice and cut and grind and salt. They cut up the fat—it was greasy, heavy, and cold on their hands, and the stove was fired red hot. All day long, pork fat boiled: their faces were red with heat, their hands red with cold. Bertha poured the boiling fat into the lard press and wound down the flat cylinder which pressed the curly, brown cracklings into a hard cake with little round impressions like a sieve. The clear liquid emerged from the funnel still bubbling. Marna thought Bertha looked like a troll around her stewpot, its vapors rising; Ingebjor looked a younger version of her.

Hams and bacon went into brine in forty-gallon crockery jars, some weeks later to the smokehouse, but that process belonged to the men. For the women, it was several days' work after the butchering, while they cooked pork liver and heart for meals and ate Bertha's *blodpannekaker*, and *blodpolse*.

Marna worked extra hard, her hair pulled back tighter even than usual. She was patient with Bertha; she avoided her father's eyes. After three days, her hands were reddened with cold and the dampness of the meat, but her eyes were clear. God had forgiven her. She had forced herself to watch the slaughter, and now, eating the blodpannekaker was the last penance Marna had set for herself. By the time the sausage was made, she would be freed.

On a raw February day in 1903, at the Stavanger monthly meeting for business, Inger Bottnen said, "The query has risen in me, what we are met here for."

"To discuss the case against Ina, here," Ole Sawyer, bellowed, nodding his head in Ina's direction. He was the leader of those opposing her ministry and her unlawful representation of the New Stavanger Meeting.

"Lena is believed by all who know her," Severine Bryngelsen said, meaning that Ina was not.

Salve's sister, Lena, had, in the previous fall, traveled to the North Carolina yearly meeting with Ina, where events occurred that neither Stavanger Meeting nor North Carolina Meeting would forget, and Lena, a staunch supporter, had become a staunch enemy. Ina's children had been ill with tonsillitis and whooping cough, and though she herself had bronchitis, her God-directed concern made it imperative for her to go to save the North Carolina Meeting from becoming Fast Friends by falling into the ways of the world. If God commanded Ina to go, He would provide for her family; Lena would provide for Ina's needs by accompanying her.

According to Ina, it was a nightmare of changing trains, jouncing on frail bones, prostrate and faint with labors of the spirit, and sustained by the strong arm and spirit of Lena. They stopped at meetings along the way for Ina to speak.

In North Carolina, Benjamin Thorsen joined Ina in the ministry.

When the yearly meeting was over, Ina had a concern that she must travel further, in North Carolina, to Ohio, to Washington, accompanied by Benjamin. Lena stayed for a while, riding unhappily in a second carriage; in the far-off mountains of North Carolina, she spoke. "Ina, thy mission is ended. Now thy abandoned babes call for thee, but thou loiterest in the company of one thou preferest to all others…" The Evil One Ina had dreamed of was made manifest: it was Lena, and it had been Benjamin who had known it, and from whose clutches he had been sent to rescue Ina.

Ole Sawyer, aged but fiery, shouted to Ina, "Woman! Look to thy children! Sundoff, look to thy wife! Thou prospereth not! Thy wife spends thy substance, yea, even that needed by the five children she had born to thee, hopefully to thee. Her spirit is not so frail to conceive of the flesh. Whether she does so from appetite or duty, I know not!"

The blasphemy was spoken. Sundoff was silent. But Ina was not. Unquavering, low-pitched, her voice spoke of the temptations fallen to the children of the New Stavanger Meeting: of Ole's grandchildren, the sins of Salve's wife, of Sigbjorn, of vanity, the devil behind their faces, that God had warned her in dream against those who took counsel against her. That God himself had prepared her for the stings and arrows. "I will suffer even thee, Ole Sawyer! I say thy soul is with the very devil!"

Ole shook with rage. "Ina, it is 'thy will be done,' even in the face of thy babes, and thy poor and ignorant husband."

"Ole, *thou shalt tremble before the word of God,* for I am His mouthpiece!"

The meeting was stunned into silence—not a Quaker silence, but that of desperation. Had the unseen Christ abandoned their meeting, and, hovering at the door, waiting entrance was His foe, the devil, in the shape of their own hearts? Had God placed before them good and evil in the body of two persons? Must they choose? They must believe one or the other!

Ina staggered out on the arm of Sundoff to their carriage. "Thou shouldst not have come, Ina," he said, as he slapped the reins on his old horse.

Through Ina's mind ran Benjamin's words of comfort, which were worth all the accusations: *Thou art gowned in gray which is to me shimmering silver, yet thou art flesh. Thy words have launched men upon dreams, challenged them to what they would not have dared without thee. Oneself is a prison, Ina, and thou wouldst free one from that prison into which we are not born but manage to place ourselves. But thy passion frees the soul and lifts the body, and thy touch is the kiss of heaven. Oh, never before has my soul and body become one as with thee...*

She asked Sundoff to stop the carriage and he, seeing her descend and kneel in the snow, knew that it was useless to stop her, that he might as well try to stop the winter from coming, the sun from rising. He was surely a man anointed, or cursed, to have such a wife.

* * *

It had been over eleven years since Kristina had died. With Christmas came the small celebrations the family engaged in: going to meeting and Christmas dinner, with roast goose. No gifts were exchanged, no merrymaking other than the quiet celebration of the birth of Christ, the Son of God, who had walked among them.

Bertha had never experienced family events before her marriage to Salve. She felt blessed enough to have Salve and his children, but she was afraid of raising them unruly and ungrateful, and she resorted to the rod as a compensation for her lack of experience. That she stifled the child in them she wasn't aware, nor was childish behavior acceptable in 1903 on the prairies of the Midwest in a small Quaker world: to have children, it was necessary to rule them with God-fearing obedience and hard work. All else was either frivolous or indulgent. Love, it followed, was frivolous.

Ina Christiansen came to the Christmas meeting of 1908 for worship, with her three children—a son and two daughters, little gray replicas of their mother. Under their bonnets were faces too somber for their years and too pale to be healthy. The brilliance of the sun through the frost-coated panes enhanced their blue eyes but made visible the near pallor of their skin. Their mother was frequently absent—no other religion appointed women ministers, and Ina needed new horizons—attending yearly meetings in New England, Canada, England, and then, her return to Norway as a minister. She was an ambassador without a country, traveling more and more without designation from her own meeting. Her children looked after themselves, although Ina said that her husband was as good as a mother. Women knew better.

Her message this Christmas was for one person alone—who would recognize herself.

Ina Christiansen stood up in the midst of the beginning silence of the meeting, between two daughters, speaking in a ghostly voice, as though she would summon the dead and not the Lord. Under her poke bonnet, her face was not visible except to the Elders facing her, who tried *not* to look. They knew her look of utter concentration, eyes shut, chin high, her attentive listening to hear God's voice, which no one else could hear: how this New World looked to be God's very pasture and they His obedient flock, that they—She said they had the greenest of pastures, abundant lambs and cattle. But that among them was a serpent beguiling, a sinner who operated under the cover of the darkness, that among their green pastures were seeds planted by the devil himself, "who hath descended to this community. Look right and left to the devil among ye! Devil, look to thy mirror to behold thy soul, how it blackens and blackens, how it dangles over the fiery gates of hell. Repent! Repent of thy crime, of the house wherein thou art usurper, thou the serpent itself who stung and stung and laid her low who has risen up!"

Bertha started and sucked in her breath in short gasps. She looked from side to side, moving only her eyes, which then swept the room: she wanted to observe Salve's face, the boys', the girls', but without turning her head, she could not see the faces she feared to see. Now Bertha knew that God had revealed her wicked secret about Kristina's death to Ina. Her fear of Ina grew into hate, and hate gnawed at Bertha's heart.

Few spoke to Ina in the socializing after meeting, fearing to be the next one denounced from the pulpit. She was a woman with the devil's eyes, some said. Her believers were fewer and fewer. Sigbjorn Rosdale shook her hand and said, "Ina, it would seem that perhaps thy children need thee more than the yearly meetings thou attends."

Ina stood flanked by her three youngest children—her son of seven, her daughters of eight and six years. Her son's trousers were too short, his jacket had holes in the elbows, her daughters' dresses were of cotton when all other children were in wool, except for their shawls, which were thin and oversized. No other children wore shawls.

"Friend Sigbjorn, beware lest thou be known for thy gluttony rather than thy Christian spirit." Ina looked at him, her eyes unforgiving. "My children wait upon the Lord and are fed with His hand. *Consider the lilies*, Sigbjorn. My children are God's lilies, and their splendor comes from within. But thou canst not see it." She turned from him, children following in unison, walking straight into Klara, who had been longing to be noticed by her.

"So, cousin! How fare thee?" She looked at Klara, the same age as her Berit. Sigbjorn saw how much better Klara looked, both in her dress, plain and badly made as it was, and her color, even though Klara wasn't as robust as Inger and the boys. Even though the Roseland children were motherless, they did have a stepmother who, although disagreeable, was at home.

Ina spoke to Klara, "Child, thou must bring thy father to God. He is stung by a serpent. But serpents die in summer." She turned on her black-heeled boots and departed with her wordless, trailing children.

The summer harvest season of 1909 was in full swing: for the women, it meant cooking for harvest crews in a kitchen already busy with canning fruits and vegetables from their gardens. Hours were long: livestock chores at dawn for men, to the harvest fields when the dew was off. Women hoed and planted and picked at dawn when gardens were cool. They prepared harvest dinners for noontime, when the men arrived from fields, sweat pungent on their overalls, the once-blue denim shirts whitened with sun and salt of sweat.

The July air was the dry smell of straw baked in the sun, mixed with the faint scent of pink single-petaled wild roses growing along the roads and under the stubble of the wheat fields. Toward evening, lengthened shadows put stilts on horses, while barns reached up to the sky, and wagons high with wheat and oats grew taller and taller, as they kept arriving and emptying into elevators, operated by horses on a treadmill.

Although Bertha was in charge of the food preparation and preservation, it was Marna who directed the household, smaller now. In 1909, they no longer had a hired girl; there were four women, and of the boys, only eighteen-year-old Johann lived at home. Karl and Knud were married and lived on other land and in houses that Salve owned: Knud lived on the farm once belonging to Bertha, Salve's wedding gift.

Marna, twenty, was engaged to be married after harvest to Emil Strandval, a member of Stavanger Meeting. Marna no longer defied Bertha: her thoughts were now occupied with a more important person. Bertha just *was*. Marna recognized the need that her father had had for Bertha after Kristina had died. Inger, outspoken and fearless, still provoked Bertha. It was Klara whom Marna worried about, who seemed to have absorbed all of Marna's self-examination and insecurity. Marna wondered if her own guilt had been merely transferred to Klara. Was it because Klara had always been torn between loyalty to her sisters and love for Bertha that made her so vulnerable? But Bertha *was* Klara's mother. She had known no other.

Marna thought about these things as she ordered Inger and Klara to baste the hams, set the tables, pick and pare vegetables, cut, slice. Her sisters were so capable that they never resented Marna's orders, content to have someone else in charge, as was Bertha. Bertha was fifty-seven years old, heavier than ever, so that the hot kitchen fired by the woodstove for so much cooking and canning was unbearable to her. She stood, red-faced and puffing in July 1909, slicing cabbage for the harvesters' noon meal. Marna glanced at her and suddenly noticed her eyes, burning bright.

"Bertha, do you feel well?" she asked, as she approached her, placing the back of her hand on Bertha's forehead.

"Ach, it's too hot. The day is too hot, the stove is too hot. Uff-ta!" Bertha eased herself into a kitchen chair.

"Bertha, I think you have a fever. Why don't you go in the parlor and rest?"

"A summer cold," Bertha insisted. But her fever grew and grew. In the middle of the summer, when there were mostly farm accidents to tend to, Dr. Barnes came to see Bertha.

"Summer influenza and congestion," he said. "Unusual at this time—I have only harvest accidents. Put on a chest poultice."

Klara, fourteen, made a poultice of linseeds soaked in boiling water and pressed in a wool cloth, running from the harvest table to look after Bertha, bringing cool cloths for her forehead and hot poultices for her chest. Her head ached, her neck hurt, her face burned, but nothing burned her like her very soul—*Ina was right! That she was dying she knew, and she knew why! Why had God waited so long?* she wondered. *Why now?*

For three days, the sisters took turns fanning her red, warty face, framed in streaks of gray wispy hair that spread out on her pillow. If Inger came, Bertha asked for Marna, who was efficient and thorough. But if Marna came, she asked for Klara. When Klara came, Bertha held her hand, and Klara bent over her, wetting her red face with tears. Bertha patted Klara's head and smoothed her cheeks. Marna and Inger didn't touch her. The girls were silent with each other.

Bertha wanted Salve. He came, he leaned over her, fanning her, but he could not make himself touch her. He stood awkwardly, smelling of sweat, grimy with chaff from the harvester, horse smell mixed with his own. She wanted to confess to Salve, but her words would not come, even to save her from eternal damnation. That it would come soon, she knew.

Malinda came, helping with all the kitchen work. Bertha preferred the girls to look after her, and Malinda preferred to be in the kitchen. She brought with her a calmness, especially to Inger and Marna—she had been Kristina's friend. But it was Malinda who stayed up with Bertha on the evening of the fourth day, when the exhausted girls had gone to bed.

Malinda recognized Bertha's crisis. Seeing Bertha's face reddened by the wasting fever, and with great efforts of prayer and resolve,

Malinda tried to stop blaming Bertha for Kristina's death. She knew that Salve was entirely unsuspecting. Even though Malinda didn't like Bertha, she had understood her longing for husband and home, children—everything that Kristina had had. Bertha's green jealousy had broken into a gangrenous heart!

In the middle of the night, Bertha cried out, *Forgive me, God, forgive me, Kristina! Salve, I wanted you so much, I could not help myself. God, have mercy! Ina, thou hast seen into my soul.* Malinda gasped, and Bertha stopped breathing.

Malinda covered Bertha's face with the sheet, and then she went to the parlor to sit, silently and alone, believing herself the first person to know as truth what she had long suspected. She did not know how long she sat, but as she rose to inform Salve of Bertha's death, she knew there would be no second person.

On July 18, the harvesting stopped, and after a simple service, Bertha was lowered into a hole dug in the Quaker cemetery where the summer grasses gave way to a black wound in the greenness. Each of Salve's sons and daughters, along with Malinda and Sigbjorn, bent down to gather a handful of earth as they filed by the grave. Klara was white-faced and silent, and she lingered while the rest of the family walked by Kristina's grave, two rows away. They paused there, while Marna looked back at Klara then turned to go back and comfort her. The family group was reminded with some satisfaction that Kristina's was a double tombstone, that space was left for their father. *He would not lie next to Bertha!*

Malinda hadn't at first recognized the figure in the long gray skirts and the poke bonnet with her arms around Klara. But when she did it was with some dread as she recognized Ina Tobiasdatter Christiansen. Malinda looked away—had Ina caught her eyes, Malinda would most surely have learned that two persons shared a horrible secret Malinda thought was hers alone.

"Lille Klara, who has lost two mothers," Ina said to her, soothing Klara's red eyes with her cool hands. "Do you remember your promise?" But Klara didn't remember she had promised anything to Ina. "That you must bring your father to God?" Klara nodded, but she didn't remember. And Ina told her that she must also promise not to listen to those who devised evil against her, because God Himself would punish them, that she was His messenger, that Klara should always come to her when she needed, and she would need to...

Klara said nothing, not knowing what to say. Then Malinda took her by the arm to lead her away. "Come, Klara," she said, and Klara saw Ina look towards Malinda, as though *she* was one of them Klara had been warned about, and Klara loved them both. But she feared Ina, too: people said she was both devil and angel in one. She didn't know what to believe. Rejoining the family group, Inger told her to stay away from Ina. Marna said nothing.

If love and respect ennoble, then only Klara was ennobled by Bertha. But Klara's love for Bertha engendered guilt toward her sisters. Marna remained loyal to her mother, Kristina, and led Inger with her to that silent shrine. Inger had laughed away Bertha's authority and said she didn't care, but the more Inger was indifferent, the more Bertha had expected of her, angered as Bertha was to see that she couldn't really touch Inger. So Inger had waited. Now she would be free.

As for the boys, now young men, they had had more of Bertha's respect and less of her authority. Their training had been in the fields and barns and mows, in the heat and long days of summer and in the bitter cold and darkness of winter farm work; that was discipline enough.

Now, with Bertha gone—she had been married to Salve Roseland nearly as long as he had been married to Kristina—the household, under the sisters' capable hands, ran as smoothly as before. Gradually, Inger and Klara had better clothes sewed by Marna who made high-necked white blouses for them, with a small lace edging and full sleeves. Marna did her best to comfort Klara, but *she* was enjoying Bertha's absence. Salve seemed neither grieved by Bertha's loss nor dismayed by his daughters' lack of grief, except for Klara's distant quietness. He liked to be alone with his daughters in an evening—Marna now came into the parlor to sew her trousseau. *Spring will come too soon,* he thought, *and Marna will be gone.*

The arrival of March 15, 1910, in the Roseland household, was looked upon with dread by Inger and Klara, and by Salve, too, although he would not say so. Now that the day was here, Marna was also infected with the general somberness of the house.

Already in the wedding dress that she would wear to meeting for her marriage to Emil Strandval, Marna stood in front of her father in the parlor. She had made a high-necked white linen dress with two tiers of fullness inset with crocheted lace and in the narrow waistband, a puffed bodice, eyelet leg of mutton sleeves. Her hair was piled up high and shining by Inger and graced with a white silk bow; Klara had helped her dress. Marna understood her sister's need to do this for her. Too much evidence of Marna's leaving was present in the house, with her quilts and linens, once laid out in the guest room, now packed in a dome-topped trunk that Salve had had made for her. Inger was occupied with thoughts of her sister's new life, wondering if Papa, waiting for Marna in the parlor, would tell her about the mysteries of marriage and what she should expect. Klara was thinking of her loneliness without Marna.

In Marna's hand was a single red rose that Malinda had got for her from a Marshalltown florist. She held it out to her father as he stood up from his worn chair, dressed in a dark suit, his vest buttoned up fully over a white shirt. His hair was iron gray, his beard silvery, his figure still strong and stocky. He was fifty-five years old, and his eldest daughter was leaving his house to be married.

"Papa," Marna began, "are you sure that it's all right for me to leave you now, now that Bertha's gone?"

Salve looked away; clearing his throat, he reached out for both of Marna's hands. He glanced down at the carpet for a moment, noting how worn it was. He'd bought it from a mail-order company when they moved into this house nearly twenty-two years ago. He could almost count the years by where and how much the carpet was worn. Marna, now almost twenty-one, was born into this house.

"Marna, you will be twenty-one in May, and Emil is twenty-five. He needs a wife, you are of age. I have Inger and Klara. They are competent, thanks to you, so of course, it is all right," he said, taking the rose from her hands. He saw that they trembled. There were tears in Marna's eyes.

"I'm sorry to leave you, Papa," she said, but he didn't dare look at her. He embraced her instead, thinking of Kristina, wishing she was there to see her daughter, to tell Marna something about the marriage bed. His embrace was awkward and hesitant. He was startled to hear Marna say, "Papa, I wish Mor were here," as she clasped her arms around his neck. Encouraged by Marna's words and her arms around his neck, he clasped her tightly for a moment, thinking how sad it was that it was the first real embrace he had ever given his oldest daughter, or she him, now that she was leaving him.

Salve released her and looked into her face. "Marna, I want you to have your mother's candleholder. I know how much it means to you. She found it in her trunk, the night she...arrived here, in Iowa, in the old house."

Yes, Marna knew, but she said, "Papa, I can't take it. Your giving it to me means everything. But—"

"But why, Marna? Why?" Salve interrupted.

"Because Klara has it now. I told her about it, how it was placed in Mor's trunk by her mother, and she, now that she's lost *her* mother, you know, Bertha, Klara is too attached to it for me to take it. I couldn't, Papa. But I thank you deeply."

Then Marna straightened, drying her eyes with a handkerchief, and looked at her father. "Papa, Emil is a good man."

Troubled by Marna's refusal of the candlestick, Salve realized it was he who should be telling her that. Still holding the rose, he held Marna at arm's length, "Marna, Kristinasdatter, you have been mother to my family. You had to grow up so fast..." He tried to control the lump in his throat by clearing it, knowing he should say something regarding a man about whom he knew a lot but didn't really know, a man from Trondelag. A man of slight build, with thin fair hair. *A closed man*, he thought. He didn't know if Emil Strandval was generous or kind. He knew that he was hard-working.

"Papa, you *do* like him, don't you?" But Salve was wondering how he could like any man who was going to take his first daughter from him. The world would never be the same for her again. All would follow: children, sickness, death. Perhaps Bertha had been luckier, raising children without the pain of childbirth. He looked into Marna's face, remembering Tollak's, a face so young, so beautiful, so capable. He couldn't wish to keep her home, just to save her from what women had to suffer.

"Yes, Marna. Emil is a good man. I'm sure he will be good to you." At the same time that he said it he realized that whether or not Emil would be good to her was something he absolutely did not know. Who knew what went on at night, in bedrooms, in bed, at breakfast time and noontime and suppertime and again at bedtime, day after day, year after year? At birthing and nursing? He was thinking of Emil's farm, so far away, isolated from all others, with Marna in the house, cooking, gardening, canning, all day alone. And then, children would come…Had he been good to Kristina? Certainly he had loved her, and she him. He remembered standing on the ship with her, bound for America. Kristina watching the wake of the water as it left her homeland. He had been too excited to think of her sorrow.

"Marna," he asked, looking her in the eyes. "Do you love this man?"

How *was* a man good to his wife? He had done what was expected of him, hadn't he? He was righteous, God-fearing. He had provided his children with lives free from poverty, imprisonment, fines, diets of rye and meager potatoes; he had brought them to the New World and made Americans out of them, when they could have remained in Norway, impoverished, harvesting stones, generation after generation. Could there have been something else he might have done? *Should* there have been something else? For what other reason did Ina Christiansen point her finger at him except that she was a crazed woman, discontent with Sundoff, a poor provider, a meek man—nay, hardly a man at all!

And Marna? What now for her? What did he *mean* by love? Did Emil love her as he had loved Kristina? Was she marrying because custom commanded, because she didn't want to be the object of scorn, a spinster? Must she suffer sex, or would she want it?

Her left hand went to her throat, and she stepped back, "Papa,

I...I don't know. I'm afraid, I guess. I think I love him, but, I don't know about the...rest." She looked at him, hoping he could tell her what she knew he couldn't. Or wouldn't. Which was it? *Women knew nothing of men. Were men equally ignorant of women? Would they couple, just like the cattle?* Marna wondered.

Salve held out the rose, and Marna smiled. "Oh yes, Papa, would you pin it on me?" His fingers fumbled, but Marna helped him. She put her chin forward, as Salve knew she would, without help from him, then went out of the parlor on his arm, to the carriage. Inger and Klara were already seated in it; Johann held the harnessed horses by their bridles, all waiting for the bride in the cold March sun.

CHAPTER EIGHT

Inger thrived under her new freedom. Klara resented Inger's response to Bertha's absence; they both missed Marna, but twenty miles was a long distance by carriage, and Inger didn't need Marna's advice and comfort.

One of their new duties, which had been Bertha's, was to hitch up the old mare, Solveig, and drive five miles to Legrand's large general store. The proprietor imported Norwegian hand knits and homespuns—housewives said the climate in America was wrong for spinning and knitting—Norwegian hard biscuits, tinned herring, lutefisk, carved wooden spoons and bowls. Farmers' tools, harness, bolts and nuts, rope, twine, were next to denim jackets and cotton flannel shirts, yard goods of wool and cotton, sewing supplies.

On a cold early March afternoon, Inger and Klara were returning home from the store, where they had bought staples, but also salt cod in small wooden boxes and *fiskeboller* in flat oval tins, some harness leather for Salve to repair harnesses, and some cotton material for dresses that Marna had promised to sew for them: a navy embossed cotton, with a pattern of flowers and scrolls that Bertha wouldn't have approved.

Inger was driving the old mare, urging her forward. Klara was huddled under the horsehair blanket. Reins in hand, Inger slapped them on the back of the plodding mare, "Gee, old Bertha," she said. "Hup, hup, hup!" urging her onward.

Klara sat up, her eyes flashing and filling with tears at the same time. "Inger, I hate it when you are like that. Don't call Solveig Bertha. You do it just to make me upset."

"No I don't. Solveig is like Bertha, that's all: old and fat and slow. And disagreeable." The mare had never been known for her good nature or willingness to be caught, and now that she was old, she refused to trot.

Klara bit her lip, trying not to cry, and Inger slapped the reins harder and harder on the mare's back. The sun, which had peeked through the cloud cover, was now gone, and with it a chilling cold was settling in. Snow had been predicted by Karl Bottnen at the general store, and Inger wanted to get home. Her arms and shoulders were beginning to feel the chill. Their carriage was the only thing visible on the flat landscape, and it crawled like a black ant over the land: dark squares of plowed field, yellowish-brown squares of unplowed stubble with small fissures from freezing and thawing, and squares with occasional faint green patches of pasture dotted with farm animals as if they were painted there—black-and-white cows, red-and-brown horses, dark silhouettes of pigs, some spotted, some with a white stripe, some coppery colored, smaller dots of white sheep. Inger's face was red-cheeked in the cold spring air, and Klara's paler one retreated again under the horsehair robe.

Inger looked at the patchwork landscape, like a quilt that Malinda was teaching her to make. She wasn't aware that Klara was huddling deeper and deeper into the robe until she heard sobs. She reached over to Klara, jerking hard at the robe to uncover her sister's face, which she now saw was swollen with tears. Klara's sobs burst forth on the otherwise soundless landscape. Immediately Inger was sorry. Klara had cried frequently, silently, to herself, ever since Bertha's death, but Inger pretended not to hear. At first she'd felt sorry; later she felt impatient and then angry. Now, she felt sorry again—she'd been the cause. Marna had comforted Klara; her absence was not filled by Inger, two years older than fifteen-year-old Klara.

Klara looked at Inger, upset that Inger had unmasked her tearstained face. "You—shouldn't do—do that," she sobbed. "You don't care at all about me."

Inger dropped the reins—it didn't matter whether she held them or not, Solveig would plod on just the same—and put her arms around Klara. "I'm sorry. Truly I am, Klara. Please forgive me."

"You don't miss Bertha because you hated her. I loved her, Inger. Don't you understand? She—she was my mother."

"I'm sorry, Klara. Please…" Inger realized how her own natural exuberance had blinded her. She hadn't meant to be unkind.

"Inger, you are lucky. It is easier for you. But now, Marna's gone, too. Oh, Inger, I'm so lonely, and my hands are so dumb, so wooden, compared to Marna's. She says Satan finds mischief for idle hands, but I think about Bertha all the time, and Mor, and then my hands stumble. Inger, we don't even talk to each other." Klara heaved a long sob and took a deep breath. Solveig had come to a dead stop, but neither sister noticed.

"Inger, you didn't even tell me about the red flag. I thought I was going to die. I didn't even know what I'd done, and then I asked Marna. She told me I wasn't sick at all, or bad. Just growing up. She said you didn't know, either. That's one thing Bertha told her about."

"Klara, I thought I was sick, too. I hid cloths in a pail under the porch floor at the back of the house. After a week, I was sure I was going to bleed to death, so I told Bertha. Oh, I should have told you, Klara, but when I knew what it was, I pretended it hadn't happened to me. I just wanted to be the way I was." As Inger spoke to Klara, she stroked Klara's forehead and pulled the carriage robe close around her, wondering why she couldn't have held out her hand to her younger sister before. She'd been jealous of Bertha's love for Klara, she knew. They'd been together but lonely all their lives, but Klara had had someone: Inger and Marna had been alone.

"Klara," Inger continued, "do you know what the red flag means?"

Klara shook her head. Her sobs had subsided into an occasional heave of frosty breath, and then a long pause. Inger looked about the horizon, to see if anyone would see or hear them, noting that Solveig had stopped dead still, little puffs of breath rising from her lowered head. "Because, well, now we can be mothers. I mean, we can have babies." She said it into the air, over Solveig's head.

"You mean, if we're married?" Klara said, raising her head, thinking of Selma and Karl's baby girl, Johanna, now a month old, Salve's first grandchild.

"Yes, yes. That's what I mean," Inger said, slapping the reins across Solveig's back again, knowing that Klara didn't know any more than that about babies. "Gee, gee, Solveig."

When the big stallion made farm rounds every month or so, Bertha had been careful that the girls were in the house. Inger loved animals, especially horses, and Johann knew all about their breeding and told her. Once she had tried to watch, and found a crack in the barn through which she saw the stallion, led shiny and snorting, to a whinnying mare. Her father just then came into the barn, and she fled.

"Klara," Inger said, "I'll try to be a better sister. Truly, I'm sorry." She slapped the reins again across Solveig's back, resolving never to use Bertha's name again—she had never said it in kindness.

The sisters rode the rest of the way home in silence, Inger feeling forgiven, and Klara unburdened. Snow flakes like fine sand were beginning to fall, and a wind was picking up, blowing the snow in little swirls across the road that cut through the middle of the flat land. March blizzards were sometimes the worst of the winter season.

At home, Solveig stood, waiting for them to unload. Inger would unhitch and unharness her and feed her—she would apologize to Solveig for speaking ill of her, while Klara made hot coffee. They would drink it by the woodstove and eat raisin cake, warming their feet, smiling at each other.

Neither knew that the months they would spend together in their father's house were numbered on one hand.

* * *

July arrived again. Marna came for a few days to help Inger and Klara cook for harvesters, and Malinda as well, each remembering last season's harvest: Bertha had died on July 17. This summer, Selma was there with her four-month-old baby, Johanna, a new life to replace the old. The sisters took turns from cooking and preserving to play with her, when she wasn't sleeping or Selma suckling her, debating which parent she resembled. Inger said she looked like a baby, and nothing else.

Inger took off Johanna's shoes and stockings and the baby smiled, doubling up her toes as the grass tickled.

"I see I shall have to repair the damage." Malinda laughed, seeing the grass stains on the white embroidered dress Marna had made, seeing the bare feet. Malinda sat under the elm with the baby, looking at the waves of heat coming from the wheat fields, hearing the bellow of the steam engine and the whirring of the thresher, thinking of how Kristina would be pleased to see her grown sons and daughters, her first grandchild. Aromas of hams and bread baking, pies, and coffee came from the kitchen. Already, there were shelves of cherries, apples, and plums in jars, and Klara and Inger piled up the root cellar with vegetables. Malinda's own children were grown; she had a dozen grandchildren. It was a good land, this America. She was content; she wondered if Kristina would still find the richness disturbing. Payment would be extracted, somehow, Kristina would think, although, at this moment, Malinda didn't see how.

When Selma developed a high fever the first of August, the sisters were upset, remembering Bertha. Selma lived for eight days instead of four, and then she died, racked by the same high fever and headache that would not stop. And so the world stopped for Salve's family, and when it began again, the lives of Inger, Klara, and Karl had changed radically. Malinda remained stunned by the swift voice of God.

Karl was a widower at twenty-five, needing a substitute mother and housekeeper. It could not be a young immigrant girl, nor did anyone know of any Berthas available, so the solution became obvious: Inger, seventeen years old, would become Karl's housekeeper and baby nurse. That would leave Klara to run her father's house.

Inger would have to go immediately. She had never cared for a baby, but girls were supposed to know how, the way nature's females instinctively knew, without learning.

After Selma's funeral, Inger, sober, and Klara, red-eyed, stood together in their father's house. "Klara, you can do it, I know you can. There's only you and Johann and Papa," Inger soothed.

Klara said that she wasn't worried about the work, it was the loneliness, and not understanding how Selma could follow Bertha, that she didn't want next July to come, ever, that harvest and canning would always mean death, like the end of summer.

Inger embraced Klara's body shaking with sobs, and her hands smoothed back Klara's dark hair.

"Now that we've become friends, too, I can't bear to have you go," Klara said, hugging her sister.

Each of them heard Johanna's cry from the carriage outside, where Karl waited for Inger, his horses hot in the sun, impatient. Inger said no more and went out the door. Klara did not follow her.

Klara went from room to room, from the pantry through the kitchen into the hallway, and then to the downstairs bedroom. She hurried out of that place into the living room, seeing Salve's Norwegian Bible in its worn, heavy, brown leather cover, stained with a spot of wax. She touched it, ran her fingers over the gold embossed letters, *Bibelen*, opening the cover to read *Det Gamle og Nye Testamentes* in Gothic letters, then *Chriftiania, 1867*, before she realized that the *s* was like an *f*. She corrected herself, reading *Christiania*, which Papa said was the old name for Oslo, the capital of Norway.

The musty odor of old pages filled the room, as she looked through a text she couldn't read in a language she could speak. In cursive scroll that she would like to be able to write, it said *Salve Knudsen fra Lyndal, Kvassogn, den 17, i niende Maaned, Idag elleve aar gammel.* After his name, she translated to herself, "On the seventeenth day, the ninth month, today eleven years old," the age when children turned the corner into beginning adulthood in Norway. They could become apprentices, which often meant leaving home, Bertha had told her. She couldn't think of taking on adult responsibilities at age eleven. *I can't even think of it at fifteen!*

She closed the cover and turned to touch the English Bible, bending over to open the softer cover where the list of family births, deaths, and marriages were recorded. The names were in different handwriting: her mother's, surely, recording all but Staale's birth. Bertha must have written in his name and Kristina's. She recognized Marna's hand, recording Bertha's death, Johanna's birth. Selma's name was not there. Was *she* to do it? Was that, now, one of her duties? She closed the Bible and touched the brass candlestick carefully, tracing her finger around the rectangle of the base, up the neck, bringing her index finger to rest lightly upon the thumb rest. She looked at the insignificance of her hands and turned them over to look at the palms, wishing they were Marna's hands. They were perspiring. She turned toward the horsehair sofa and knelt on the worn carpet, her elbows resting on the seat, her hands clasped together. She bowed her head, wanting her throat to unknot, wanting the day to pass, the week, a month. Wanting July never to come again.

* * *

The plinkety-plink sound of the merry-go-round was heard all over the fairgrounds, and its location was a favorite meeting ground for young people from the farms who could otherwise meet only in church. They preferred the atmosphere of the brightly painted wooden horses charging round and round and up and down, next to the Ferris wheel's high rise and fall. From the Ferris wheel, farms for miles around were visible, and couples would look for their own rooftops and barns fading endlessly into the blue horizon of Indian summer. In mid-September, frost would soon arrive so that the nights were cold, but the days were intense with honeybees in goldenrod and silver threads of cocoons spinning in the air. There was a lull in farm work, before corn picking and after the summer threshing and haying, when young men dressed up in their store-bought three-piece suits and hats, to look over the crop of unmarried girls, in black skirts and lacy white shirts or all-white dresses, straw ribbon-trimmed hats. Girls grouped together, self-conscious and expectant.

Many of the Norwegians were Quaker, but, as long as they "observed moderation and temperance on all occasions," as written in the queries, attendance gradually became acceptable for the young of Quaker families, and the merry-go-round was matchmaking territory.

But the fair was not acceptable to Ina Christiansen who, despite being disowned from the Stavanger Meeting, led protests against fairs and circus shows, against the beer-drinking Germans, calling out for all to "see the devil's face inside each bottle, who will eat the soul."

September 1914 gave Ina double ammunition against the Germans and their sinful polkas and beer drinking. She shouted how traitorous they were, but that war-making was not surprising from those who "killeth the prophets and stoneth the children." Others cheered Ina's anti-German tirade, because of the German declaration of war on France and Russia, and cheered their defeat at the Marne only last week. The Germans, many born in Germany, gathered together, and spoke in subdued voices—there was nothing to celebrate and everything to fear. The Norwegians boycotted them.

Klara and Inger went to the fair and to the merry-go-round with Johann and his bride, Siri, hearing its muffled and tinny music; music of any kind was unusual for them. All three young women wore white dresses; a row of lace fringed each high white neckline like a calyx, their necks rose like stems to the flowers of their faces. At each throat was a cameo pin; their waists were narrow, their natural-straw hats small and jaunty.

The sisters were just under twenty and twenty-two years; Klara was slight, her face looked both worried and innocent. Inger had seen already what love could bring for women: care, children, more work. And she was still Karl's housekeeper; he hadn't thought of another bride. Inger had all the household care without the compensation of a husband. She lived like a spinster. Klara had become good friends with her father over the four years they'd been alone together, especially after Johann married. Inger was a little jealous of that, but more so of Viktor Endresen.

He is tall with dark hair and pale blue eyes, like an early spring sky, when winter is still at hand. His bushy eyebrows are as dark as the bare spring branches, his nose very straight. He has such large hands. This is how Klara had memorized Viktor Endresen.

"Papa," she said that evening at home in the parlor after supper, "I met Viktor Endresen today." Salve was deep in his usual chair, studying the accounts of his four farms, occupied now by his three sons and himself. His face was younger-looking than he'd looked for years, the lines around the mouth softened, his eyes full of humor. Klara was on the sofa, embroidering a pillowcase.

Klara knew that there was no Norwegian man whom her father didn't know or know about, and she hoped he'd volunteer all he knew. Salve looked at Klara with an amused smile. "Have you and Inger spent the afternoon at the merry-go-round?"

"Papa, I just wondered if you knew him. Johann introduced us, Papa, that's all." Klara looked away from her father so that he wouldn't see her flush.

"Well, let me think. I know *of* him." He glanced at Klara who had just pricked her finger and was sucking it, waiting for him to continue. But he didn't.

She looked up, and then back quickly at her work. "What *of* him? Papa?"

Salve didn't take his eyes away from his ledgers as he spoke. "His mother emigrated to Amerika when she was a little girl. Her father had been a skipper. She came to Legrand with her mother and her uncle."

"Who was he, and what happened to her father?" Klara stood up from the horsehair sofa and then sat down again, putting her embroidery aside. She wore a dark dress and a white apron, brown button boots were visible under her skirts. They were small and narrow, with tiny buttons up each side requiring a shoe hook to button.

"Her father was lost with his ship. Her uncle was a Quaker merchant from Stavanger, often the interpreter for the English Quakers who visited Norway regularly."

"Did you know him then, Papa?"

Salve glanced at Klara over his spectacles. "I remember him in Norway."

"But, if that's true, Papa, then why don't they come to Stavanger Meeting?

"Because he quarreled with the Friends in Norway about something, and this uncle—his name was Reier Reiersen—wrote a paper against changes some people wanted. Just like here: Ina calls it heart-preaching versus scriptures-preaching. Reiersen took the opposite position from Ina. The meeting didn't want to hear him, so Reiersen emigrated, coming here to Legrand. But he never stepped his foot inside our meetinghouse."

"Where is he now?"

"He died here before I returned to Norway for your mother. But he's buried in the Stavanger churchyard. Klara, why all these questions?" Salve turned around to look at her.

She picked up her embroidery. "Oh, so Viktor didn't know him either."

Salve was amused to see Klara so eager to know about this Viktor. "Not unless he was born before that." Salve winked at his daughter. "But why such a great interest?"

Klara countered her father's question with a question. "What about him, Papa? What about Viktor?"

"Well, both his mother and uncle had some property, that is, money, from business and shipping. They weren't farmers. They bought quite a bit of land here. His mother, the one who came as a little girl, married a Norwegian named Endresen, from near Stavanger. His first name was Endre. Here they call it Andrew."

"And?"

"And!" Salve emphasized, meaning enough questions.

"What is it, Papa? Don't you like his father?"

"I don't really know Andrew Endresen." Salve laid down his pencil and crossed his arms.

"But you know about him, don't you?" Klara was now standing in front of him, demanding to know what he was holding back.

"Ja, I suppose I do."

"But what? What is it?"

"His mother is a fine woman, this Andrea, Marthe's child."

"And his father?"

"His father?" Salve shifted in his chair, eyes on his books again. "Well, it is said that he drinks. That the farm is semineglected. There. Is that what you wanted to hear?"

Klara looked at her father sharply in the bright gaslight. He looked back at her, saying "I've never seen it, Klara. It's only what I've heard, ja. And people get the truth mixed up. Be careful of what people say, Klara."

"But Papa, are *you* careful, telling me this?"

"Maybe not. But you would be wise to be careful."

"Careful of what, Papa? The son is not the father! You've always said that!" Klara didn't notice how her father studied her face, wondering, perhaps, if it were already too late to warn her.

Two Sunday afternoons later, Viktor Endresen came to call, driving a spirited horse in a light carriage. *Has he come from the Lutheran church, where Papa said his mother goes?* Klara wondered. *Did he go to church? Papa will want to know that.*

Salve invited him inside and into the parlor, where Klara sat on the sofa, ill at ease, and thinking that this man was handsomer than she'd remembered. He sat in a straight chair opposite her father. She smiled wanly, ill at ease for what her father would say.

"What is your church, Viktor?" he asked.

"The Dillon church, Mr. Roseland."

"You mean the German Lutheran church?"

"Ja. My mother and my grandmother were Lutheran. My mother doesn't think she has to go to a Norwegian church. We are all Americans, she says."

"So we are," Salve said, who had already spoken more to Viktor than Klara ever had.

They talked farms and crops. Klara knew that her papa was interrogating Viktor to find out if the rumors he heard were true—that the Endresen sons and their father were not very good farmers.

"What crops do you raise? What is your yield? How many horses?" Klara knew all the questions her father would ask. He leaned forward, looking intently at Viktor Endresen, who did not flinch. The questions would go on and on, and Papa would call it a conversation.

"We have six draft horses and four others."

Klara sat straight up on the sofa, understanding that *four others* meant driving or riding horses. She was ill at ease, knowing her father would think that *two* driving horses were all a farmer needed, that the Endresens cared more for their horses than for their crops, that the horses had to be chosen and trained to care for the land.

That no farmer should want horses too fast or too spirited, too untamed for farm work—doing so would merely be an expression of his own feelings that he, too, would not be harnessed any more than necessary. To be a farmer, the land must harness the man before the horse. It was the land that mattered.

Her father wouldn't understand that she and Viktor were born in America where land was unending and limitless, that neither she nor Viktor had ever known Røyseland of the stones. She'd only seen the rich black earth of Iowa.

And then Viktor rose and said that he must leave. Klara hadn't spoken to him; Viktor knew that Salve Roseland was deciding if he was suitable to call on his daughter. The men shook hands by the front door, and then Viktor was off, driving his spirited horse faster than Salve thought horses should be driven, except in cases of emergency like fire or injury. Even death must drive slow.

"Papa, you didn't like him, did you?" Klara walked to her father, where they both stood by the open door. She put both her hands on his forearms.

"Klara, Viktor is a farmer, but his people are not. Not even in Norway." How could the grandson of a skipper and a merchant have a feeling for the land? Could anyone, just anyone, learn to understand land who hasn't come from generations of farmers?

"Does that mean you don't like him, for that?" Her eyes narrowed, and Salve knew that underneath this slight and lovely daughter was a will of steel.

"I didn't say that, Klara. But I—"

"Then don't say any more, Papa, if it can't be nice."

Klara thought how different Viktor was from all the Quaker boys with their stiff gait and awkward words and lumpy dark clothes, but she didn't know if she liked him—she'd never talked to him. The moment passed when Papa would have asked her *not* to see Viktor so that she saw him nearly every other Sunday afternoon, in the parlor.

Salve was always in the house, not always in the parlor. Viktor talked about his mother, his younger brother, Fritchjof, and his sisters. He never mentioned his father. She talked about her sisters, and about Bertha and when she died, and Selma. He invited Klara to meet his family.

November, crisp but sunny: the back of Viktor's horse was shiny as a horse chestnut and the same color. Viktor drove carefully and once reached over to touch her hand. At the Endresen house, his family waited for them: his mother, Andrea, with a kind face, two sisters, dark-haired Ida, the eldest, and the youngest of all, Sigrid, with yellow hair. Three brothers were Orrin, Leonard, and Frichjof. Viktor was next to youngest, after Sigrid. Viktor and Frichjof looked alike. Mr. Endresen was tall and thin with a heavy mustache, and the baldest of heads; his dreamy eyes seemed to say: *If no one cares who I am, I won't either.* Andrea's presence commanded the family.

There was a soberness about them that seemed inspired, not by the fear of God, but by the fear of what might exist around the corner. In the midst of this intangible insecurity Andrea sat, in a high-necked ,black silk dress, wearing a gold filigree pin with two small pearls.

Klara was offered a seat on the oak sofa like her father's, like everybody's, upholstered in patent leather with the simulated flaws of leather. The house was smaller and plainer than the Roselands', but some things were finer—the heavy Bible, gilt-framed. "It was presented to my father when he was eleven. See," and Andrea opened the cover. *Johann Ommund Andreas Jansen, Stavanger, den 10 i ellevte Maaned, 1829, idag elleve har gammel,* written in beautiful calligraphy, the same inscription as her father's.

Klara touched the scrolled calligraphy of Andrea's past tentatively—the Bible was the Old Country, it was still *home*. She looked at the *Bibelen* in a kind of wonder because it seemed to hold for Andrea a favored but lost past—the reverse of what America was to most immigrants. Her past had a lost father, a widowed mother, a long sea voyage when she was just a child. She felt united with Andrea by loss of a parent.

As Klara saw a faded blue chest with a rounded top painted with faded rosemaling of branching trees, stiff with flowers, Andrea directed her to a framed, aging certificate on the wall, dated April 7, 1856, a license from Stavanger designating her father, Johann

Ommund Andreas Jansen, a skipper, and another one, Andrea explained, for her uncle, as merchant: a second framed gold-sealed document, the name, Reier Reiersen, December 23, 1854.

Andrea's eyes looked into the distance for a moment, then she said, "Now, my treasures are in America, my children…" Her proud eyes swept over them all. Andrew saw it; he looked away.

And afterward, Klara and Viktor left. Klara listened to the clip-clop of the horse's feet on the road and wondered what kind of scenes may have taken place behind the closed door of the family. No one would ever tell, not even Viktor, who didn't have to be the son of his father. This was America.

In early December, Klara and Salve sat at supper of potato dumplings with corned beef in the scrubbed kitchen, their white plates on a spotless blue-checked cloth. Salve broke his bread in half and swirled it in the sauce from the dumplings. His spectacles—small oval lens framed with silver-colored wire—lay beside him on the tablecloth. The blue of his flannel shirt under his black-striped vest seemed to deepen the color of his eyes. He looked up and smiled at her as Klara cleared his plate and brought canned peach halves, raisin cake, and coffee.

"So, my daughter. And what plans do you and Inger have for Sunday?" Often, Inger and Karl and Johanna came for Sunday dinner, or she and Salve went to Karl's house. No one needed to remind her that they would butcher on Saturday at Karl's house—Klara was spared the squeals of the pigs. There would be fresh liver, but no one, since Bertha's death, made blodpolse or blodpannekaker.

Klara hesitated, standing over Salve as she poured his coffee out of a blue white-spattered enamel pot. "Papa, I think on Sunday Viktor will ask me to marry him."

Still standing behind him, she waited for his response. "Klara, do you want to marry him?"

"I think so, Papa. Didn't you know that you wanted to marry Mama?" Klara sat back down at the table; her lower lip quivered slightly, her eyes were clear and steady. Had her hair not been swept up on top of her head, she would have looked fourteen. Its darkness emphasized the whiteness of her skin; her ears were small, curled like a perfect shell. Salve turned around to look at her, thinking how diminutive she was; Kristina had been sturdier.

He looked at her face, "Ja, Klara, Kristina was thirty years old, she had lived away from home. You are only twenty, you have lived only at home, with me."

"Papa, it's something you have against Viktor. It's about his father, isn't it?"

"Ja, Klara. I'm afraid of men whose fathers have been known to drink."

"Viktor hates liquor even more than you, because he has seen what it does to people. But anyway, he hasn't asked me yet."

"Klara, you must decide what you think."

Do I want to marry Viktor? Klara wondered. Did she want to stay with Papa always, taking care of him when he grew old, growing into an old maid herself, who didn't belong anywhere, a misfit? But did she want a baby with diabetes like Marna's Christina Anna had? Could she bear to have a child die, even bear childbirth? Even bear what marriage brought? What she wanted to know most of all even women wouldn't talk about. Marna had once told her, "Wait till you find out what it is to be a woman." She wouldn't say more. Bertha had once told her that in order to have children, a woman had to couple like a dog! Klara had never forgotten that.

Klara put the blue pot on the side of the stove and returned to her place at the table. "Papa, don't you want me to marry? Or is it that you don't want me to marry Viktor?"

"I think you are very young, Klara." Salve placed his hand on Klara's arm. He thought of the cares of marriage: babies, sickness, grief, work unending from morning till night, day after day, seven days a week. But unmarried women had nothing. He didn't want that for her either. There was no alternative for women.

"Papa, this is America. It isn't the Old Country. You can be different from your father. You were the first to say it! Viktor can be like his mother, Papa. But anyway, he hasn't asked me."

"He will. I would ask you, too." Salve picked up his spectacles and fingered them. Then he put them on. He looked out the window toward the horizon.

The next Sunday, Klara wasn't looking forward to Viktor's afternoon visit. But when she heard his carriage and his horse whinny to their horses in the barn, and when she saw Viktor striding toward the house, hatless, his dark hair combed back, his eyes chicory-blue, tension on his face, she knew that she could never keep her promise to herself to stay with her father.

On the ninth of March, 1915, Klara was with her father for the last evening of her girlhood. Her throat was large and tight, and she had never felt more alone. She loved two men who did not love each other; how could she, then, love each as totally as she needed to?

The gas lamplight shone on Salve's face and Klara saw his eye movement. He really *was* reading through the glasses that sat on the end of his nose, and he was *not* thinking about her leaving on this last night together. In the light, his hands looked bigger than they were, and the callouses were magnified. Klara wanted to take her father's hands in her own and shake them, to find out what they knew about a woman that could help her, to tell her what she needed to know. She hadn't ever seen a man naked! She couldn't even tell the man who was going to be her husband that she was frightened, or ask him where she should put the pail of bloody, briny cloths? Should she hide them so he wouldn't find them? Maybe he doesn't even know that this monthly thing happened to women. How could he know if no one ever talked about such things? His sisters wouldn't ever tell him. And not his mother, Andrea. Did men have to learn it from their wives?

We are all supposed to know by instinct, she thought, *the way a bird builds a certain kind of nest, lays eggs, sets on them until they hatch, the way they bring food to their egg-shaped hatchlings, unraveling themselves from an oval into a small bird, and whether they could digest insects, or only seeds.* But she was not a bird, or a woodchuck, or any of those creatures, not even a horse or a cow, and she didn't know as much as they did. No one would tell her anything about her role as a woman, as a wife or a mother.

You will find out what it is to be a woman! Klara heard Marna say. And Bertha's words, *Women have to couple like a dog,* she heard over and over as she watched her father read the paper. Klara ran to Salve, kneeling and putting her head in his lap, her arms around him, "Papa. I don't want to leave you. I want to stay here."

He stroked her hair and cheeks with his large, gentle hands. "Klara, you've done a woman's work since you were fifteen Klara. It will be all right, you must believe." But Salve's large hands were more soothing than his words. Klara felt them, hard but gentle, on her face, the callouses catching in her hair.

Her sobs subsided, and she relaxed, her head still on her father's lap. He said, "Come, I have something for you." Together they rose and went into the spare bedroom where Klara's linens and clothes were spread out. Inger would come to help her pack them in the morning. He took an envelope from under the mattress, "I didn't want you to find it," he said, handing it to her. "Open it."

Inside was a check for five hundred dollars. "For a team of horses," he said. "I have found some for you." Before Klara could respond, he added, "Wait," as he went out, to return with a package in brown wrapping paper.

Still standing, Klara took the package and untied the white string, feeling something hard and familiar underneath. The paper fell away, and there was the brass candleholder. "I thought of putting it in your trunk, Klara." Her tears fell on her dark dress along with her father's. He realized it was a thoughtless thing to have said. He was back in his first house in Legrand with his bride, who unpacked this very candleholder and tried not to cry. But it was his youngest daughter, Klara, who held it, and it was thirty years later.

Tomorrow came, and the marriage service was held in the Marshall County Courthouse, with its high Palladium gold-leafed dome, because Viktor was not Quaker and Klara was not Lutheran. The service was simple, like the Quaker service, like Klara's dress of white net over silk, narrow waistline and fuller skirt. She wore satin slippers with a beaded bow, her mass of hair piled up looked bouffant. She carried a bouquet of loose red roses; Viktor wore a blue serge suit, a buttoned vest, a white shirt: Salve, Andrea, and Andrew and Klara's brothers were chiaroscuro. Viktor was nervous about his father. They had a family dinner at Stone's Restaurant Under the Viaduct, Inger feeling an old maid to have Klara marry first, Karl thinking of Selma, Johann and Siri happy to be eating out, and Knud uncomfortable with Aline's possessiveness of him. Only Marna couldn't be there because of Christina Anna's constant illness.

And then, Klara listened to the clippety-clop of Sport's hooves marking the twelve miles from Marshalltown, thinking of how much she had wanted to spend the first night in her father's house where she could sleep in her own room, and Viktor could sleep in the guest room with the crocheted bedspread and decorative lace pillow. Then it would seem as though she had Papa's blessings.

Too soon, they arrived at Viktor's own house with the brass bed from Andrea and the round oak pedestal table from Karl and Knud, the white plates in the unpainted cupboard in the kitchen, the linens in the trunk that Karl had delivered that very morning with the brass candleholder safely inside. Viktor would have to take care of Sport and feed the cows, the pigs, the ewes, soon to lamb. Klara would start a fire in the woodstove, although it would be bedtime. The bedroom wasn't heated, and she would dress warmly for bed, and they would be tired and, she hoped, go to sleep.

On the early morning of March 11, Klara dressed after Viktor had gone out to do his chores, thankful for the darkness: she didn't want to see or even to touch her shameful body. The house was cold and unfamiliar, and there was no recognizable sound at all that she could hear, the way a house speaks with its sounds: the creaks on the stairs, the shifting of the eaves in the cold, even the scratches of mice or squirrels audible during the night and in the early morning hours of darkness.

Klara shivered, washing herself in cold water in the dark, fumbling with her clothes, laid out the night before in her slow deliberation before going to bed: garters and wool stockings, cotton-knit underclothes, a flannel dark-blue dress and wool cardigan, a striped apron. She moved slowly, numbed with remembrance of her wedding night and the cold. She went down the stairs and into the kitchen, to find that Viktor had already started the woodstove before he went out. Its heat added to the flame already in her cheeks, the shame burning in her face. She cooked oatmeal. She fried eggs and made coffee. *You will find out what it is to be a woman!* Marna's words burned into her with a revelation. She knew why Marna wouldn't say more.

She hadn't even seen him, or looked into his eyes—were they black at night? How long was it that she lay on her back while Viktor thrust at her roughly? Was it minutes or hours? It *was* hours that she lay silently afterward, when she felt Viktor turn his back and within minutes was snoring. She had got up and come to the fire, here in the kitchen, where she had sat and cried. Viktor hadn't even known.

Now she heard his steps outside in the darkness on the frozen ground that would thaw partially during the day and freeze hard again at night. Perhaps all of March would be like that. Viktor entered the kitchen, took off his blanket-lined denim jacket and hung it on a peg before he sat down. She poured his coffee. They did not look at each other. What they had to say was to themselves only. *His eyes were once so warm*, Klara thought.

Viktor ate silently, his eyes focused on his plate. She wondered if *he* wondered if she was happy, if she was homesick, if she was hurting, ashamed. Was he, too, ashamed? Or were they simply—married?

Viktor finished his breakfast and then put on his working jacket and cap. "What time is dinner. At noon?" Dinner was always at noon at every farmstead across the land. There was no need for the question. Now Viktor could go to the barn and find solace in the horses, in the warmth of the wide-eyed calves, in the sweetness of the guileless lambs.

Klara kept her eyes tearless at breakfast, but after Viktor went out, she couldn't stop them anymore. Why, to be a mother, must one be defiled by an act from which girls were kept in ignorance and left only the knowledge of its sin? An act done in the dark, secret and dutiful and without witness? If she were now pregnant, how could she even love the baby? How could she live through the day, with such dread of another night? Day after day and night after night! Couldn't she ever sleep like a child again?

Klara's thoughts were a paralysis to action, but her hands didn't hear them. Her hands carried plates, emptied coffee cups, waited to know what to prepare for dinner. Her hands remembered what Marna said: *Idle hands are the devil's tools.* Their knowledge must be her salvation now, hands that had been so well-taught that they now unpacked, arranged clothes, made order in the house, and made note of what to do, to clean, to launder, to cook. The pantry was filled with canned and salted food that Klara had made at her father's house and the sod cave had enough potatoes and carrots until a new crop would grow; Klara's hands knew how to select and prepare everything, without her.

She remembered how her father had said she must believe, but did he then know what it would be like for her? Must she make this her house and invite God in, after such a night when her body was not hers to command but, by some promise made, not in front of God, but in front of a county official, had become somebody else's to do with as they would? Was it that her body was no longer hers, even to cry with?

Viktor came for noon dinner and smiled at her. The March sun in the noon sky filled the kitchen and shone on the white plates, on Viktor's face. Klara saw how little he had to hide and how evident his simple hunger. He ate and said that the lambs would be coming soon, today even. He knew that his bride would understand that he might be up with the ewes perhaps all night, if there were birthing problems.

Since yesterday, he had a home of his own and a wife of his own who shared with him all that he had. That is all. And as he finished eating, he placed his arm on Klara's, and as he stood up, he leaned to kiss her forehead, half turning to go, but lingering. Then, almost as if he reprimanded himself for being womanish, he took his jacket in his hands and went outside, walking across the barren thawing earth between his clapboard house and the red-painted barn, still holding the jacket in his arms. He walked slowly and twice looked back toward the house as Klara watched him, but he saw only the glare of the glass in the sun.

Klara knew then that she would have to get used to the terrors of the night, knowing that no woman would tell another what to expect on her wedding night, because she had no vocabulary for it, and that having one would be the end of marriage.

In July, the earth was cracked and dry in the cornfields; row after row, acre after acre of the dark rising and falling leaves were turning brown and wilting in the sun. Even if there were enough water in the well, Viktor had no way to water his corn; without rain, the corn crop would soon be lost. Viktor stood in the garden, watering with a hose. He liked to watch the lettuce, the heart-shaped leaves of the green beans and wilted tomato vines spring back to life—he could almost watch them stiffen and slowly raise their leaves like arms. His pale-blue denim shirt was nearly white from the sun, his sleeves were rolled up above his elbows, and his denim overalls were his softest and most worn. He kept a pocket watch in the bib pocket tied to a black shoestring, but he used it only to verify what the sun had already told him. In the winter, he used it more.

Klara watched the plants, too, and pulled up weeds in a nearly weedless garden, wordless under the shade of a straw hat.

"You are so quiet, Klara."

"I don't know what's wrong, why the corn is dying," she said, without looking up.

"It's simple: no rain."

"I don't mean that," Klara said. "I mean—why?"

"Klara," Viktor asked, "do you think we're being taught something by the corn drying up?"

"You believe in good luck and bad luck, Viktor. There is no such thing."

Viktor believed that drought and disease, flood and fire, tornadoes and blizzards are chance happenings of weather, that being a farmer meant trying his skill against the disasters that occur—that some you win, some you lose.

"Klara, am I supposed to sacrifice a lamb or a calf?" He smiled at her, as a man could when he wasn't worried about leading a godly life. He lived one day at a time, each day following each. Klara added the directions she went: two steps ahead and one back was progress. But two steps back and one ahead was disaster. Viktor didn't know of anything in his life that would cause him to worry about how he lived. Klara cared about the past, which was always present, measuring her standing with God by events in her life that had already happened; the future was unknown.

Klara discovered that the cloudless sky was farther away than she'd ever thought the sky to be. Clouds were never infinite distances away, and she could read the sun in them, read the rain, the wind. But the infinite depth of the pure blue began to seem ominous, as though the very pathways of God would take her so deep into the distance that she could never return.

Then, as the weeks and months had passed, she was pleased to discover, however slowly, that if she went anywhere—to visit Papa, Marna, or Inger—that she wanted to return, that what she really wanted was to be where she was, right there, firm on the earth, with Viktor.

And then rain came in the form of a dark thunderstorm; spidery lightning etched itself like quicksilver across the sky, and the responding crack of thunder was like the splitting of heads. Even though most barns had lightning rods it could still mean fire. Klara and Viktor were outside together, watching the storm come. Each had, at least once, heard shrieking whinnies from trapped horses too terrified to be led through the wall of smoke, bawling cattle, the silly screech of chickens scurrying as the dry hay crackled, hay laboriously put up, load after load, sling after sling, all summer long—a year's worth of hay lost in minutes, perhaps all the horses and all the milk-cows if it were milking time. No one ever forgot the stench of burned animals—each animal known and named—it offended one's heart. So Klara's small hand gripped Viktor's large relaxed one, but the thunder and lightning stopped, followed by the rain that came quietly and earnestly after the short storm, watering the land long and gently.

By October, the ears of the corn were fat and orange, the leaves and stalks were pale and crisp, and whispered loudly as the wind played across them. Frost had blackened the garden. All that remained of the climbing green vines was black string wound around bean poles; tomato vines huddled like ghostly hulks, their produce gathered long ago, eaten or canned. Carrots and potatoes, cabbage and turnips were in gunny sacks in the dark root cave, behind the apples.

On her twenty-first birthday in late November, Viktor brought Klara a cradle, carved with scrolled hearts and flowers, made by a Norwegian carpenter. He carried it into the house from his sleigh—the snow already deep enough for sleighs—as his horse stood and shook his sleigh bells.

"Klara," he said, as he opened the door, blowing in snow and weather and the warmth of his smile and the cradle he put on the floor. Klara knelt down, ran her hand over it, tracing the scrolls with her fingers while she looked in Viktor's eyes; she touched his face, wanted to touch the blue in his eyes to tell him it was the blue of the summer sky. Instead she looked down at her belly and blushed. Viktor noted her embarrassment, grasped her hands, put his head against her chest, and said in a voice gone husky, "Klara, my wife."

Kneeling there together in the kitchen by the cradle, the door was still open to the outside but they didn't notice. Then Klara heard Sport's impatient whinny. "He doesn't thank you for keeping him waiting, Viktor," she said. "Go and put him inside."

When March came, the cradle was lined with embroidered linen and filled with a down comforter and baby clothes. Marna and Inger had come after Christmas for a few days to sew with her. Marna brought Gerald and Kristina, and Inger brought Johanna.

On the evening of March 20, Klara held a baby girl in her arms, and in Viktor's presence she unwrapped the blankets Marna had swaddled her in, looking at tiny toes like baby mice in a row, two sets of them, and ten fingers that curled around her index finger, two seashell ears, dark soft hair, puffy closed eyes.

"What a long journey she had, Viktor. And what a small miracle." Her face was white and tired, and she looked away from Viktor and her baby for a moment. "Viktor, I'm glad it's now, I mean 1916, instead of 1915." And Viktor knew what she meant, remembering their early nights together with some shame. "Viktor"—she looked at him again, putting her hand on his arm—"God has blessed us, truly."

CHAPTER NINE

"Doctor, she calls out to me, but she doesn't know me!"

"It's the fever. She is delirious."

"But why, Doctor? What happened?"

"Mr. Endresen, you are a farmer. You deliver calves, colts. You know what can happen."

"I know. I know that I know. But everything was all right, the delivery, ja!"

"This infection doesn't show up for a few days. But it's there."

Viktor Endresen and Doctor Barnes stood in the green-painted hallway of the Marshalltown Deaconess Hospital, Viktor in his blue serge suit, with a blue-check flannel shirt, the doctor, tall, heavy-boned, and balding, in a short white jacket and steel-framed glasses.

"All we can do is wait," Dr. Barnes added. "Her temperature is nearly 106!" The doctor turned from Viktor, leaving him with that ominous reminder outside the door of Klara's hospital room.

When Viktor entered, he saw how small Klara looked in the white painted metal bed that cranked up at the bottom, its S-shaped handle protruding from the frame under the mattress. A curved half-moon basin with a thermometer sat on a metal nightstand.

Viktor sat down by her bed on the single metal chair, his face in his hands, hearing the ticking of his own pocket watch and Klara's garbled words crying out from somewhere Viktor had never been and didn't want his wife to be. In delirium, she called for Salve, begging forgiveness for leaving him, for wanting her baby too much. Her hands kneaded each other. Viktor would rather watch his own barn burn, with Sport and Bess inside, than hear and see his wife like that. He had already driven Sport like a madman coming here, going back each day, twelve miles one way. Today was the third day he had sat here like this, listening to her, hearing the same words from the doctor, not daring to leave but having to care for the lambs, the farrowing sows. In two days, it would be April, and the muddy roads were heavy on the wheels of the carriage. Sport was spattered with mud each time he arrived at the livery near the hospital, so he'd tied up Sport's tail in a knot. But how could he think of a knot in Sport's tail when Klara was lying on the pillow with her hair cascading wildly around her face, her braid loosened?

Inger and Salve came together and stood, silent, grim-faced, at the foot of the bed, until a nurse brought another chair, reminding them that their visit must be short. Another day and the scene was the same: the silent watchers, the fever-tossed daughter, wife, sister, and mother. Marna had taken Klara's baby to care for.

Two days later, Viktor hurried down the bare hallway to Klara's room, meeting Dr. Barnes on the way. "She is better, Doctor?"

"Mr. Endresen, we had to move your wife, to—to the wing of the hospital with security."

"Security? You mean…bars?" Viktor asked him, unbelieving.

Dr. Barnes explained that in the night she had gone to the next room and put her hands on the face of the patient, calling *Salve, Salve*. "Who is Salve? That's not your name."

Viktor wanted to take him by his white coat lapels and shake him that he dare have done such a thing, without consulting Viktor. "It's her father. Who did you think?" He grasped the doctor by the shoulders.

"The man screamed, so the nurses found her there, *feeling* that patient, they said."

Viktor tightened his hands on the doctor who said that her high fever made her mind stray, he hoped she'd recover from that—her mind, he meant—and he looked at Viktor's hands on his upper arms,

"Please, Mr. Endresen, restrain yourself. We're doing all we can."

Viktor released his hold on the doctor, apologetic at his sudden gesture, convinced that Klara had been told her father was next door. Salve had been there yesterday, when Viktor left. He regretted that he had put his hands on the doctor—he'd always thought that doctors were unimpeachable. His own brother Leonard had something called epilepsy that had required restraint.

On May 20, exactly two months since her birth, Kristina Andrea died of pneumonia. Klara had been in the hospital for those two months; she was getting well. She knew that she had had postpartum infection—it was called milk fever—but she had no sense of how long or how ill she was. Her calm was strange; she hadn't asked for her child.

Viktor stood in the doorway of her room on the afternoon of May 20, heavy and silent, wondering if his wife had forgotten the baby he didn't want to remind her of, wondering if her memory would return—if he wanted it to, when he had to break the news. He had arrived at the hospital late because of it; today they would have little time together. It would be better, he believed, if she never remembered the baby.

From the doorway, he saw Klara raise her head from the pillow, her braid neatly redone, her face calm. "Viktor, Viktor," she called, and he rushed to her, grasping her in his arms. Viktor wet her face, her hair, her gown with his tears, and his chest heaved with the grief he had tried to control those many weeks. He couldn't even say her name, his throat was so constricted, from joy, from the grief she didn't know.

"Viktor," she said, the first she had mentioned his name in all these weeks. Was she at last his, not Salve's? He brushed her long brown hair back from her face. How dark it looked against her white face, white sheets, her thin body.

"Viktor, where is Inger, and Papa, and Andrea, and—my baby. How is my baby, how is Kristina Andrea? Viktor, oh Viktor, I want so much to go home now. I want to take care of my baby. Marna has enough to do. Kristina Andrea must have grown so much. Viktor, how long have I been sick?"

Viktor buried his face in her neck; he could not answer. She thrust back his arms. "Viktor, speak to me. When can I come home? Viktor, let me see your face." But he hid it next to hers. "Viktor, you ask the doctor when I can come home."

He heard the nurse rattling the keys as she opened the door which she had locked behind him. "It is time for you to leave," she said. Viktor wanted to strangle her.

He staggered out of the hospital, a wordless and lumpen man with a clay tongue. *If only my whip could reach you, God, the way it reaches Sport.* Viktor wanted to break the world and himself. How could he, *they,* he and his Klara, go home? Why, if the devil himself greeted him at his own door tonight, it would be no more than he expected. Klara is right—there is a devil. He hadn't seen her God, but he had seen her devil.

The next morning, Viktor stood in May's warm sunlight in the gray Quaker churchyard, hearing the words, "The Lord giveth, and the Lord taketh away." Blasphemous words! It would be better *not to give*! Viktor was too angry to cry as the tiny coffin was lowered into a grave behind the Quaker meetinghouse, and in it, a baby dressed in clothes made by Klara's hands. Knud, Karl, Johann, Salve, Marna, Inger, Andrea—all pressed their hands into Viktor's as they left, turning tearstained faces away from him, knowing that Klara didn't know. Marna was crying openly, blaming herself for the baby's pneumonia and death. Marna and Inger stayed with Andrea to watch the earth spaded in. Viktor watched and thought of Klara, who would again lose her senses when she heard that her baby was dead. "There will be no more children," the doctor had said.

As the four turned to leave together, a woman walked toward them, backlighted by the sun, so that her face was unidentifiable. Startled, Marna and Inger stopped and put their hands on Viktor's arm, guarding him, when they recognized a poke bonnet and shawl they knew and feared.

"Marna, you don't like to remember me, do you?" she asked. "Or you, Inger. But you will pay, too."

"Ina, we have nothing to do with you here," Marna said and turned to Viktor. "Come, go around her."

"What do you want here?" Viktor asked her.

"To remind you that the wages of sin is death." Ina Tobiasdatter stood firmly planted in front of them.

"What sin are you talking about, woman?" Viktor stormed, stepping forward to her, looking her in the face. "Speak!"

"Thou wouldst defile me: look to thyself!" Ina's face was ghostly.

Viktor thought he imagined it.

"Ina, we have nothing for you. Go!" he said, trembling, more in anger than fear.

"Look to your wife! To Salve! All of you who forgot God! Do you know about Kristina, about Bertha? You, you will reap his fires for denying me, son of a drunkard!"

"Ina, you are the devil himself. You are always where you ought not to be." Inger's face was white with anger as she moved forward, raising her arms in front of her as though to part the way.

"Woman, get out of my way!" Viktor took Marna and his mother each by the arms, following Inger. "Move," he commanded, "or I'll move you," and he pushed her aside in an anger that Marna had never seen in him. His eyes flashed, his voice shook. He helped his mother, Andrea, mount his carriage. Inger stood with her arms around Marna as Ina shouted how the wrath of God would fall on them, how God wrote down the wickedness of those who would not listen to His word.

Viktor drove off, hearing the words, "Repent, now!" that were as out of place on this soft May day as the scene he had just been a part of. He'd heard from Klara that Ina often appeared in the churchyard, pale and condemning, that she was the conscience of them all. He feared she would visit Klara only to blacken Klara's soul with her accusing finger, so that Klara would never recover. He would never tell her he had seen Ina, if ever the day came his wife would know of this burial.

He made an effort to drive Sport sensibly; Sport tensed for the whip in Viktor's shaking hands, which didn't come. Andrea said nothing, frightened of her son's anger, which she had known too well in her husband. She did not know who this woman was—she did not ask—but Andrea feared her.

That afternoon, Viktor entered the hospital, heavy-footed, grieving. The nurse let him into Klara's room. Her large, dark eyes questioned him.

She leaned forward, eager to speak. He watched her, standing in the doorway. "Viktor, I had a dream last night. You must tell me if it is true." She kept her eyes fixed upon his—he couldn't escape her eyes. "I dreamed that the baby, the baby"—and she lowered her eyes—"the baby died. Viktor, you must always tell me the truth. Tell me that it was a dream." She was so calm that Viktor didn't believe she knew what she was saying. He turned away, but she had already read the answer in his eyes.

"Viktor, come here," she held out her arms, and he went to her, clasping her in his. "Viktor, I want to go home. We have each other. We will have more children. Viktor, it was God's will. We must accept it. Something may have happened to her, and God saved us, and her, from it." She did not say what *it* was. Viktor was stunned: he could not understand the ways of God, *if* they were God's ways. He remembered Ina's words at the cemetery.

Just after Klara went home, and after some years of accusations against Ina, the Stavanger Quaker Meeting presented to Ina the verdict that she was "guilty of insubordination, indiscreet conduct and ill treatment of her husband, for which she has been dealt with and disowned."

Ina stood in meeting, appealing her disownment, directing her eyes at the Elders, at Lars Stangeland, clerk of meeting, at Ole Sawyer, who resembled a spring potato, at Sigbjorn Rosdale, Nicholas Larssen. It was a face they knew well, as she knew theirs. She knew how, year after year, she had revealed their petty jealousies and faced up to their hypocrisies. And now, *they* felt fit to judge *her*. She began.

Jealousy and persecution are suffered by God's handmaidens: Christ on the cross, I too, Ina said. *They said I took money: I am an invalid, and a rich Friend gave to me; they said I threw out my husband and arranged to sell his goods. I need to warn sinners, so that I have not their blood on my hands! Ye who interfere with God's handmaiden, will be struck down. Ye will hang on your own gallows for earthly sins, and burn in hell for sins against me which are against Him. The good suffer, the evil are not granted that to live is to suffer….*

Viktor did not tell Klara what she would soon learn; she needed no bad news, not now. Ina's disownment was upheld, though she appealed, but some vindication came her way later that year. Ina had her own premonitions, and her grievances were not single.

* * *

By the end of 1919, there were ten Roseland grandchildren. One of them, born in September, was named Viktor Bernard Endresen. Since his arrival, his father, whose names he had, believed less in the power of doctors and more in the power of God. He had wrestled Him in his anger when he'd heard his wife pray to be made worthy of a son he knew she couldn't have. When Bernie was born, he was, quite simply, awed.

Inger, who had married in the spring following Klara's illness, now had a boy and a girl; Karl had married Helga and had a girl, in addition to Karl's Johanna, who was ten. Marna would have a third child in January; Johann and Siri had three. Only Knud and his wife, Aline, had no children.

The sisters lived four and twelve miles apart, but babies and the constant housework and food preparation kept them at home. By 1919, their horses encountered Model T Fords along the roads and frequently bolted and ran. Inger could handle horses, but Klara was frightened: Viktor would drive her to Inger's house and, together, the sisters would drive to Marna's. Special occasions called for sisters' visits of two to three days, children and all, during harvest season, or canning, or birthing, or illness: the flu epidemic was not over, as they had thought.

Emil was attacked by the virus on New Year's Day, 1919, when his eldest daughter, Christina Anna, was just getting over it. Marna went from sick child to sick husband in the light of the kerosene lamp, her dark shadow heightened against the walls like a giant bat rather than an angel. Christina Anna was a weak, diabetic child, now with the flu. Marna rubbed her back and put a hot water bottle in her bed. Her breathing quieted, and she returned to Emil, whose temperature seemed uncontrollable, despite snow packs she had placed on him.

But Emil was lying with his eyes and mouth open; one arm dangled over the side of the bed. "Emil," she said, and her hand went to her mouth. She touched his face, but his eyes were staring—

she knew he was dead.

The clock ticked on and on. Why couldn't it have said that there were just so many minutes, so many seconds, left in their lives, so that they could have said good-bye, that they could have said they had truly loved each other? They had never spoken of love: they had had lifetimes stretching out in front of them to say it…Marna didn't know how long she stood there in her flannel nightgown. She didn't ask the clock what hour it was—it ticked as though nothing at all had happened. She crossed her husband's arms and closed his eyes, pulling the covers just up to his chest, straightening the bed. Then she sat with him the rest of the night, in a rocking chair next to his bed, telling her heart to be still. Before daylight she awakened her son, Thomas, and sent him on the horse to her neighbor's house, and then to Inger's house, the closest distance of the two sisters.

Marna's hands were limp and empty, waiting for her to come back inside them. The sisters came. Inger and Klara became her hands, cooking and cleaning, speaking love and grief at the same time, preparing the simple ceremonies of the dead at the same time as they awaited the birth of Marna's third child.

The day Emil was buried, his son was born. When he was placed in Marna's arms, her hands came back to her. "Klara, I have lost Emil, who was a good man, but God has given me his son, and his name will be Emil." And the three sisters cried together, as Marna's hands comforted Inger and Klara, as though Bertha had just died, and it was Marna who mothered them, Marna who taught them about hands.

That same January, the gavel echoed its hollow sound in a courtroom of Marshall County, furnished only by wooden benches and tables and the higher seat of the judge. The accusers were seven men whose testimony lay before the judge, a signed document addressed to the Commission of Insanity of Marshall County, Iowa. The men were farmers and small businessmen from Marshalltown, Iowa, and a former Quaker schoolmaster, now a small farmer and Quaker minister. They stood in a row, the farmers easily determined by their sun-tanned faces and white foreheads, their hats now in their hands—not even the Quakers anymore insisted on keeping their hats on, at least in a courtroom. Their suits of clothes looked less lived-in—accustomed as they were to overalls—than those two who were businessmen: proprietors of a hardware and a feedstore. They sat, as the judge was seated.

On the opposing side of the chambers, facing the men, was the accused, a woman dressed in gray and wearing a gray poke bonnet.

"Would the Board of Commissioners please enter," the judge said. In the room came four men, one of them a medical doctor, who took their seats at a table between the opponents.

"Read the charge," the judge said, nodding to the clerk of court.

"To the commissioner of insanity of Marshall County, Iowa: Gentlemen: Your informants respectfully represent that one Ina T. Christiansen, now in the said county, is insane and a fit subject for custody and treatment in the hospital for the insane, that the necessary steps be taken to investigate as provided by law—"

"Proceed with your first witness." The Judge nodded to the commissioner. Nicholas Larsson stood, was sworn in, and testified that Ina Christiansen was disowned from Stavanger Meeting and stated upon what grounds, as he cast angry looks at Ina, silent and stony-faced.

"You are saying that she is insane for the same reasons she was disowned from Stavanger Meeting?" The commissioner was perplexed. Ina Christiansen was known to the community, because of her antiwar and temperance activities—at least, she had not taken a hatchet into saloons, like Carrie Nation. She had marched for women's suffrage; she had filed for divorce, then retracted it, in an age when no one divorced. Her private life was the subject of gossip, but no matter what they thought, people hated to be her enemy—all these things, he knew.

The commissioner found that Ina's accusers had endless grievances against her behavior as a woman. They feared her and wanted to get even, for *her* exposure of what she called *their* misdoings. The judge next called upon the accused. She strode, fearless, to the witness chair. Yes, she had fled to Canada. Yes, she had refused to be accompanied by the constable who had gone to her house to read the summons and escort her to the court. She looked at the commissioner, but at the same time, she looked through him and beyond. The commissioner's final question to her was, "Mrs. Christiansen, do you know why these men have accused you of insanity?"

"Yes," she answered softly, breathlessly, as she looked beyond the room, her eyes calm, fearless. "They would discredit me. 'Blessed are ye when men shall revile you and persecute you…'" She said that she was reminded of Mary Dyer in Boston, hanged there for her faith. "I say to you, a prophetess has been among you."

Ina Christiansen stood tall and alone in the courtroom's echoing silence. The judge and the commissioner looked at each other, not wanting to be among her enemies; it would be to be the enemy of God. The court was dismissed, and the verdict on the following day stated that neither the board nor the court-appointed doctor had found evidence of insanity in Ina Christiansen.

Klara read the verdict in the *Marshalltown Times-Republican*. She did not call Viktor's attention to it, but rather she said a quiet prayer of thankfulness. After all, Ina was her cousin.

Klara looked out of her kitchen window at Bernie, two years old, playing with a puppy on the green, fenced lawn of a summer day. Pride thickened in her throat; a small fear entered somewhere at the edge of pride, in stealth, like a rodent in the hen house. She wanted Bernie to grow up, but more than that, she wanted him to stay a child, needing no one but her. Not even Viktor.

Klara stopped packing green beans into Mason jars and went outside to Bernie. She saw a small boy with eyes as blue as Viktor's, his dark hair. "Puppy hungry, Bernie hungry," he said. She scooped him and the puppy up in her arms, hugging them both, as she saw Viktor coming early from the barn for the noonday meal, to spend some moments with Bernie. She would have to hurry.

"Playing with Bernie?" Viktor asked, but it wasn't a question. "He might like to go with me on the manure spreader this afternoon."

"But he has to have a nap."

"After his nap."

"Viktor, it's dangerous. You are busy with the horses and the machinery, and—"

Viktor interrupted her. "How is he going to be a farmer without learning young?" Viktor smiled.

"Maybe he doesn't want to be one," Klara answered. "Maybe he wants to be a doctor or a lawyer."

"Nothin' better than farming, Klara. Does my son need more?" He settled down to buttering his bread, cutting his boiled potatoes and roast meat with a fork and knife, and eating with his fork in his left hand. "Like they do in Norway," Klara said. He didn't see anything wrong with it.

Viktor placed newborn lambs in Bernie's lap and rubbed fuzzy piglets on his cheeks. That spring, Bernie wandered into the poultry incubator, squeezed baby chickens with the all the force of love, each one lifeless when he put it down gently. Viktor did not scold him. Bernie loved to sit on Viktor's lap in farm wagons, holding onto the thick black reins of the big horses that were Salve's wedding gift, saying *Gee! Ho!* Viktor never let him hold the reins of Sport or Bess. Viktor let Bernie sit in his lap as he drove the Model T, which now most farmers had, to drive in good weather only: in 1921, they cost $290. But country roads were not built for cars. The rich, black soil without stones was thick mud in rain that sucked up the wheels of the light Model Ts, it was frozen ruts in winter.

Klara always watched to see if Bernie was too close to the horses, to the pigs, if the cattle would step on him, if he was buttoned up from the cold, if he was covered from the sun, if the water Viktor gave him from the well was from a clean cup. If he caught a cold, she thought it was pneumonia, or meningitis, or influenza. She knew she was wrong, and she prayed for another child, so that Bernie could be free. She knew that she loved Bernie more than God. She feared that God might test her. She remembered Abraham and Isaac. But God had already tested her, taking her Kristina Andrea.

Klara sat by Bernie for a few minutes while he went to sleep, thinking of how she must think of others besides herself and Bernie: of Karl's sorrow, *because Johanna looks like her mother, Helga rejects*

Johanna, Inger said. *Helga is jealous of Selma, even dead,* adding that Karl couldn't remove the jealousy from Helga's heart. *She will have him even in death,* Inger said, *because she made Karl promise to be buried next to her, not Selma, even though the empty half of Selma's grave stands there, waiting for him.* Inger, so long in charge of Karl's house, must know the truth.

Klara reminded herself how she should think of Marna with three children, one ill, her husband dead. But her thoughts returned to Bernie and herself, *her* need for another child.

In May 1923, in the hospital where she had spent so many weeks long ago, Klara gave birth to a baby she knew was dead: it didn't cry and she saw the head fall over the doctor's hand, the small limbs hang limp. He handed the baby to a nurse who took it away, and Dr. Barnes, in his stained surgical gown, stood over her, saying words that confirmed what she knew, "Mrs. Endresen, the baby, you know, I think you know, the baby was stillborn. I'm so sorry."

It was four years since Bernie was born and four years that she'd prayed for pregnancy. What was God telling her now? "Dr. Barnes, is...was the baby all right?" He had not shown it to her, as though it was some fearful thing.

"Well, Mrs. Endresen, he—it was a boy—he had a harelip."

"But that's not serious."

"And a cleft palate," he added. "Viktor is waiting. Do you want to tell him, or shall I?"

"I will, Doctor." No one but the divine surgeon could repair a cleft palate, and that he must do in the womb. No, she didn't want her child laughed at by other children, an ugly hole where his lip should be.

Viktor entered the hospital room, hat in hand, his thick brows knitted, waiting for Klara to tell him.

"Viktor, he was—stillborn. A son, with a harelip and a cleft palate."

Viktor sat down, next to her, his face in his hands, but Klara pulled them away. "Viktor, I wouldn't want him to live—like that. Viktor, it was for the best."

"Klara, you lost your first baby, now—" but he suddenly stopped. It was she who had carried this baby and Kristina Andrea. If she could accept his death, and hers, why should he make her find it unacceptable? But he could not believe even the biblical rule that a mother was supposed to accept loss after loss *because God had forgot to pay attention!* To lie down and let a train run over you, to say it was God's will was wrongheaded, was all he could think, the way his father's drinking was wrong! Was Leonard's epilepsy *right*?

As for his father—Viktor had thought that prohibition would cure him, but all it did was strain his mother's resources, emotional and material. He'd even grown to admire Ina Christiansen through prohibition, her gray-clothed figure with the poke bonnet and the will of the devil himself marching into beer parlors, smashing every bottle in sight with an umbrella, chasing the men out into the streets. Andrea could never speak of her husband's drunken shame, but Viktor couldn't speak of it either.

His fists clenched automatically. Klara saw them. "Viktor, you don't believe in God's will, because you don't believe in God. You fight the truth!"

Yes, he did. The truth was wrong! "Not like you, Klara. You accept—everything." He stood and walked into the hall before he said more, hiding the anger in his flashing eyes, resolving at the same time that there would be no more pregnancies. Abstinence was the only method he knew, and that might be beyond his ability, maybe even Klara's. When he was tempted, he would try to put a dead baby with a cleft palate and a deformed mouth in front of his eyes.

* * *

Berit Vinje sat on her front porch, next to Salve Roseland's new house and garden in Legrand. To Salve's twenty-two grandchildren watching, crazy Berit was the chief occupation for the Sunday afternoon of his eightieth birthday. Rumors of her craziness were confirmed to them as they watched her, knees apart, apron sagging with bread she tore in pieces and tossed to birds. Imaginary birds, the children said, because they never saw any, and everyone knew that birds were fed by God. As the sun lowered on the horizon, children compared the lengths of their stilt-like forms on the grass; the house became full of little stucco hills in the evening shadows, like rosy mountains of the moon. The birds retired for the night so that Berit Vinje went inside with her bread and the children into Grandfather Roseland's house.

A store-sized jar of lemon drops and a large cookie jar of sugar cookies sat on the oak buffet. Girls could touch a china doll with black-painted hair and a pink taffeta dress; boys would look through the stereoscope to view camels from the Holy Land, pyramids from Egypt, faraway places with baked landscapes, and men dressed in long robes like nightgowns even Jesus himself wore. It was a world to wonder at, a world where seas split open and swallowed people who lived in evil ways, where whales regurgitated men up on the shores after swallowing them, where fiery furnaces and lions in dens consumed bad people.

Grandfather Roseland had built this house for himself and his third wife, Ingrid, and for family gatherings. The dining and living rooms were united by a wide square open doorway, its heavy oak furniture now set aside for tables put together to make places for fifty persons. Light inside, already darkened by window drapery and shadowy floral carpets, filtered through lace curtains.

Presences were felt: Great Aunt Lena in a long black dress and white apron, a white cap on her gray head; forbidding Nicholas Larssen, former head of Stavanger School, his white hair a halo for his ruddy face, an unsmiling St. Nicholas. Sigbjorn and Malinda were seated together, looking less Quakerish than Nicholas and Lena, but looking their eighty-plus years, their faces framed in white hair, watery blue eyes. Few of the old Quakers remained; most had given up the severity of their dress.

Inger's hair was the only bobbed hair of all the women present: Klara eyed it carefully. Not one of the three sisters had graying hair. Salve had accepted Inger's husband, Thomas, but because his mother was divorced, acceptance had been slow. The three sisters and three sisters-in-law had thickened at their waistlines after years of pregnancy, their limbs strengthened with years of hard work. Marna had remarried a man who had been her hired hand. That he was short-tempered and from nowhere, everyone knew. Whatever else he was, they didn't know, although Marna's sober face seemed to tell them. Klara, who once mourned the death of two babies, now had four children, two boys, Bernie and Manley, and two girls, Martha and Andrea. Martha was next to Bernie, then Manley. Andrea was the youngest.

Except for Ingrid, who wore a long, pale lavender lace dress and tea-rose face powder and had cobwebby hair, the women wore medium-length dresses, rather straight and loose, of rayon or cotton fabric, in colors from light blue to navy. Aline wore a purple so dark it looked harmless, but it was still purple. None had ever worn the short dresses of the twenties.

Over all the multiple aromas of food brooded the smell of lutefisk, loved by parents, hated by children who knew better, and who could easily reject the past they never knew by their noses.

"Sit down, women. Eat your dinner," Viktor said, but no one heard him as Inger carried in a platter of steaming lutefisk which shimmered and shook, translucent and rubbery. Klara followed, carrying a bowl of melted butter and boiled potatoes. The children would eat ham and scalloped potatoes, chicken and peas, beef with noodles, and wait for dessert. Coffee, like the wine at Canaan, poured from a bottomless blue-marbled enamel pot by aproned mothers. Transformed from their daily work, they shouted and laughed and poured and passed, sitting down at intervals, only to jump up to fetch something again, and then again.

Fifty dinner plates were removed and placed in families' food baskets. A Norwegian who had never heard of Quakers played "That Silver-haired Daddy of Mine," and "In My Heart There Rings a Melody," and hymns from churches now attended by Salve's children and their families.

Viktor had bought a Victrola at a farm foreclosure sale in 1931; Klara had objected less to the fact that it was music than to foreclosures—they already had a radio, for news and market reports, Viktor said. When Viktor brought it home, and she saw its great shiny cabinet, she protested. "Viktor," she said, "you have taken advantage of someone's loss."

"Klara, what happens if no one buys at the sale? Aren't they worse off?" Viktor said. Bernie had examined it carefully: the records in the cabinet, the turntable, the faithful white dog with the black spotted head listening to His Master's Voice. Music became acceptable in the house when Bernie played the record, "I Love to Tell the Story," and his mother heard the clear, angelic voice of Alma Gluck singing it.

That same year, 1931, when Bernie was twelve, the Tilman High School inaugurated an orchestra by offering free music lessons on strings and brass and woodwinds to any pupil who would buy an instrument.

"Bernie should play in the new school orchestra, Viktor," Klara had said at the noon meal—only Andrea had been at home. It was September; school had begun for Martha, Manley, and Bernie. Opinions about the school orchestra had varied from enthusiasm to outright opposition. Any citizen of the town would be invited to play who could play; high-school students would get free lessons.

"Why don't I instead, Klara?" Viktor had said, adding that her cousin Ina would be shocked.

"Viktor, you always make light of what I suggest."

"But it's always something you want Bernie to do. Maybe he don't want to."

"He wouldn't think of asking for a violin."

"A violin, is it? Now Klara, you know hog prices are rock bottom!" They were six cents a pound, and they were drinking ersatz coffee Klara made from parched corn, not because Viktor couldn't afford to buy coffee in these bad times, but because Klara was too frugal to buy it. But a violin!

But Viktor had bought him a violin at the same time he'd refused to burn his corn—at ten cents a bushel—or kill his baby pigs: he'd said he'd rather give them away to starving people.

* * *

Now, in 1935, Salve and most of his children hummed along with the violin, until the violinist played folk songs from Norway that no one else knew. Hearing such tunes played on the thin strings of the violin, Salve Knudsen stood once again in Kvaas, an awkward boy whose feet had wanted to dance. He had wanted to taste forbidden beer, fiery acquavit—he wanted to be anyone but himself, a clod of a boy in *wadmal*, cursed by the priests, looked down upon by officials, by neighbors. Was it because he was poor and badly dressed or because he was a heretic, a *kveker*? he had wondered. *If they could see me now,* he thought. Where were the boys his age who had laughed at him, who had stayed? Still-poor farmers, gone to Oslo, to Stavanger to find work? He had been in America for sixty-one years—he had forgotten the Old Country. *If you don't like it here*, he'd said to those who complained, who missed the old ways, *go back*! *But if you go back, you have to leave your land behind, your new ways.* All of them wanted to go back for a visit. Few did. Those who did came back with new stories about the Old Country, how it had changed, how backward it was.

Harald Gimre went when he was seventy and returned a changed man: "Salve, they don't even understand Norwegian anymore," he'd shouted, spitting saliva through his teeth. He'd promised himself one return trip, *to go hjem til Norge befor ligge pa doden,* not understanding that his language was foreign to anyone except the Midwestern Norwegian Americans. It was not even written. Ever since his return he was heard muttering to himself, brooding. He was no longer Norwegian. Who was he then? He couldn't even understand his own grandchildren, who were clearly ashamed of him. They hung back in his presence, until the children's mothers or fathers—his own sons and daughters—thrust them forward to speak to him. Some of them were teenagers who ignored him completely. He muttered, from memories deeper and deeper inside him; he raged. When he died, his family was relieved. They did not visit his grave.

Salve looked down the long table of his children and grandchildren and old friends, knowing he would never make that trip to Norway. Home was here where he was no stranger, nor to English. He had no desire to go back and let ghosts loose upon his declining years...

Kristina: he whispered her name. Even for her he had built this, his third house: his first house, his second house were built for her alone. *All of it had been for her. Everything!*

Salve leaned forward in an effort to rise. He wanted to say how the land, the houses, coming to America—this house too, were all for Kristina. He looked at Ingrid with her white spidery hair as though she were a stranger, until he remembered. He eased himself back in his chair. He was getting like Harald Gimre.

He imagined Kristina now, her hair white, too, like Ingrid's, her face framed with it, looking with wonder at her children, her grandchildren. Would she smile? Would she say, rather, that they came to America to be Quaker without restraint? Would she ask when the boarding school was discontinued, the queries stopped, the monthly meetings stopped, when the music began. Since when did they have paid musicians enter *her* house, since when did her children have phonographs, radios, telephones in their homes? She wouldn't even know what they were, cars, even, all of them now common as earth. What would Malinda tell Kristina? That her children now went to churches of whatever denomination was the closest to their homes, that he, Salve, had married a Lutheran? Would she learn that Klara married the son of a drunkard, a man whose sister was divorced, Inger a man whose mother was divorced? Would she ask why they had left Norway? *To become rich,* that would be her answer to Salve Roseland. And then she would ask if Ina Christiansen, too, had been dealt with in the ways of the New World, if they had removed her bonnet and gray dresses, if they had silenced her who was their conscience, who came at death, if not before...

"I will not kill baby pigs and burn corn," Viktor's voice boomed out, awaking Salve from his memories, "when people are going hungry!" Salve heard the talk of the New Deal over and over again. All the men here were farmers, and now that the music was over, the real subject of the evening began. All were anti–New Deal and anti-Roosevelt; sons old enough to talk about it echoed the politics of their fathers.

"But don't you understand why the New Deal wants farmers

to do that?" It was Thomas, Inger's husband who spoke, leaning forward in a conciliatory but superior manner, trying to explain. "I mean, it does make sense."

"Vik is right, Tom. It *doesn't* make sense. Why, I'd rather give mine away, at least they'd feed somebody." Johann responded, and Knud and Karl backed him up, glaring at Tom. Viktor was pleased to be supported by Klara's brothers. Marna's husband said nothing but sat there, dark eyes clouded, scowling. He never said anything at these family gatherings. He lived off Marna, her farm, her family, and his rejection by them was obvious, and it was that knowledge which angered him, and that they knew he took it out on Marna. He had been her hired man, and she needed him, as Salve had needed Bertha so many years ago, so she married him.

Even those in agreement could argue with each other, until the women decided that enough was enough, that it was late, and that politics was always unpleasant, so they gathered their picnic baskets and their children and gathered their husbands to depart.

Bernie was medium tall when he wanted to be tall; he had Viktor's blue eyes and dark hair, but his face was rounder and softer than Viktor's angular bones, and his mouth was full, like his mother's, but something about him was ill at ease. During the years when Martha, Manley, then Andrea were born, Bernie had helped his mother in the house, with babies, with laundry, with canning. Viktor wanted Bernie to learn farming: horses, hogs, planting, harvesting, and not spend his life changing diapers, but he felt Klara's need was too severe for him to insist. Because Bernie was so competent, Klara didn't get a hired girl.

When Martha was over ten, it was her turn, and Bernie was free to work outside. Coming next to Bernie, her mother's favorite—her father's favorite being her younger sister, Andrea—Martha felt insecure and often unloved. She tried to compensate by work; she preferred cleaning to cooking. Manley was called the peacemaker between all of them, and he was often needed: Martha and Andrea quarreled, Bernie and Viktor quarreled.

Viktor was closest to Andrea because she was the boy he'd

wanted in Bernie. She was with him summer and winter, in the barn, in the fields, sitting on his lap as he harrowed or ploughed, later on the broad sweaty backs of her father's horses, holding on to big brass knobs on the harness. As she grew, she learned to unhitch the harness's heavy link chains from the whiffle tree, unhitch cross reins that made the two horses a team. She put the buckles in the right place in the harness, high up on the inner rump, reachable by standing on the tongue of the wagon. She led the towering team to the water tanks, stepping aside with her small bare feet so that the horses' dinner-plate sized hooves didn't step on them. Then she stood, diminutive, in the mangers, next to the horses' massive heads to remove their bridles. With brass decorative studs and thick blinkers made of layers of oiled leather, they were too heavy for her to lift; her father would later hang them up.

When Andrea, now called Johnny by her request, waited for Vicktor to come for the noon meal, she would stand by the wire woven fence of the house yard, draped in whatever bit of odd harness her father had given her, a hitch strap tied to her harness and snapped into the wire fence. Her legs twitched real flies away and her imagined burnished tail switched at them. She snorted and pawed the ground, stamped her feet and shook her head, blowing through her lips, *brrrrrr*, with a little explosion of air. "Klara, we have a filly for a daughter," Viktor had said.

Farmers' work was usually alone, the day-to-day work in the fields, mowing weeds along fence rows between planting and harvesting seasons, the work with farrowing, lambing, calving, feeding livestock, the work mending fences, harness, plows, wagon tongues—all the repair that took up time Viktor did and did alone. The horses were his companions, and the birds and the fields of clover and wheat were also, the corn leaves whispered to him, the wheat stalks sighed. Now he shared them with his youngest daughter, Andrea. Because she did not want to be a girl, she chose the name of Johnny. Viktor added *Jump-up*. She smelled of the sweat of horses, of clover pastures and moist walnuts and salt; Martha's smell was of soaps and ammonias and cleansers.

Then she, too, was in school, and Viktor was alone again.

"Next?" the barber looked around, as he brushed the hair from a customer's shoulders and shook the cloth that draped his customers. Klara rose to take her place in the barber's chair. "And now, what would you be wanting?" the barber asked her.

The barber shop smelled like steam and shampoo and macassar oil and liniment and men's wet hair. Posters of women in bobbed hair with red lips were taped on the wall-length mirror, as well as full-length slim men with thin mustaches and slicked down hair, holding top hats, wearing spats. Ads were tacked here and there for hair oil and shampoos, a pile of thumbed magazines and newspapers were scattered on a small nicked table by the storefront window, now steamed up from the inside.

She sat down in the chair, and took out her bone hairpins so that her hair cascaded down across her shoulders and the chair itself, reaching her lap. Only Viktor had seen her with it down.

"I will have my hair bobbed."

"Aw, lady, I can't," the barber said. He wore a white shirt with a dark buttoned-up vest, and a black apron from the waist down, his head was balding.

"My sister said that she came here."

"Ah, yes. Mrs. Sawyer, was she? I remember. I refused her, too."

"But you cut it."

"I don't want husbands in here accusing me of enjoying cutting their wives' hair. I *don't* enjoy it. Do you want to look like that?" He motioned toward the poster of the woman with the bobbed hair and lipstick.

Klara blushed. "No, I don't," she said.

"Does your husband know you are doing this?" he asked.

"Well, it's going to be a surprise."

"Some surprise."

He put his hand on her heavy hair, raising a portion of it, his scissors poised in his right hand. In seconds, the barber held up high a lock of hair four feet long, shorn from Klara's head. Klara looked at it, and put her hand over her mouth.

"Stop!" shouted a new customer, standing, waving his hands. He left, slamming the door behind him.

"He is right," the barber said. But the rest he cut off quickly, just above Klara's small eartips.

She drove the four miles in the Ford carrying her hair in a brown paper bag. Her head felt strangely weightless. She shook it and looked right and left at the frozen winter landscape, the fields flat and unending, bent-over cornstalks dusted with hummocks of snow, making the horizon look like endless egg crates. Klara convinced herself that Viktor would like her to be more modern: *I never thought you'd have the nerve to do it,* he would say, proud of her.

Bernie greeted her at the door offering to carry her groceries. He stopped to stare at her. "Mother! What happened to your hair?"

Klara laughed and hugged him. She kissed Martha and Manley. "Here it is, Bernie. Right in this bag." And she gave it to him. Bernie opened it, looked in, and touched her shining hair in the paper bag, freshly washed, fragrant.

He put his hand in the bag, feeling the hair, and then withdrew it quickly, as though he were touching something freshly and mysteriously dead. "Mother, how would you like it if the Belgians' tails were naked?" Manley and Martha, then Johnny, stared down at the floor.

The meatballs in the green glass Mason jar looked sickly, so Klara hurried to get them out of the jar, adding carrots and green celery. The pie had nearly finished baking when Viktor entered with Bernie—she could see that Bernie hadn't told him. Viktor smiled at her, but his smile fell off his face: he stared.

"Whatever did you—do? Your, your hair!" He walked to her and reached for her head, but withdrew his hand, quickly, without touching it.

Viktor didn't come to the family supper table. He went to bed and lay there, blinking into the darkness. Klara sat at the table with the children and the only sound was the room-filling tick of the cuckoo clock, and the harsh caw of the cuckoo when eight o'clock was struck. When she went to bed, after stoking the stove and tidying up, Viktor was still awake. But he said nothing to her. Klara felt like Magdalene before she repented.

They never talked about it. Viktor bought her a box for her hair made of black-stained oak lined with fluted pink taffeta. Had the lining been white it would have a resembled a tiny coffin.

CHAPTER TEN

Early in the morning on January 6, 1936, Klara was awakened by a voice, she said.

"It was a dream," said Viktor, who hadn't heard it but was awakened by Klara.

"No," she said. "It was a voice, speaking to me."

"Go back to sleep, Klara," Viktor said. "You're just having a dream."

But she got up then, at five o'clock, an hour earlier than usual. She dressed in the dark and went to the kitchen to fire up the stove. Viktor got up as well, too awake to go back to sleep, knowing something had upset his wife. He heard the house creak with cold as he dressed. In the kitchen, Klara was setting the table for breakfast, cooking oatmeal, trying to be calm.

"Klara, answer me. What's the matter?"

"Someone said to me, 'Go to thy father.'" She didn't look at Viktor. She stood there, vigorously stirring oatmeal.

"But you know he's well. I've never seen him look better than on his eightieth birthday." Viktor always tried to make light of Klara's now-and-then voices.

"God speaks," she said, and he knew she believed it. *Ina's doing*, he thought.

"Call him up, then. Your father, I mean." Klara had two fathers: her heavenly father and her earthly one. Viktor meant Salve.

"It's too early."

"Well, later then."

At seven-thirty, Bernie, Martha, and Manley were off to school, lunches packed, but Andrea stayed home with a cough that wouldn't stop. As the children left, Klara called her father on the telephone.

"Papa?" she said. His voice was the same as ever, a little high-pitched on the telephone. Sometimes you couldn't hear anything on the party lines without shouting.

"Yes, Klara? Is something wrong?" Salve asked his youngest daughter. In the past there had been.

"Oh, no, Papa. I…I just wanted to, to hear your voice." Klara didn't know what else to say. He wondered why she had called. She felt foolish.

The day was planned for soapmaking in the washhouse, a separate building near the Endresen's main house that contained a Maytag gasoline washing machine, numerous galvanized washtubs on legs with casters, a cast-iron cookstove, and a heavy, black-painted iron lard press.

By midmorning, clouds of steam and the strong odor of lye and tallow permeated the washhouse. The cold window panes were steamed up from the heat of the boiling and accumulating frost inside, and Klara's face was red from the woodstove and the stirring. Wisps of her hair circled her face, curled from the steam. The washhouse was cold by the door and windows—only outside clapboard covered ribs of two-by-fours—but by the red-hot woodstove, heat would hover in a big arc: whoever stirred the cooking fat, would burn in the front and freeze in the back.

Polly, the wife of Viktor's hired man, Bill Cullens, helped Klara with the soapmaking. Both lived with the Endresens: Bill and Polly needed shelter, living as they did in a flimsy tar-paper shack on a quarter acre of land they had managed to buy in Tilman. Polly was illiterate, good-hearted, and red-faced with large pores, teeth missing from her smile, and dark, thin hair that was pulled back in a knot no bigger than a walnut. During soapmaking, it hung like strings about her face. Bill smelled of old sweat and faint urine. The children hated for their mother to correct their grammar, because she didn't correct Polly, and they objected to sharing their meals at the table—Bill leaned his chair back on two legs, slurped his coffee, and belched—and they objected to giving up a bedroom to them so that Manley and Bernie had to share.

Martha and Bernie and Manley were at school. Johnny hated wash Mondays, her mother gone to the washhouse most of the day. Soapmaking day was even worse. Johnny was feeling like Andrea, playing with a laughing/crying doll—a gift from Grandmother Andrea for Christmas when she wanted to be Johnny, outside with her father in the barn with the horses; her dad was mending harnesses in the machine shop. She liked the doll, although she didn't play with it when Manley was home. *Just like a girl*, he'd say. She brought Martha's pink-painted doll bed downstairs to the living room, just for the day, without Martha's china doll. She saw her mother's candleholder on a bookshelf and picked it up. It was black and ugly.

In the afternoon, Andrea went into the washhouse to watch the soap poured. The smell of the tallow rendering was like the smell of burning candles as it boiled down to a clear bubbling liquid, the white pieces of fat turned into brown cracklings floating on the bubbling surface. After the lye was added, the tallow was creamy and yellowish, an evil-smelling porridge. Her mother poured it into a wooden box lined with a washed feed sack. When the soap hardened, Polly would cut it into squares for the gas Maytag washer and for dishes.

Klara and Polly cleaned up the hardened droplets of tallow from the cold wood floor with lye and boiling water. Andrea had been sent back to the house so the lye wouldn't splash on her and burn her skin or eyes. She sat by the kitchen window and looked out at the cold, thinking of it as a great white bear, the straw stack its snow-covered back, its claws tines from the hay forks, its eyes small unfrozen pools in the watering tank. Only a hole big enough for the cows' and horses' muzzles wasn't frozen, kept open by a kerosene burner. Andrea picked out the bear's parts, one by one, a jigsaw not put together.

The telephone rang two shorts and one long. She answered and heard Aunt Inger's voice crackle and spit with static. The hot acid smell of lye and steam poured out of the door of the washhouse into the bitter outside air as she opened it.

"Mother, Aunt Inger is calling."

"Can't you see what she wants?"

"I can't hear her very well."

Klara looked around her, wiping her hands on her apron over her sweater, and looking at her rubber boots. "I guess I'll have to come. Why she would call now?" she asked of no one. Andrea went back in the house with her mother, who took off her boots at the door and entered in her stockings. She picked up the receiver and shouted, "Inger, this is Klara. What? Speak louder. I can't hear."

Andrea saw her mother clutch her neck—she did that when she was upset. She clicked the carriage of the receiver up and down and up and down in a frenzied effort to get the operator. The receiver told of tragedy, of death and barn fires, of fatal or maiming farm accidents in the lives of the country people whose telephone lines criss-crossed through the operator's small second-floor office in the old brick building in Gilman, Iowa, that looked out upon the grain elevator, the small bank, and Inez's Groceries, places that took care of most all the business done in Gilman as the operator plugged her cables back and forth into the holes that connected and disconnected her parties. These lines told the operator everything: why Inger had called her sister, if the Halversons had saved any livestock from their barn fire the week before, who went bankrupt, who had babies, if Nettie Crandall would bring mince or cherry pies to the church supper. The operator was Millie to everyone outside of her telephone life, but in the role of lifeline to the community, she lost her name and became Operator.

"Operator! Operator!" Klara cried into the black fixed horn, immovable in its oak cabinet, while its two black-bell eyes stared out upon the faces who received its dire messages. "Operator!"

Finally, the upward click of release, that febrile connection of human contact with the pulse of a wire.

"Yes," said a voice, maintaining its operator, not its Millie sound.

"Operator, did Inger just try to call me? Did she call me?"

"Yes, Klara. What can I do for you?"

Now the voice was Millie's. "Do you want to call her back?"

"Yes! Yes!" But Millie could not connect the line.

When one wanted most to connect the lines, the wind blew the frail wires too hard, or lines were crossed.

"Klara," Millie went on, "I...I am terribly sorry about your father. Inger said it was a quick heart attack, that he didn't even know what happened."

Klara staggered back from the telephone. Andrea froze and looked at her. Klara grabbed her boots, and staggered halfway to the barn in her socks, trying to put boots on, running at the same time.

"Viktor, Viktor." She ran to the barn.

Andrea followed without her oilcloth sheepskin, shivering, and Viktor came out of the barn, just as Klara sank to her knees in her apron with its hardened drops of tallow. "Viktor, Viktor," she cried. "Remember the voice I heard this morning? You thought I was hearing things!" and she put her face in her hands and sobbed. Andrea had never heard her mother cry so hard.

"Viktor, my father called me, and I didn't heed him. He was mother and father to me, and...and I have killed him."

Viktor said nothing. He raised her to her feet and put his arms around her, walking her back to the house. Andrea stood, unnoticed. The school bus came from school, and Klara never acknowledged her four children standing around her now, as fear prodded their skin, jabbed into their pores. It entered the house, filling the very air with its cold, sweaty scent. Even Bernie was shut out from her.

Martha set the table and prepared bacon and scrambled eggs and applesauce for supper. The children ate with their father, silently, and then they went to bed, not knowing what else to do.

Salve's funeral was at the Quaker meetinghouse. It had not been filled to such capacity for many years. During the opening silence, feet shuffled noisily on the bare floors, so many had to stand. Sigbjorn spoke. Others gave tributes. Then Salve's sons and sons-in-law carried his body to the Quaker graveyard. He was buried next to Kristina.

The smell of coffee in Salve's house after his funeral brought hope to the Endresen children that their mother would come back to them and their father would stop looking grim. Aunt Marna, too, and Inger were crying; seeing cousins on such a day gave no pleasure.

They drove home in silence. Klara's face was empty and distant.

Martha was tense, Bernie was tenser; Andrea and Manley took comfort in each other, exchanging wordless looks, sitting close together, conscious of the fact that while they had their parents in the flesh, they did not have them in spirit.

Viktor thought of his own family, of how sorrow was no stranger to him but was something he tried not to let in the door. It had come too many times to him, and still he didn't speak of it to Klara, of how sorrow pried open his door without knocking: of how his brother Frichjof lay in an unknown grave in a city known to him only by its stockyards, those miles of railed pens where cattle were brought from all over the West and Midwest and slaughtered, including his own. Where in that city of slaughter did Frichjof lie? Was there grass on his grave, a tree to give him shade, a quietness around him like the countryside he grew up in? Dead from tuberculosis, his wife didn't even bring him home. Had Frichjof been ashamed to come home, ashamed of his father's drunken violence before his death from an alcohol-ruined liver? Next was Leonard, whose wife reported his epileptic seizures to the state commissioner: she was threatened with violence, she never knew when she was safe. He was crazy, she told the commissioner, who confined Leonard to the state mental institution. *Independence? You mean the loony bin*! people would say. There, Leonard hanged himself with his sheets. And as for his father, Andrew, his funeral was small and meant nothing but relief to his family. Orrin and Viktor, who by then missed two brothers, were among his pallbearers, carrying their father's body into the church to that small and hopefully unnoticed funeral. They had both felt blasphemous entering the church of a God to whom they couldn't pray. They did it for Andrea, their mother.

His father's funeral was not like Salve's, with hundreds of people, with flowers stacked up the walls in his house because they weren't allowed in the meetinghouse.

At home, Klara read the Bible and went to bed, dry-eyed, wordless. She lingered over Kristina's brass candleholder, which she kept in the living room on a bookshelf. She held it in her hands, rubbed it; Bernie noticed that it only made her cry more. Her children hunched over books, a game of caroms, but so halfheartedly that Bernie said, "OK, kids, go to bed." He could be bossy. But this activity repeated itself. A week passed. Ten days that the house was half-alive.

"Klara, this has gone on long enough," Viktor said, lying awake, hearing Klara awake, hearing the clock tick and the cuckoo strike eleven times, twelve times, then once, wishing the silly bird would drown out the sound of Klara's crying.

"What has gone on?"

"This grief."

"I can't help it. Viktor, my father was *buried*. Have you no understanding?"

"Klara, you have a family to look after."

"But I failed Papa."

"Are you now going to fail your children?"

"That's not fair. Just because you didn't grieve when your father died."

"That's not kind, Klara. I've never known you to be like that."

"But I don't see how you could have felt sad when he died, such a man as he was, a drunkard!"

"Klara! Why do you say such things?" Viktor's voice rose.

"Papa was such a good man. He was—"

"Not like me or my father, you mean?" Viktor demanded.

"Papa didn't even want me to marry you!"

Viktor didn't say any more. He shifted his covers, and then there was no sound but the clock ticking.

In the morning, when the children came to breakfast, Viktor's place was empty. "Where's Dad?" Bernie asked.

"He ate early. He had some work to do," his mother said.

But Bernie noticed that his father's plate was clean; it had not been touched. Klara saw that Bernie noticed. She saw the yellow school bus come, saw Andrea watch Bernie, Martha, then Manley climb its two steps, Manley lingering, looking back at the house that he couldn't see into because of the frost on the panes. Andrea's cough was still too bad for school—whooping cough lasted for weeks.

Toward noon, Andrea stared out of the kitchen window, making a hole in the frost with her breath, the frost refreezing in broken stars. Viktor entered the kitchen where her mother stood, preparing the noon meal. She turned to him, wiping the corner of her eyes with her apron, and said, "Viktor, I'm sorry." Viktor looked away, saying nothing, still hurt by Klara's accusations.

Klara knew that Viktor could not know how Salve had been mother and father to her; his existence had given belief to her doubt, courage to her frailty. He was the way she thought of God, but accessible—God was remote—while Viktor's father was his Achilles heel, his shame. Andrew's shadow was behind her and Viktor's quarrels, as was Klara's father. Their quarrels were about fathers. And sons.

The cuckoo clock struck eight times. By the time the doors had opened, and the first of the eight sounded, Manley and Andrea stood in front of the wooden bird that flapped his rigid wings, hearing strident notes coming out of his red wooden throat, watching both the bird and the cone-shaped weight which lowered visibly on its chain. The cuckoo bird was painted blue with a white breast and a red tongue, and every half-hour he came out of his wooden house with its pitched wide roof and carved gingerbread trees, right out of Hansel and Gretel's forest. Martha and Bernie didn't bother to watch it anymore, but no one could miss hearing its tinny, harsh cuckoos counting the hours.

By eight o'clock in January, it had been dark for so long that it seemed late. The hour usually meant Bible story time—when the children were younger, it was seven o'clock, but since Salve's death nearly two weeks ago, Klara had read to them only sporadically. Viktor turned pages of the *Chicago Daily Drovers Journal*, checking the grain and pork markets, although he had nothing to sell in January, Bernie was looking at small animal traps in the Sears catalogue. Martha wiped up the kitchen sink for the second time since supper as a matter of habit. Manley and Andrea were watching their mother mend socks by the gaslight, wondering if she heard the clock strike, wondering if she would read to them, if she heard the wind howling outside. They thought they were getting too old to be read to and felt abashed to ask her and cheated when she didn't volunteer.

Over the years, they had listened over and over to words they only partially understood, preferring the Old Testament stories: Joseph in his coat of many colors, the lean cows that ate the fat cows, the bravery of David, trying to imagine Isaac's fear when his own father stood over him with a knife. Klara read the Bible by habit and because of its moral truths, important for her children's instruction and for moral reminders to herself. Her children liked the stories for themselves. Seeing Andrea and Manley, Klara put down her mending and went to the living-room table to get the Bible.

"Do you want a story tonight?" she asked them. They nodded. Motioning for them to sit at the oak pedestal table with her, she leafed through the pages, stopping at Hebrews. Manley noticed and was disappointed. He didn't like Hebrews. Martha came, too, and stood next to her mother.

"My son, despise not the chastening of the Lord, nor faint when thou art rebuked of Him. For whom the Lord loveth he chasteneth and scourgeth every son he receiveth," Klara read. On and on she read, about the Reubenites and the Gadites, about he who *shall be put to death if he will not hearken unto thy words...*

The clock ticked loudly, punctuating the sound of the wind. Viktor's newspaper rustled. He said nothing at all, but he looked at his wife and children, scowling in a way known to everyone. But no one was looking at him until he said, "Klara, stop reading all that stuff about punishment to the children. If you have to read it, read it to yourself."

Andrea and Manley knew, and Bernie and Martha as well, that the willow switch of their father was not half so painful as their mother's reproach, either of them or of herself—it was the same. They were branded by it, like the cattle from the West with singe marks burned into their hides that had festered then healed. While the willow switch stung their flesh, it was quick and short, but their mother's scoldings they never forgot, nor her hurt when Grandfather Roseland died. It was a scar on them all.

Martha didn't care as much about what the Bible said as what Mother said, and brandishing their mother's wishes, she made

Andrea and Manley feel guilty, even if they weren't. Martha filled the kerosene lamps, swept and dusted, and polished furniture with a linseed oil and turpentine mix. She made beds and said to them, "Pick up your coat, put away your games. Help Mother."

Martha's and Bernie's lives centered on cares that weren't those of their younger brother and sister. They noticed the things that upset their mother: fatigue, illness, grief. "Don't do that! You'll make Mother sick," Martha said again and again to Andrea and Manley. Bernie punched them, with his tongue between his teeth, anger somewhere lodged deep inside of him directed at something other than them. But Manley and Andrea were there.

Andrea and Manley noticed the loaves of bread fresh from the oven that their mother made, that she smiled at them and sang sad songs, that she was there as the sun was there every morning and as it went down in the evening, that they were a family—in the large outside dark and cold of January—snug inside a warm house where the flickering of kerosene lamps and the one bright gas lamp on the table made their shadows large against the walls.

But now, as she sat there in the bright yellow light, her reading halted, her face in her hands, the clock's ticks seemed unconnected; each one seemed to be the last, until after waiting, another tock came to the relief of the listeners. Then the sound of the bird scolded with one strike that echoed in the room. Martha advanced a step and put her hands on her mother's shoulders, gingerly at first, and then she kneaded them lightly.

Viktor rose. "Time for bed," he said. He stood, putting on his blanket-lined jacket from the kitchen. "Guess I'll go check the livestock. I think there's a lot of snow on the way." Manley and Andrea filed up the stairs silently, leaving Martha standing behind Mother, Bernie seeming to look at the Sears catalog, all of them wishing for the frequent comments of their parents about each other's sleep, instead of such silence.

"Viktor sleeps like a log."

"Klara is restless."

"I couldn't keep Viktor awake if I tried."

"Klara may be restless, but she doesn't wake me. It's a good thing, or I wouldn't get any sleep."

The morning sounds were muffled by snow that kept falling, determined to fill in crevices between the house and the woodshed, to close the space to the washhouse, the yards between house and barn, and to obliterate fence rows along the country roads so completely that one unfamiliar with the roads would need a map and compass. The snowplow had come in the night, but the operator, had already called a general ring, consisting of a lengthy ring, followed by the punctuation of little ones, to announce school's cancellation. The winds followed the snowplow with a ferocity as though it had forgot to come for too long and must make up for lost time. The temperature dropped to thirty below zero.

The blizzard alternated with the snowplows for days, as though the weather were stuck in a broken cogwheel, or the wind felt the snow to be lonely without it. Every night, it howled and filled up roads plowed that day. No one ventured beyond his farmstead: being lost in the storm was to be suspended in white space, walking in the sky with no point of reference, no sense of movement to tell where one was, or who. Even on home territory, no one could find a pathway out of the swirling whiteness, and stories were told of Norway and the old days on the frontier when men froze to death ten yards from their own doorstep, where they had been walking in a circle.

There was no school for a few days, and then no school for a week, and then the week stretched into two, three, four. There was no mail delivery, no shopping trips. The children had permission to stay up later than eight and savored the later hours as a treasure, until they discovered that the hour of ten o'clock in January, if their parents were in bed, was cold and lonely.

At night, the family was confined to the house like hibernating bears, so they played anagrams and Monopoly and Authors, and games with cards that their mother said were learning games, not gambling games. Klara's grief gradually became less visible; she told them stories of her mother, told to her by her father, she said. When she could talk about him, they knew that his place in her heart was less of a wound, that he would always be there, even for them, through her.

She told them stories of Ruth in a strange land, and Manley and Andrea thought she was talking about Kristina. But she *was* talking about both, Martha said later. Then their mother talked about Bertha, how she, herself only fourteen, lost a second mother without knowing the first. She filled in Røyseland before their eyes: a white clapboard house with gingerbread trim, a roof with sod growing on it, hills covered with stones and with sheep—they weren't certain which was bigger. There was a noisy waterfall somewhere, and a man with a white beard and a strange name: Tollak Torgrimsen, a photograph of him that made him real, unlike Rachel. She talked about Kristina's ocean voyage, and coming to America with Salve, about Stavanger and the Quakers and Elias Tasted—Kristina had been his housekeeper, she said—and she talked about seven years of waiting, and Manley thought it was Jacob waiting for Rachel, and Andrea thought about the seven lean cows and the seven fat cows, trying to remember which ones ate the other, that it was the reverse of common sense. They knew lots of stories about the number seven. Andrea and Manley asked Martha how their mother knew so much if she'd never been there or known her mother, and Martha said they were from Salve, from *stories*.

During the day, Viktor and Bernie and Manley had to spend hours with snow shovels to clear paths for the cows and hogs to watering tanks, to keep their kerosene heaters filled. They carried grain in bushels that couldn't be brought with wagons. Andrea helped with the chickens and sheep but lingered with the horses, climbing up on the mangers, brushing their manes. Viktor had brought them into the barn in the first days of the storm—normally they stayed outside in winter, burrowed up into the strawstack in the pasture for warmth. The barn was filled with the sounds of its inhabitants. Horses snorted in the darkness of the barn, whinnying at feeding time, stamping their big shaggy feet, while the cows mooed or stood placidly chewing.

The cellar was filled with food, and Viktor cleared a path to the root cellar for the root vegetables. Martha made taffy and popcorn balls, while Andrea and Manley made snow tunnels near the house, among the Norway spruce. Andrea and Manley stayed there until they were bitterly cold, playing Job *whom the Lord chasteneth*, enduring the cold as long as they could because of the intensified pleasure of getting warm by the kitchen stove, warming their hands on cups of hot chocolate. Bernie fretted over not being able to check his traps at the farm creeks—he collected fifty cents for each muskrat pelt, skinned and stretched over a wire frame.

The battery radio and the telephone brought news, although many of the telephone lines were battered down by the wind; snow covered them much of the time, and static often interrupted the radio. It was a dangerous time for tenant farmers who sometimes lived in thinly-built houses, tar-papered on the outside in winter, like Polly and Bill. Inside would be a potbellied stove or a space oil burner with its red interior glaring out of the cataract eye of the isinglass window, which would cry, "Too hot, too hot!" too late. Then the red-hot fire crept hungrily into the thin, tar-papered walls and erupt into a brief and small and soon forgotten holocaust.

Valentine's Day brought the first clear weather, although it was bitter cold. Viktor hitched up the Belgians to a grain wagon box fitted with sled runners to drive the four miles to Gilman; the roads were still not passable by car. He filled the wagon box with clean straw and blankets, and Klara made thermoses of hot cocoa and coffee and a basket of corned beef sandwiches that they would eat at Grandmother Andrea's house. She sent a cherry pie and a chocolate cake to Andrea.

The first sunshine in a month came on blinding to a white world; luminescent shadows curled into crannies of snow folded over into tents and towers and curves and caves, sculpted by the wind. Bernie stayed home, wanting to find his traps; Martha had cramps. So Manley and Andrea went to Inez's market with a list of staples for their mother, and to the drugstore for aspirin and Valentines. Viktor went to the feedstore for a salt block, to the post office with a feed sack to collect weeks' accumulation of newspapers and mail.

At Gould's Drugstore, Manley and Andrea bought Martha a *To*

Our Sister Valentine and one *For Our Mother*, on which they would allow Martha to write her name, too. They bought another, *To Grandmother*, which they delivered to her. Manley bought denatured alcohol to use in the burner of the steam engine Grandmother Andrea had given Manley; Manley and Johnny used the new gas kitchen range to melt pig-iron ingots of lead for the lead soldiers molds she'd also given him.

The big Belgians stood in the street outside Grandmother Andrea's gray stuccoed house with the wide verandah; she watched her namesake and grandson from behind the oval glass in the front door as they climbed out of the wagon and up her front steps, Viktor behind them. She was seventy-five, dressed in black as always, with a ecru-colored lace collar. Sometimes she wore a black beaded cap with strings that tied under her chin. At the dining room table, she served the children hot soup and olives; Andrea loved olives. Manley looked into the glass china cupboard behind him while Grandmother stood, shuffling as she did to the cabinet, pointing out the boat which her father had carved, with ribbed sides, oars, and oarlocks, sitting in a boat trestle, smooth and polished. A *snekke*, she said, adding, "He knew that sea, Andrea, and the sea was his grave."

"But do you remember him, Grandma?" Manley asked, shifting in his baggy knickers, which Mother had made him wear and he hated. He would not wear them to school.

"Uff-ta!" she said. "Uff-ta! I was only your age when he went down with his ship. He was the captain, you know, and he was on a voyage to Australia." She gestured with both arms, outward to Australia, but not back; her silver wire-framed glasses jiggled on her nose.

"But do you remember him, Grandma?" Manley wondered.

"Ja, I remember him." Her eyes grew watery, beyond the mist of age, until they were brimming. And that was all she said.

At suppertime, each Endresen found a valentine cookie with his or her name written in red frosting that Martha had made. When Manley and Andrea presented Martha with the *To my Sister* valentine, which was very special because they had bought it with their own allowance, she hugged them.

That night in the double bed that Martha and Andrea shared, Andrea said, "Martha, it was cold in the wagon. You wouldn't have liked it." Martha said nothing. "Martha," Andrea said, tentatively, "you were really nice to make the cookies. Martha…"

"I'm glad you're here, Andrea." And they snuggled together, deep in the winter feather bed.

In April, Andrea Jahnsen Endresen lay in the guest bedroom counting the years of her life, counting her children, counting her grandchildren. She asked to see her namesake granddaughter. Lying in a lace-trimmed nightgown and a pink bed jacket, she didn't look any different to Andrea-Johnny except that she was in bed, and not dressed in her black dress with the white lace collar. A crocheted bedspread lay folded neatly across the bottom of the bed, and the down comforter covered her from the waist down. Viktor saw the fever in her eyes, which were hard and bright, her cheeks flushed from pneumonia. Iva, who lived across the street, stayed with her.

Grandmother Andrea put her hand on little Andrea's head, "You won't forget me, will you? Now go home, Viktor. Take my namesake home for her sleep. I don't want mourners around me. I am saying good-bye. Now, until we meet again."

Out of earshot, Iva added, "She means it, Viktor. And that there is nothing here for you to do. I'll be here."

On the way home, Klara said, "She is a fine woman, Viktor."

"I'd rather be there than Iva."

"Viktor, you can cry if you want."

"It's not for me—it's for her. Her life was hard. But I never saw Mother cry."

"All women cry, sometime."

"My mother didn't. She was, is, one of the brave. She lost two grown sons, and I never saw her cry. Even when—"

"Even when what?"

"I didn't mean anything."

"Viktor, you mean even when your dad…I mean—"

"Forget it, Klara. I mean that without Mother, well, who would I be?"

"But we will meet again, Viktor. You will meet her. And she will see her father, as I will my mother. Viktor, you do believe that, don't you?" But Viktor didn't answer.

There was silence the rest of the way home. Andrea slept in the backseat, wrapped in a blanket. The house was dark and still when Viktor carried Andrea inside, but the strident cuckoo greeted them with eleven strikes. And it struck five before the telephone jangled its unnerving ring, but Viktor was awake. He knew it would be Iva, and Andrea Jahnsen Endresen would be gone forever.

And then spring came. It covered two new black graves with greenness; it came as a rebuff to a bitter winter's endless cold and endless white and grief and death. It came dizzy with nonsense, the dizziness of just being alive.

Aunt Bessie, Uncle Orrin's wife, started it from where she stood at the end of her grassy lane where she went shortly after noon to get her mail. Johnny and Manley heard the rasp of her mailbox door opening; they waved. "What's two times a hen?" she called.

"What's three trillion times six million," Manley yelled, and Johnny repeated, to see if their silly voices meant anything in the fineness of the spring air with the pinkest tip of apple blossom nestled in the bud.

"Forty quadrillion!" she called. "What's three times a bee?" Her print dress was light and flowery in the distance, but her hair still looked like winter, tied up tightly in its little nest of hairpins.

"Ask her what two times *fuck* is," Manley said to Johnny, and so she did, shouting it through the virgin apple bud, not once, but twice.

Viktor appeared from nowhere; Manley had already fled. When Johnny saw her father's face, she did, too, knowing she'd said something bad. Viktor found her in the washhouse where she went to grind hard winter wheat with a hand grinder—it was something she and Manley never wanted to be asked to do; their hands and shoulders and arms ached for days afterward. By the time her father found her, Johnny had ground nearly two pounds of it.

Viktor lifted her bodily and wordlessly, his black brows hovering over eyes like a thundercloud; his words were a willow switch which left her buttocks smarting and red and her heart burning from abuse. Her mother contributed to her shame: without mentioning her daughter's crime, she took a clean rag, dipped it in kerosene and wiped out the inside of Johnny's mouth. "There!" she said, as though she had scourged the devil himself.

Klara punished evil to thwart him, and Viktor punished disobedience for its own sake. But Johnny never knew what she'd said wrong; she never asked Manley if he knew.

Manley never mentioned it, and Johnny never blamed him. But he was sorry. He made it up to her by feeding the chickens she was supposed to feed, and by cleaning out the hen house while she sat and watched him.

CHAPTER ELEVEN

Something between Bernie and Viktor hovered in the air like a bird that didn't want to land—it just kept circling and hovering. Bernie graduated from high school in May, a month after Grandmother Andrea died. He was just under seventeen years old, with adolescent skin and behavior: he was both cocky and confused, not knowing what to do next. He had taken some pride in not being a brilliant student, of not having been taken advantage of, he'd said, like the good-grade seekers who went for girl stuff. "Nobody can put anything over on me!" he said. Klara believed that the teachers were incompetent or bad-natured—whatever was responsible for a poor school record wasn't Bernie's fault.

In mid-June, Klara had stood in the kitchen kneading bread dough, Bernie sat next to her on the paint-chipped metal kitchen stool, hands in the pockets of his overalls. He was looking for a way out of having nothing he wanted to do.

"Bernie, I think you should stay home for a year, help your dad, then maybe you'll know what to do." Klara was pulling the dough toward her with her fingers, pushing it away with the heel of her palm. She didn't look at him.

"Dad doesn't want me. Not sure I want to either." Bernie leaned against the kitchen cupboard, still on the stool, and Klara reached up to his cheek, dusting it with flour. He brushed it off, feeling for the hope of a beginning beard, but his cheeks were as clean as Manley's.

"But what else would you do? You haven't even thought about college. Maybe..."

Bernie interrupted her, "I don't want to go to college. I'm not a good student."

"It doesn't mean you couldn't be. You'd probably find college more challenging than Gilman High."

"Well, I don't want to stay with Dad, unless he'd let me run the hog operation." He looked intently at his mother, a look which meant, *Would you ask him?* Bernie always asked his mother to intervene for him in affairs concerning his dad. He always had. By now, neither he nor his dad thought anything of it.

Klara asked Viktor that night in their double brass bed. She knew when to ask Viktor to grant favors: favors to Bernie were favors to her.

Viktor wasn't so certain Bernie's staying was a good idea. "Klara, we don't get on too good. You know that."

That they had differences of opinion about farming, Klara knew. It had started with the pigs. Especially the Berkshire pigs. Viktor's pigs were Hampshire crossbreeds, black and big-boned, ringed with a white midriff, long snouts, big bacon sides and a lot of fat, and he chose the best ones farrowed each year to breed for the next. He kept them all together in a big hog house, losing a number of baby ones from mothers lying on them—the sows were so big and the piglets so little that the sows couldn't tell they were lying on anything.

Bernie's all-black Berkshires had pug snouts. They were small-boned with legs shorter than the Hampshires and with bigger hams. Bernie wanted to keep the farrowing sows in individual houses hauled out to alfalfa fields with the tractor. But Viktor didn't raise alfalfa—he raised clover. He didn't grind the corn—he fed it on the cob. He didn't scrub the sows before farrowing. He didn't notch the ears of each litter to keep track of how many farrowed and how many survived in order to weed out nonproducing sows. "Don't interfere with my farming," Viktor warned. *Don't tread on me!* was what he meant.

"I don't interfere with the household, Klara."

"Bernie could be a real help to you for a year. There are new ways, Viktor. Bernie has learned a lot at school, and from the county agent, and 4-H. You should be thankful for it. You didn't get to go to high school, and there wasn't any 4-H when you grew up," Klara said.

"The day a 4-H kid tells me how to farm is the day I quit." But how could Viktor forget the tiny lamb he chose for the gravestone of his first and, he thought, only child. Then Bernie came, and after Bernie, another child died. Klara was hardly to blame for spoiling Bernie.

"Klara, I can't refuse him, if he's bound and determined. But I want him to know I'm the boss." Viktor realized that he had given in, almost without a struggle. Of course he would be the boss. Then he turned to go to sleep, Klara's arms around his waist, her knees tucked under his.

The next morning at breakfast, before the family was up, Klara poured her husband's coffee and then stood with her hands on her hips, chin stuck out in a way he knew when it came to Bernie. "Viktor, I think you should let him *run* the hog business, just for a year!" Klara said it all at once.

"Over my dead body!" Viktor's eyes flashed. "You don't know what you're asking." He went on to say how he was a good hog man, how he wasn't into some delicate newfangled breed that needed intensive care, how *all the money he earned came from his hogs*. "I'm not going to have my son ruin my business, and that's that."

Klara knew when he meant it, but she stood facing him, her anger matching his, each waiting for the other to make some concession. She couldn't. Viktor would have to. He knew it.

"Tell you what I'll do. He can stay and raise as many Berkshires as he wants, and I won't interfere. As long as he leaves my hogs alone."

Bernie accepted. But Viktor wanted promptness and unquestioned loyalty. *Because I said so* should be enough: Viktor wanted obeisance. Bernie had agreed to help his father farm, in exchange for freedom to raise his Berkshires. But what kind and how much help was never specified. Before a month had passed, Viktor was already beginning to be sorry.

In June, Johnny was hunting eggs in the machine shed that housed farm implements in winter and in summer when they weren't in use. It was the home of the ancient Model T, abandoned to time and rot in favor of the 1932 black Ford they now had. Peeling upholsteries of a cutter, a four-wheeled buggy, and a Model T were invaded by mice that further unstuffed the stuffing. Sport had pulled that buggy. Viktor would never get rid of it, like Old Billy. The shed's dirt floor accumulated odors of the years, dust mixed with nesting mice, chickens, old grease from machinery, the barrel of axle grease with its long wooden paddle.

Every week or two, Johnny hunted there for eggs: runaway hens trying to nest would lay their eggs in the rotting carriage seats, or in the old sheepskin-covered seats of the ploughs and harrows, the reaper in the farthest corner. Off to prison for the hen, where two to three weeks confinement in a small coop would cure her of mother instincts and start her laying eggs again. If the eggs were found every week, Klara used them for baking, otherwise they were thrown to the pigs. But unfound eggs, abandoned to time and rot, if cracked, were a fouler smell than the ruttiest billy goat and worse than a skunk. Throwing one, not *at*—as bad as murder—but *near* someone so that it broke was the greatest insult possible, reserved for the most extreme quarrels with Manley. Johnny wouldn't dare do it to Martha or Bernie. She hated hunting the eggs under nasty hens that pecked any hand that reached for eggs, or flew out from the darkness with wings and beak and claw.

This time, the odors were mixed with smoke from the attic shed. Johnny climbed warily up the ladder, to find Bernie lying by the open window, smoking. She eased herself down and ran to her mother, hastened by recognition of a sin that needed to be revealed, especially since it was Bernie's sin. Her mother was picking strawberries, her apron red-dappled, her fingers strawberry red. A sweet and pungent strawberry odor promised shortcake and whipped cream. Klara offered Johnny a berry. "You could help pick, if you like."

Johnny ate the berry, looking down at the basket full of them, and reached for another as she said, "Mother, do you know what Bernie's doing?"

At suppertime, Bernie stood in the kitchen in front of his dad, hoping his father's abrupt anger had been soothed by his mother, the bridge, the fence-mender.

"Bernie, you know I don't allow smoking in any building on my farm, barn, sheds, hog house—anyplace. You ought to know better. You've been to barn and machine shed fires before. Why, a fire would wipe me out, nearly. I'd have to quit farming." Viktor paced. He said how he'd offered Bernie the chance to raise his own hogs his own way, and now, how did Bernie suppose his dad felt about it?

Couldn't trust him for five minutes!

"Bernie, how could you be so deceitful, smoking?" Klara turned to her husband. "Viktor, you care more about the fact that he smoked in a farm building than about the fact he was smoking!"

"Damned fool son of mine ought to know better! And Klara, you stay out of this!" Viktor walked to the sink in the kitchen where his razor strap hung on a hook. He grabbed it, but Klara rushed between Bernie and Viktor.

"You whip him, you whip me instead," she declared in a such a quiet voice that Manley and Johnny were frightened.

"Mother, don't!" Martha appeared from nowhere, it seemed, and went to her mother. "Please, Mother." She began to cry.

Viktor put down his strap, and went outside, but his anger remained in the faces of everyone. Bernie, shamefaced, said nothing.

Suppertime was silent, and Bernie was missing. No one asked where he was. Viktor's eyes watched his plate, his bread as he buttered it, as each crescent bite reduced it.

The next day, Johnny suffered swift retribution. She felt something strange in her panties, something squirming, tickling, and itching at the same time. She squatted where she was in the orchard, the light filtering through the apple trees in a dappled, moving symphony of soft, feathery edges of leaves, shadowed and lighted, and a shaft of light settled on her for just a moment, illuminating something that looked like spaghetti, alive and moving. She had seen it before in Queenie's puppies. She sneaked away from Manley, who was supposed to be calling her with his new water-bird whistle from Sears Roebuck, and ran home, breathless and frightened and crying. Klara took her to Dr. Parson.

"Has she been playing with kittens or puppies?" he asked.

"Yes. We live on a farm." The doctor's last name was Parson, but since his son joined his practice, his patients called him Dr. O by his initial; no one knew his given name.

Johnny knew that she sneaked the puppies into her bed at night, kissing their soft baby noses, mouth to mouth. Manley did, too. She had to drink a bitter syrup and go to bed without supper.

Manley called to her in the soft dark, the smell of hay and roses drifting up to her.

"Johnny," he whispered, and she felt comforted, for that was her pet name. "Johnny, what's the matter? Do you have worms?"

She wouldn't answer but lay sniffling quietly, her tummyache, that night and the next day, enough to cure her forever of the sin of tattling. And to teach her about punishment.

Bernie stayed home for a year, consoled by his mother and put to the plow by his dad, whose teachings were explained by work and in silence. But Viktor had Johnny; even though she was inseparable from Manley, she was still his Johnny Jump-up: not a girl, and if not a boy, somewhere in between. Viktor could count on her for errands, for helping with the horses. She would stay in the barn watching them eat, hearing the grinding sounds of the grain, the snorts from spirited Dan and Kate, and the relaxed *brrrr*'s from the placid Belgian offspring from Salve's wedding gift—Viktor Endresen was late to give up his horses for a tractor. She watched the light in their amber eyes. The darker yellow iris and the deep pool of darkness in the pupils and in the corners of their eyes looked to her like a little pile of sand under glass. She could inhale their smell and then ask her father the same question: "When can I have a horse of my own?"

"You have old Billy," Viktor would say.

Johnny would sigh and wait. The only thing she liked about old Billy was his bright red sorrel color, the white blaze down his face, and his two white feet. She respected Billy—different from liking—because he was her father's tribute to his brother who had ridden him daily, twelve miles to and from Grinnell College. There, at the livery, Billy had maneuvered himself out of his halter to tramp in gardens, eat the growing plants, until the livery discovered a single slipknot held him. When Frichjof went to Chicago, he'd asked Viktor to keep Billy until he came back. When even Frichjof's body didn't come back, the horse was the last link between them: seeing Billy was to hear the last words his brother spoke to Viktor.

Once since then, Viktor had loaned Billy to Rusty Malcolm, whose only possession, besides a ramshackle house, three ill-clothed children, and a frightened wife, was a black Percheron stallion. Rusty peddled the talents of his stallion to deserving mares, leading him from farm to farm behind a carriage pulled by Billy.

"*He* will only work for love." Rusty Malcolm roared as he winked and laughed heartily, spitting tobacco juice over his shoulder. So He, as Rusty called the stallion, was never put to harness. He had wild white crescents in his eyes; he was a vast trembling shadow in the eye of the sun, and Billy had been his slave. Because Billy was a spirited horse and because Rusty Malcolm was lazy and didn't wish to spend time driving a spirited horse properly, he resorted to such a severe curb bit that Billy's tongue was sawed half into before Viktor learned of it.

CHAPTER TWELVE

The dew was almost dry. Johnny mounted old Billy, climbing up from a maple stump in the barnyard, her straw hat sitting on her back, its ties resting on her browned throat, water jugs on either side of the Western saddle. The burlap around them was dry—it felt OK against her legs. Mother came outside to say good-bye, as she did every morning.

"Johnny, when Inger and I worked in the fields we covered up our arms with long-sleeved shirts, caps over our eyes, like Dad wears. We didn't want to get brown." Klara noticed Johnny's half-bare brown legs, bare brown arms and sun-streaked hair.

"Must have been hot," Johnny said.

"We didn't think so—it's what we wore."

"Oh, yes, the *olden* days." They both laughed. "Bye, Mother." Manley appeared on the way to his pigs. "Bye, lazybones," she said to him.

He gave her a sheepish look. At fourteen years, he was old enough to work like a man around the farm, but too young to handle heavy bundles for eight, nine hours on the threshing run. His job was to do the many chores at home, and the milking. Manley hated milking, and he wasn't very good with a team of horses. He knew it.

"Don't let that old nag run away again," he said. Old Billy was skittish—every time he saw a stray piece of paper, he bolted and ran. After his mouth was injured, Dad wouldn't let her use anything but a straight snaffle that wouldn't hold a flea, so he ran until he felt foolish, seeing nothing to run from, Johnny said.

"Well, see you later," she called, urging reluctant old Billy out the gate and down the roadside to the Anderson farm four miles away. He moved sideways, turning his head toward the barn. She kicked with both feet and slapped the reins on his neck, then kicked again—it was always his way. When he started forward, she sighed.

Sometimes she would have liked to change places with Martha.

"Hi, Water Monkey," neighbors greeted her as they converged from all directions to the threshing site which moved from farm to farm. She hated to be called water monkey. She'd inherited the job at age eleven from Lyle Thompson, who'd grown up enough to plow—he was good with horses—and she'd like to have inherited his gray pony as well. Even old, Billy was a handful.

She pumped the water from the well, filling the stoneware jugs, wetting the burlap wrapped around them. For the rest of the day, her legs would be wet and clammy and chafed by burlap. Her first stop was to men in the fields. One, on the ground, pitched bundles of grain up onto the hayrack; the one on top caught each bundle in midair and stacked it, stubble side out.

"Water?" she called. Either they motioned her on or stood, leaning for seconds on their pitchforks, waiting for her. Shocks dotted the fields of stubble like sheep grazing, twelve to fourteen bundles stacked together in each shock; the flattened places left in the emptied fields were like a wool carpet textured with polka dots. Taking water to the field was easy—Old Billy had no objection to men and horses, but the threshing machine threatened him, except when he was tired and forgot to care. The roar of the machine was constant, the puffs of white from the steam engine were ghostly to old Billy, the holocaust of straw emerging from the long funnel was to him a tornado. At first, he had bolted so suddenly that the leather strap holding the topmost water jug loosened, and the jug flew away in the air and split apart on the ground, like a halved peach.

Now Billy was wary, snorting into the air like a colt. "When is your old man going to buy you a horse?" Ira Stonewall queried, shouting it into the thresher's roar out of his tobacco-stained face and four-day beard, nodding at Viktor pitching bundles into the thresher belt opposite him. To Viktor, he said, "Nice leg on your kid, there, Viktor."

Finally, there was Adolf and Mr. Vroom, the owner of the machine and his assistant. One or the other of them, or both, watched the lumbering giants—the steam locomotive and the thresher itself—for the inevitable breakdowns, hoping they would be small, that they would have the parts to repair it. Both men were grease covered, their hands blackened. Adolf wore a wad of tobacco in his mouth tucked behind a smile, the brown juices evident when he spit at a spot, usually somewhere behind him. His belly overhung his trousers which he constantly hiked up with both hands. Mr. Vroom's face was lighted by gold teeth gleaming out of a greased and sunburned darkness, but he still seemed deserving of the title *Mr.*, until one realized that the Mr. indicated that he was a hired mechanic and not the owner. He behaved accordingly, one step behind Adolf.

Adolf took the water jug in his left hand, removed the cork with the right, sloshed a little water out from the depths, cradled the weight in the crook of his elbow which he elevated to the required height and poured in a mouthful then spit it out. Then he drank thirstily, letting the water spill over his mouth and down his chin. He wiped his mouth with the back of his right hand, handing the jug back to Johnny at the same time. Johnny tried not to see Adolf's ritual. She brought him the water last, and as she refilled it, she remembered his teeth juicy with brown tobacco, his tongue as black as his greased hands. She dumped out the jug, sloshing water all over it, and filled it again.

The last man to drink was the one stacking the strawstack. His job was to make steep, weather-shedding sides out of what would otherwise be merely a pyramid of chaff and straw, soaked by every rain until the straw molded or blew apart by the wind. The finished strawstack, slightly crescent-shaped from the back-and-forth movement of the funnel in its arc, would shed rainfall and snowfall, provide shelter for wintering cattle and horses, who burrowed up into its sides as the wind howled and made it eventually look like a house with an overhanging, thatched roof. A farmer's skill in everything he did could be judged by the shape of his strawstack. The stacking of one's own would be enough punishment for a year. Throughout the long winter days, a farmer could remember how he'd earned these moments of sitting in a chair by the kitchen fire, leaning back, remembering summer.

Johnny's father stacked his own, his movements a duet with the vortex of the spewing funnel, his mouth blackened by grime, rivulets of sweat making pathways through the black riverbed of his forehead, denim shirt stuck to his back, caked over and over again with sweat and dirt and chaff. He lunged back and forth with his fork, wresting form from a funnel-shaped tornado, his arms flailing like windmills as the Leviathan took shape, growing sides straight up after endless wrestling, until a straw castle of unassailable embankment was created in three days out of a storm subdued by sheer will. When it was over, Viktor said, "I stacked it," and that was all he spoke.

At noon, farmers unhitched their horses, tied them under trees or the shade of a barn. They washed outside on a bench under the trees, pouring from pails of water into enamel wash basins, lathering with Packer's tar soap. They washed up to their elbows, rinsed their faces with their hands, piled up rough brown linen towels in a heap on the ground. After using a communal comb in front of a mirror tacked to a tree, they presented themselves at long tables—planks atop sawhorses—under the trees, their hair plastered back from now-exposed white foreheads, the rest of their faces patinaed by all the weather of the year, frost to harvest. They ate, looking down at their plates, they broke bread and wiped up bits of ham, turkey, stuffing, roast beef, creamed onions, home-baked beans, scalloped potatoes, roasting ears, raspberry jam and gooseberry jelly, Waldorf salads, and blackberry, cherry, lemon, green apple, and chocolate pies and white cakes high with frosting.

They ate, while the horses waited somewhere in the arrested quiet of the barnyard. The landscape-filling roar of the thresher was temporarily hushed, and the small sounds of summer could again be heard through the heat waves, shimmering on the horizon, women's voices humming like the distant cicadas.

The men were shy and wordless in the presence of so many women, as though they would say things meant for the machine shop, or as though they were afraid their voices would disrupt the momentary quiet and boom out in the volume they used above the roar of the threshing machine and grain elevators, when directions were shouted here and there instead of spoken. Mostly, they ate.

"Hello, Andrea," the women said, and Johnny hesitated between being Johnny or Andrea. She waited for the men to finish before she washed—she would have preferred to wash under the pump, or in the kitchen.

"Git in there and wash up, girl," Ira said, making room for her. She never knew where to sit, hoping always that Adolf wouldn't come again and make her sit next to him. She didn't look for her father—she had to be a regular—but she sat like a gap between two men, feeling like Andrea without a trace of Johnny, and while she wouldn't have traded what she was doing for what Martha was doing, at mealtime she was a stranger, belonging neither to the men, nor to the women.

Her work itself was mind-filling, hour after hour, day after day. She watched the shades of day wear on; the combination of heat, light, and body fatigue of herself and Old Billy told her what time it was. It registered firmly in her subconscious as she looked forward to the end of each day when she could go home, and put away the one dollar she would have earned. At the end of the summer, she would be able to buy another baby pig from Manley, feed it, and then sell it. With that money she would buy a calf. Someday, a horse.

"Now I can buy a calf, Manley," Johnny said, counting thirty-eight dollars and forty cents in a coin purse.

"You ought to stick to pigs. You'll earn more money. I can help you feed them." Johnny helped Manley, because her pigs remained with the sow and then with the weaned pigs. Ownership was merely a matter of having paid Manley a small amount for baby pigs.

"I hate pigs. They smell. I want a calf. And anyway, Dad doesn't like your Berkshires." Because of Viktor's attitude, Johnny felt traitorous helping Manley with his Berkshires; she felt worse if she didn't help.

She tried to join the boys' 4-H Club rather than the girls' club. "Why would you want to join the boys' 4-H?" asked the area leader and the county agent, both looking at her quizzically. Their eyes asked, *Who are you to go against the rules?*

"Because I have raised pigs, and—and now I want to raise a 4-H calf. And maybe a colt." Girls had Saturday lunchtime meetings and practiced cooking, canning, baking, setting tables, getting stains out of clothing, washable or dry-cleanable. They refined home remedies, but all of it was to take care of the men of the house.

"Girls can raise animals through the girls' 4-H. You can attend the boys' meetings to learn how, but you can't be a member. Anyway, your brother is the one raising pigs, isn't he?"

She went with Manley to one meeting. Compared to the girls' club, the boys' was large and crowded and met in the evenings, because boys worked on the farms on Saturdays. One other girl, Tina Schmidt, was there—Manley had described her as "indistinguishable from her Chester Whites," meaning she was fat and pink underneath her grime; she entered the show rings with scrubbed and powdered pigs, but their dirt had been transferred to her in the process.

Tina picked Andrea out. "I hear *you* breed Berkshires!" She didn't ask but looked directly at Manley, reaching for brownies as they were passed by. Did she expect him to deny it?

"I...I thought I'd raise a calf," Johnny answered, watching Manley. He'd never say she didn't raise pigs.

"What breed? I mean, you have to know what you want."

"I hadn't thought."

Tina gave her a scornful look and turned away to chat with the county agent. Johnny never went back.

She bought Ludwig, a white-face out of Viktor's feed lot, choosing him from the calves her father bought, usually in Nebraska, sometimes in Kansas. Like many corn farmers of the Midwest, he bought feeder calves, grass bred and raised on land too poor for corn, then fattened them on corn for a year in feedlots, where their only activity was to stand and eat. Then off to the Chicago stockyards they went, accompanied by the farmers who stayed in the Stockyards Inn with other farmers and brokers, occasionally a woman who dared feed cattle. She was a spinster for obvious reasons, she was too hard, too tough, meaning she wasn't like a woman. Johnny had heard the tales.

"I'll tell you, Johnny, that calf will never win a prize, no matter how well you feed him. He's too narrow in the flanks, too high-backed, too shallow in the chest, too large-boned." Manley said, being very conscious of the large-boned Hampshire-cross hogs that their dad had, his small-boned Berkshires.

"I don't care," Johnny replied.

Her dad never fed or raised animals he had to pamper. If she was going to pamper a 4-H calf, she'd have to do it on her own, she knew.

She got up in subzero winter mornings to feed and water her calf, who didn't seem to appreciate what was being done for him. He blinked his calm eyes dispassionately in the dim, cold light. And then, during that long winter, she got her first period.

It happened on a Sunday in January and required stealth to keep it from Martha, who would tell Manley. Then she could never be Johnny again. "Just you wait, Andrea. Just you wait till it's your turn!" Martha had once said to her. "It's not going to be my turn," she'd said.

On Monday, it hadn't gone away, so she went to school with Kleenex stuffed in her panties. The wad of tissue soaked with blood fell out on the gymnasium floor during basketball practice, and Johnny joined the other girls who stopped playing to look at it, "Who would have done such a stupid and dirty thing!" she said, her heart pounding.

When the girls' locker room was empty, she put a nickel in the Kotex machine and hurried to pin the enormous pad to her panties with the safety pins that were in the packet. The locker room smelled of girls' sweaty socks and girls' monthlies because the girls *mustn't take showers during their period,* and the girls informed their exasperated teachers that their mothers had forbidden it, sweaty or not. They would get pneumonia, or fevers, or hemorrhages.

She hadn't grown into the girl she didn't want to be: a girl in a world that was built for boys and men, who left their wives, sisters, and mothers in the kitchen and in the chicken house and in the milk house and the garden, who expected women to aid and succor those who were entitled to go out into the affairs of the world. Even Jeanne d'Arc had worn men's clothes to indicate that she should be considered someone with a man's job to do in the world of men. How could she have gone into battle flowing with menstrual blood? In the heat of battle, did she say, "Excuse me, I have to change my Kotex?"

Ludwig couldn't understand her cramps on cold winter mornings when she hated caring for him. When summer came, she taught him to lead, she washed and curled the hair on his flanks with a row comb as she'd seen 4-H boys do, preparing for the show-ring.

She didn't care that he wasn't purebred, or even a good calf, until she took her place in the early August show-ring with Ludwig, named by cousin Johanna. She led him proudly, wishing Tina Schmidt would see her, his white face whiter still from bluing, clean as a washed baby. There were twenty-seven calves in her 4-H class for medium-weight Herefords. Around the ring they went, parents of sure winners watching the judges, watching the best purebred and registered calves from their herds led by their sons, burnished brass on polished-leather halters, shiny brass chains under the calves' jawbones. Johnny's halter had no ornament.

Ten calves were picked out to line up in the middle of the ring as she and Ludwig kept walking round and round, as the judges felt and punched and bent over and felt and eyed and rubbed the calves in the center. A wink would move a calf to the front of the line. Ludwig had not had half a glance. She looked at Manley, hoping she wouldn't cry, as ribbons were passed out: blue, red, white, then the lesser colors of pink and yellow—even paler colors for lesser prizes. She did care when she led Ludwig out of the show ring, twenty-fifth in line, and Tina Schmidt caught her eye and smirked. After a year of special care, Ludwig didn't look as good as Viktor's steers from the feed lot, just as Manley had said. At least they'd had companionship. *You'd be better off to feed good hogs, even just one, than a lousy calf.* Manley's look reminded her of his words.

The next day, she led Ludwig into the auction ring where the meat-packing companies vied for the prize winners. No one competed to buy Ludwig, sold as all 4-H calves were, except for the very best ones that would go on to the state fair. His incredibly blue blinking eyes, ringed by the washed wavy hair of his white face, looked at

Johnny, she was sure, as he was led away, and she fought back tears, knowing what was going to happen to him. She could already see him stagger with a blow on the head at the stockyards, then they would string him up by the hind feet and cut his throat and slit his gut while he'd be still alive. How could she have wanted a calf?

She had made no friends among the boys, because she was a girl trying to do boys' things, and none among the girls because she was trying to behave as a boy. The boys would have been friends with her if she'd won or even placed, but now, she wasn't even worthy of their attention. They admired fat and red Tina Schmidt because she won first in her class of Chester Whites.

The summer after Ludwig, when she was thirteen, she would take canned tomatoes to the county fair, and whole spiced pears and a hooked rug to the girls' 4-H booths, and give a flower-arranging demonstration in the hated uniform of the girls' 4-H: blue middy sailor blouse with its black necktie, a matching blue pleated skirt. In this uniform, she would walk the long buildings of the cow and pig barns, seeing the boys in cowboy boots or high-topped shoes and denims. She would see Tina Schmidt, disheveled as usual, herding her immaculate Chester Whites, chatting unself-consciously with the boys, and would know her failures as a knot in her stomach, an ache in the chest. She would want to bolt from the flower demonstration and run away, like Old Billy ran.

She would bite her lip while she placed stiff calla lily leaves on a needlepoint flower holder—like a fan. Bernie had planted them for Mother. She saw the arrangement in a book, and would have duplicated it. "You should cut the leaves, everything, during the demonstration," the judge would say, did say, a heavyset woman with a hawk nose and hard eyes. "Didn't someone teach you how to arrange flowers?" Johnny would have laid them out exactly as she was going to place them, all cut, so she wouldn't miss.

"Yes. I—I mean no." Her face reddened.

The worst of it was that she knew the judge to be right. She hated the flower-arranging, because doing it was a statement that she had failed to be a boy, failed both to be Johnny or to be Andrea.

Her feeling about the arrangement was as stiff as the leaves. She was glad that Adolf and Mr. Vroom wouldn't see her trying to arrange flowers—hers weren't even flowers. Just leaves...

In mid-August, after the fair, Manley stood in the cottonwood grove with neighbor boys, Bob Edwards and Jon Andersen, headed toward the timber—the woods around part of the creek that wound its way through the permanent pasture. He carried a rifle. They were going hunting for squirrels, hawks, rabbits—any one of them they could find and shoot.

"Andrea, Mother has something she wants you to do. She told me to tell you," Manley said.

"Liar! Mother isn't even home." Johnny stood, deprived of her name, Johnny, by Manley, her hands on her small hips, chin out, angry. "And don't call me Andrea!"

"That's your name, isn't it?" Manley said.

"Yeah, go on home," Bob echoed. "We don't want girls." He towered over Manley, although they were both fourteen. Jon was Manley's height—both no bigger than Johnny. Manley wanted to reject her in front of his friends, he didn't want to admit that he'd ever played with her.

"I can shoot as well as you can!" she shouted. "Better, even. *And* ride!"

"Sure! Girls can ride better," Bob the bully said, nudging Jon. "They don't have *something* to get in the way."

Johnny fought back angry tears. The sun invited her, this late summer Saturday, to the creek, the pasture drying from the sun, the woods with leaves not yet turning sere. She would like to have wrested the rifle from Manley—she was just as strong—but touching it in anyone's hands was absolutely forbidden. Their father had taught his children how to handle guns.

Jon was a sissy and Bob a bully, and she hated them both. Bob had dared her to poke the bees' nest, he had urged her on, while he and Jon *and* Manley stood a safe distance away cheering her, the bees swarming around her head, stinging her face, her arms, her legs. Manley was sorry when she was sick afterward, but he'd stood and watched.

Now, Manley had abandoned her altogether. Johnny went back to the house. All things were contriving to separate her from being *as good as a boy,* Manley said once.

The next Saturday, the old warrior, old Billy, stumbled and fell down with her in the cottonwood grove. He was getting old, his bright red sorrel whitening with age, his teeth lengthening, the cavernous temples above his eyes deepening, one knee grotesquely enlarged from arthritis. Before Johnny could extricate her left leg that was through the stirrup, Billy stood; he spooked and dragged her; she watched his rear hooves rise and fall next to her head. She could see the clean frog of his left foot and its "V." When her shoe came off and her foot was free, Billy ran to the barn where Manley found him, saddled and bridled and riderless.

He called her name in ever wider arcs, until she answered from under the tall cottonwood trees. He ran to her.

"Manley, it hurts," and she pointed to her black-and-blue ankle. Her face was smudged with dirt mixed with tears.

"What happened?"

"He fell, just stumbled and fell. My foot was stuck in the stirrup." Manley carried her a quarter-mile to the house. He could be nice to her when his friends weren't with him.

"Viktor, that horse is dangerous. He's too old!" Klara said, that evening at supper, after the doctor had casted Johnny's ankle. *Six weeks with crutches,* he'd said. *And maybe you'd better get rid of that horse.*

"I guess he's thirty," Viktor said, sipping coffee.

"Well, she can't ride him anymore."

"He's got more pep than the rest of them, even now," Viktor remarked.

"How much money have you saved, Johnny?" her mother asked.

"Everything I've earned."

"How much is that?"

"One hundred and three dollars and fifty cents." It wasn't enough for a horse, Johnny knew.

"Maybe we should look around for a horse, Johnny. Maybe we can help," her mother said.

"We'll have to see," Viktor said, which was the most promising answer he had ever given to Johnny's endless question: *When*? So she matched hope with watching livestock sales for horses in the *Times Republican*. She found a scheduled auction of horses, in Marshalltown, shipped in from the West.

"You don't want horses like that," her dad said. "You got to know their breeding. They'll all have shipping fever, distemper, and you won't know how they've been handled. You got to handle a horse right, right from the beginning."

But they went anyway. Manley, too, but he was scornful. "Are you really going to get one of those hay burners?"

There were eighty horses or so, all colors, all rough, ungroomed, frazzled-looking. Dad was right, Johnny thought, not wanting his face to tell her, "I told you so!" as they saw one after another ill-bred horse.

Off to the side of the auction ring, a crowd of men circled around a single horse, a white filly, wild-eyed, untethered, trying to rope her. She was whinnying on her hind legs trying to dodge the ropes and the men. Johnny remembered Jeanne d'Arc's white horse on the front of her book and grabbed Manley, "Look at her! I hope they don't catch her!" They being men who *broke* instead of *trained*, always having to break something, subdue it, control it. Everyone watched. Everyone commented:

"Mean little devil. I'd take that out of her."

"Why do they bring such a horse here to be sold?"

"I want to look her in the mouth. Can't believe them fellahs that bring in horses like this."

Ropes finally pulled down her head and rough hands forced open her mouth. Johnny stood watching beads of blood oozing against the white skin like sweat drops on the heads of the men. A tight rope grazed her nose. Her legs were long and graceful, sinewy and tensed under pearly-colored skin, blood vessels were outlined on tensed muscles. Her nose and eyes had black skin, not the pink skin of albinos; her dark eyes were luminous in the whiteness of her face. A number was tagged to her tail, and she was tied to a post.

Viktor and Manley were beside Johnny as she counted her money, earned from her and old Billy's labor on the threshing runs, from the blue-blinking eyes of Ludwig led off to be slaughtered, of the cold mornings before school caring for him, cleaning pigpens, and carrying buttermilk to them.

"Dad, I think she's an Arab."

"Oh you do, do you?" Viktor smiled.

"Dad, please, would you bid?"

"If you want her, you bid, Johnny," he said. But he was smiling.

So she pulled herself up on one of the posts around the ring, pigtails sticking out, and she said, "Here!" shouting it in her strongest voice, knowing, because her dad told her to bid, that he would lend her what money she didn't have. Her face was red, and her heart beat somewhere in her throat and wouldn't go back to her chest. What she remembered afterward was the loss of something she'd never had and a voice saying, "One hundred seventy-five dollars to the girl with the pigtails!" In the next few minutes, she slid down from the post, crying.

"Just like a girl," Manley said, but he was smiling. At the very moment when she should have been able to stand up to the men, and say, "Yep! I picked that one out, and now I got her," she was behaving like a girl.

"Never thought you'd buy a white horse, Johnny," Viktor said, as they went to the secretary to pay. "I'll pay, Johnny, for now." He didn't protest bloodlines, shipping fever, nothing. Manley knew about bloodlines, even if they were Berkshires. Somewhere in this mare, they were there. Viktor had taught his children about bloodlines.

At midnight, the trucker unloaded his gangplank near the Endresen's barn to unload the filly. She came off the truck jittery and jumping, but the solid ground under her feet calmed her. The truck roared off, leaving them in a warm autumn night watching a filly, silvery in the moonlight. Pegasus, Johnny thought. The filly's eyes mirrored the black star-studded sky, mirrored the eyes of the three who looked at her. "A horse that color will get blotchy when she gets older. She'll look like any old flea-bitten nag," Manley said. But Manley was smiling in the way only Manley could smile.

"Well, about time to go to bed, don't you think, Johnny?" Viktor said. "Better get her in the box stall."

"Dad, she's beautiful, isn't she?" Johnny answered, her eyes shining at him, at the filly, at Manley. She turned toward the barn, holding the lead rope, tugging on it slightly. The filly reared up, wheeling on her hind legs, her front legs striking out at the stars, at the barn she wouldn't enter, a barn invaded by gasoline smells, grease and petroleum on the clothes of the farmers once permeated with the odor of horses, a barn emptied of sweet hay and nutty droppings and sweaty leather harness. Only Billy remained.

"Try again, Johnny," Viktor said. But the filly reared up, then dropped hard on her front legs, again she reared higher and dropped harder, whinnying. "Stop a minute. Pat her." But she snorted and blew through her nose, stamped her front feet.

"Maybe she's *loco*," Manley said.

"Oh no, the way she was handled would make any horse seem loco. No. I'll teach her."

"Then teach her quickly so we can go to bed," Viktor said. "I'm not used to such hours."

For an hour, Johnny tried to lead the filly into the barn. And for an hour she reared and whinnied, and Johnny tried hard not to cry. Viktor went to bed, and Manley promised to stay. "Johnny, take your time. It's nice here, under the stars," Manley said, and Johnny wanted to hug him and cry at the same time. But she didn't.

"Maybe she *is* loco, Manley. Then what?" Suddenly the filly stopped fighting and walked in.

"Told you so," Manley said, smiling. "She's not as loco as you were!"

Before breakfast, Johnny groomed the filly and filled the box stall with yellow straw. Her mother and Martha looked in from the top door, seeing the sun shine blindingly on a horse of silver standing deep in golden straw. She whinnied and moved toward Johnny, pushing her with her black muzzle. Martha stepped backward, and their mother reached forward to touch that nose. "What will you call her, Johnny? She's so beautiful, she must have a special name."

"Call her Silver, Andrea," Martha said.

"No. That's a cowboy horse's name."

"Isn't this a cowboy horse? It came from the West, didn't it?" Martha asked.

"I'm not training her like that. I'm getting an English saddle." Johnny turned to her mother, "What shall I call her?" thinking of Jeanne d'Arc's nameless white warhorse on the book cover, wishing she knew what Jeanne had called her.

"How about Maud? Maud Muller? Because she's so pure-looking. It will be a good-luck name."

It was the name of a book her mother liked about a woman. Johnny liked it, because she didn't know anyone with that name. It would be Maud Muller, instead of usual names like Bess, or Kate, farmers' horses names, but she would call her Maud.

So Maud Muller stood knee-deep in the straw that Viktor had wrestled before balers took over, while Old Billy stood in the cottonwood grove thinking of his past, holding no rue for Rusty Malcolm who turned his tongue into a grape cluster. Andrea knelt in the barn, brushing the belly, the legs, fetlocks, mane, felt the firm muzzle that was the mare's upon her head, her shoulder. She cupped the mare's muzzle in her hands.

The mare was high-tempered and difficult to train, and the whiteness of the mare reflected any omission of daily grooming; her white flanks could stain with neglect, like the mark of sin, her mother said.

Martha said, "But I too want to ride her."

Johnny smarted with possession, angry with the idea of sharing. "No!" she cried. "No!"

"You are selfish. You are always in the barn, never in the house. I want to ride."

"But she will not behave, she will just stand there and not move…"

"How do you know? How do you know when you are so selfish you have never let anyone try?" Martha said.

"Johnny, you must share, even your Maud," Klara said gently, looking at her defiant daughter. "If I'd known…"

"Mother, Martha will get hurt. She doesn't know how to ride. She doesn't know Maud."

Johnny looked at her sister, who said, "Please, Andrea," knowing it wasn't that Martha really wanted to ride—she was afraid of horses—but to be a part of Johnny's life, away from the house and its endless cares. Johnny felt her own selfishness touch her like an icy hand, and she felt ashamed.

"Here, Martha, let me help you. There's no saddle horn, you know." Whenever she rode, which was rarely, Martha held on to the horn of the Western saddle with both hands. Martha held to the reins. Up, up rose Maud, and Martha held the reins tighter, pulling the mare backward.

"Put your hands around her neck! Grab her neck! Go forward on her neck!" Johnny screamed as Maud went up, as the reins supporting Martha's weight pulled the white mare's head over backward, as she fell backward, with Martha. Johnny saw in her mind the crushed body of her sister and the mare with a broken back. Hearing nothing, she looked and saw both Martha and the white mare getting up, unhurt. Martha's face was as white as the mare and both wore traces of dirt.

"Johnny," Mother said, brushing off the dirt from Martha's face, putting her arms around her anxiously, "you must not be so selfish with Maud. You must teach her to let others ride her."

"Mother, Andrea can ride her. I don't want to anymore." She brushed off her clothes and examined herself, expecting to find a broken bone under her clothes, unseen.

"I'm sorry, Martha. I really am." Johnny was. But even her father never asked to ride her. He remembered when he had traded his proud-spirited horses for the patient Belgians by Salve's wishes when he had married, then traded Dan and Kate for the reeking Allis Chalmers tractor, traded the expectant whinnying at feeding time for silence. Now he could pay homage to Maud.

The summer passed too quickly. Labor Day was celebrated by the annual Leif Erickson Picnic, where Norwegian immigrants and their descendants waved Norwegian flags and ate *varme polser,* or hot dogs, hamburgers and lefse, and the old settlers talked about the Old Country while the Viking band played and Norwegian Americans danced Norwegian folk dances in native costume. The costume was mostly that of the Hardangerfjord, because many of them didn't know what their regions' native costumes were, and the Hardangerfjord's costume was easy to copy: black skirt, red vest—embroidered, beaded, or even plain would do—and a white blouse with a high neck and silver filigree pin with silver dangles, and any man could find a white shirt and black trousers made into knee pants by tucking the lower half of the trousers into white knee socks. The Quaker Norwegians called it "Lars Larsen Day," although they acknowledged Leif Erickson as well. The difference was that those who celebrated only Leif Erickson Day did the dancing and maybe some fetching something from the car, out of sight of wives and women and Quakers.

Klara was always anxious to go home, because Leif's day won out over Lars's day, and although there weren't many who called themselves Quakers, their legacy was a sobriety not known to the other Norwegians. It was too irreligious a gathering with music and dancing and other things, Klara thought, who didn't realize the importance of the celebration, that it truly was Leif Erickson, son of Erik the Red, who discovered America, and not Columbus, nor that once, deep inside every Norwegian had been the blood of the sea:— sea-skimming swift ships with helmeted men, marauding, raiding, discovering. Viktor the silent one became Viktor the gregarious, laughing and chatting with the old boys, friends of his father and mother, who otherwise lived mostly with the godly Roselands, hard on the spirit and not easy with good times. The Endresens had believed in Vikings more than in men in black suits and black wide-brimmed hats that cast shadows on ordinarily conscientious men. But Viktor remembered the sins of his father all his life.

By four o'clock, Viktor looked at his watch to announce chore time, but both Johnny and Klara had already been longing to leave. Full of hot dogs and soda pop, the Endresens climbed into the black two-door Ford; Klara went home to her roses and raspberries, Viktor to his chores, Manley to his pigs, Martha to Mother's house, and Johnny to the white mare.

CHAPTER THIRTEEN

When Bernie went to college the next year, everyone was happier except for Klara. Bernie hitchhiked home most weekends to check on his Berkshires. Viktor said he was going to sell them, but Bernie was teaching Manley how to take care of them. Manley liked pigs.

Bernie came home for Thanksgiving, content with college, pleased at how happy his brother and sisters were to see him. His mother's fried chicken he didn't have to kill. He brought his laundry home in a cardboard mailable case covered with canvas duck but it was never mailed: his mother washed and ironed everything before he returned. Manley wanted to talk about the Berkshires. Martha and Johnny were proud of a brother in college, the second of all of Salve's grandchildren to attend. Viktor was relieved to have him gone. All six of them stood in the kitchen, fragrant with pumpkin and apple pies baking, and a dressed goose in the sink, eager to hear Bernie talk.

"Mother, did you know that Ina Christiansen has been involved with this bank robber they finally caught, after seven years? The one that killed a cop in Tipton?"

"It's all over the papers, Bernie," Viktor said. "That woman has to rile up something—she can't just stay home."

"Why? What about it, Bernie?" Klara asked.

"We're studying this case in government class."

Of course she and Viktor read about it daily in the *Des Moines Register*, but they did *not* discuss it. They knew Ina had appealed to the governor personally, driving her old Ford to Des Moines, appearing before him with two daughters, all in Quaker bonnets. Klara wished she had such nerve. She had talked about it with Inger until even Inger said Ina *only* wanted notoriety. Marna hadn't taken a stand.

"He's been given the death penalty, and Ina's converting this criminal. She wants his body to bury. Some of the class think she's right, except for burying him. Others think she's crazy."

"Just what I always said, Klara," Viktor said, thinking of how good college was for Bernie.

"Some just don't believe in the death penalty," Bernie went on.

"Bernie, no Quaker believes in taking a life for a life. I don't either," Klara said. "Ina is only doing what the rest of us don't have the courage to do."

"Rot! Klara, you don't really believe that, do you?" Viktor demanded, pacing back and forth in the kitchen. "Let Bernie finish, anyway. Stop interrupting him."

"I'm not interrupting, Viktor. I'm just saying what I think."

"But that's just what the argument is about, Dad, if she's crazy or a fanatic devoted to a cause. There's some story about neighbors that once tried to have her locked up."

"Klara knows that story. Ask her about it, Bernie."

"Jealous neighbors, Bernie, tried to commit her to Independence, and they lost the case, that's all." Klara hadn't waited to be asked. She pushed stuffing into the goose. Martha held its cavity open.

"I could have told them a thing or two, if she hadn't been your mother's cousin," Viktor said. He remembered Ina the day he buried his baby; he remembered Ina cried out for punishment, for him, for Klara, for the world. Her voice had haunted him ever since. He was happy to hear what Bernie said against Ina.

Klara turned to the oven to take out her pies, her face reddened both by the discussion and by the stove. Manley and Andrea listened, leaning against the kitchen sink. They knew enough not to take part in this discussion. Bernie said he didn't tell anyone he knew her, or that she was his mother's cousin, which made her his, too, didn't it! "You're the only safe one, Dad," Bernie said, smiling.

Klara was more pleased that Bernie and Viktor discussed something than she was upset because they ridiculed Ina. "Bernie, tell me"—she bent over the goose Martha held, closing the cavity with skewers and thread—"what do *you* think?"

"I remember long singsong sermons at quarterly meetings—I didn't understand a word she said." He added that then he'd believed what she told him.

"Klara, I've had enough of that crazy woman's ideas. I don't want her mentioned anymore in this house."

"Viktor! She is your conscience, and mine. She is the conscience of us all!" but Klara's sentence was halved by her husband's anger.

"Klara, I say *shut up*!"

Five stunned faces heard the hiss and curve of the *s*, the *t*'s finality, of words never before heard in the house. Bernie, defiant, moved to stand next to his mother, a supporting arm around her. Viktor put on his farm jacket as his eyes made a final and disdainful sweep of the room. No one moved to follow him, not even Johnny. Martha ran out of the room, but everyone knew she would be back, silent, with red eyes, setting the table. Bernie went to the shed behind the washhouse where the shotguns were kept. He would go hunting for pheasant. Johnny and Manley went quietly outside, Manley to his pigs, Johnny to the horses. Viktor was already there, rubbing old Billy's nose.

* * *

Before dawn on Monday, January 24, 1938, two young men arose early on a wintery day in Iowa to coffee and rolls, brought to them on trays. They changed from identical blue broadcloth into blue serge suits, white shirts, and navy polkadot ties. Each tucked a white handkerchief in his left breast pocket. Twenty-one-year-old Allen Wheaton put a yellow rose in his right lapel. He did not speak to John Mercer; neither spoke to the men who guarded them. There was nothing to say.

Governor Krashel sipped black coffee, hoping that his telephone would ring before dawn, giving him reasons for last-minute executive clemency. He was not in favor of the death penalty, but too many people demanded it. He had denied the request of a mother and two daughters who appeared in his office in black dresses and black poke bonnets tied under their chins in wide bows. As it was, the telephone would ring for him shortly *after* dawn; by then it would be too late.

Many would witness the executions in Fort Madison. One hundred permissions were granted to *see the process of justice in action*, they said. Hundreds were turned away. Ina Christiansen had arrived in Fort Madison, Iowa, the night before, asking Sheriff Christian permission to spend at least part of the night with John Mercer in his cell. "Now that is a request we can't grant, Mrs. Christiansen. Don't you know this is a prison?"

She leaned into him, her arms on his forearms, trying to pass. "I want to see him before he goes. I want to hold him in my arms once more and call him my son!" Sheriff Christian was not moved.

"This is no boardinghouse, Missus!" He resented the woman who had turned his courtroom into a prayer meeting, she and her daughters kneeling down in front of the judge, chanting prayers while the prisoner stood in front of them. Sheriff Christian had been furious and wanted to arrest her for court disturbance, but the judge had held his hand to him for silence. He had stood, red-faced and angry while she prayed. Now she was here to claim his body—the state had granted it her—and she wanted to spend the night with him.

Ina stood as tall as she could, a monochrome in black, her chin thrust out, her eyes small points of steel. "I will see him again one day in heaven!" Before dawn, she was at the prison gates, hoping John Mercer would see her. But his eyes looked only at the nothingness ahead of him in the darkness of predawn and pelting snow, which disguised dawn's precise arrival. But timing had not been determined by meteorologists, but rather by the dawn that would not give up the dark.

Two sheriffs mounted the scaffold with the sentenced men. The hangman placed the nooses, already knotted by a rope company in Chicago, around their necks; he placed straps around their legs and arms, tightening them so the ropes would control their death convulsions. Wheaton faltered visibly, swaying toward Mercer. The hangman steadied him before placing black hoods over their heads; each sheriff asked his prisoner if he had anything to say. Two hoarse nos were audible to them.

At 7:24, Warden Glenn Haynes dropped his hand to signal. One hundred witnesses watched the two men's eight-foot falls, the quivering bodies, feet twitching in black, prison-provided shoes, until the feet were still and the black hoods limp. Something like snowflakes fell from under a hood: the hangman said they were yellow rose petals. At 7:40, prison doctors pronounced the two men dead.

Guests filed out of the courtyard prison into the presence of two hearses, where in one, the white lining of a Quaker bonnet framing a white face was visible. All else was black: bonnet, dress, hearse. After the doors of the hearses closed with their still-warm cargo, there was nothing else to see. The hundred witnesses departed, contemplating what they had seen. The consensus, were it taken, was that justice had been served: an eye should be paid for with an eye, for a life, a life.

Ina Christiansen, fifty-five years old, rode with the body of John Mercer to the family farm. Fourteen family members gathered in the family living room around the black-covered coffin with its silver handles, in a plain room, sparsely furnished. The coffin rested on a linoleum floor. A woman in a cloche hat holding two borzoi hounds watched them pray from her photograph: John Mercer's mother. A letter read, from Mercer written before his death, stated that, through Ina, he had found a *true* mother, and a heavenly Father.

Family members carried the coffin to the orchard and lowered it into the ground, under the barren branches of an apple tree. The body inside was seven hours' dead.

Viktor was in the house for a Saturday noon September meal, reading the morning papers delivered by Ralph Hobbs, the mail carrier. Seeing Ralph, or hearing the door of the metal mailbox open on its wooden fencepost, Viktor would take out his nickel-plated pocket watch from the bib pocket of his overall where it was tied with a black shoestring, to see if it was a minute or two before or after twelve noon. Viktor would go in to dinner carrying the newspapers. Andrea heard the mailbox and appeared from the barn. Martha had gone to Marshalltown with a classmate. Manley was with his pigs.

"Ring the bell, Johnny," her father said. She pulled the chain on the dinner bell which could be heard a half mile away. She waited for

Manley, but when he didn't appear, she shrugged and went inside. She looked at her hands, dirty from currying old Billy.

"Wash them," her mother said. She was, Andrea said.

"Klara, you ought to see what's in the paper today."

"Whenever you say that, I know it's not good." Klara knew what it was: Ina had asked the state for another body.

"Well, Klara, now what do you think of your cousin? The state won't give her another body to bury. Now why, do you suppose? It would be easier digging in the orchard now than in January!" Viktor read the headlines aloud: IOWA REFUSES QUAKER WOMAN'S REQUEST. Ralph had pointed out that news to Viktor; he knew about Ina.

"*Why not* is a good question, because it calls attention to the state's cruelty," Klara answered him. "An eye for an eye is what the state practices," Klara said, serving Viktor meat and potatoes, pouring coffee, telling Andrea to help herself, asking where Manley was. She prepared meat three times a day, even when the children were all in school and ate sandwiches for lunch. Viktor insisted on meat at noon and bacon or sausage for breakfast, and the children needed it for supper.

"About time the state got wise to her, Klara. They probably didn't know that she was disowned by her meeting, then her own neighbors declared her insane." Viktor rattled the *Des Moines Register* in his hands, pointing to a column.

"Viktor, she was acquitted," Klara reminded her husband. "And all those good Christian men from her West Branch Meeting were put in their places when they heard the verdict, signed by a doctor and chief of court!"

Andrea hated to hear her parents argue over Ina, but she wanted to know what they thought. "Mother," she said, "how well do you know Ina?"

"Well enough to allow her to meddle in other people's lives, but not well enough to know better," Viktor said.

"She didn't ask you, Viktor."

"What's one doctor's verdict against the testimony of eight

good men who'd known her for years? The doctor never heard her crazy sermons!"

"Viktor, you once said you didn't want to discuss Ina Christiansen in this house. Well, let's not!" Klara banged the dirty pots in the sink. "But!" She stood in front of Viktor and Andrea, her arms straight and rigid at her sides, fists clenched. "There is something I want to say first! If God hadn't made someone like Ina, men would have to. But God has done it for them, so they can have a scapegoat and someone they can laugh at, too. Just like you do. But *you*, all of *you* who deride her will one day come against the face of God, and you will not be acquitted!"

CHAPTER FOURTEEN

"Johnny, I have something to tell you…" Klara said, when her daughter came home from school one day in the fall. Andrea always hated things that began, *There is something I must tell you* rather than the telling itself. She thought of the worst things that could happen: Maud died; her dad had a fatal accident with the tractor, the corn picker; he cut off his hand in the mower; Manley had polio—but Manley had come home in the school bus with her—Bernie had quit school to come live at home; Martha had come down with infantile paralysis. Nothing had happened to her mother, because she was the one telling it. But it couldn't be too bad, because her mother called her Johnny.

"What? Tell it!"

"Johnny, old Billy died this morning. You remember we told you when you got a new horse you'd have to part with old Billy. But now, he's gone."

"Mother, I was feeling sorry for him, honest. His teeth were so long he couldn't chew his grain or hay very well." Johnny bit her lip, thinking of his ribs showing more and more, thinking of…"But what happened? He didn't choke or anything like that, did he?"

"No. Dad went down to the barn about noon—he'd left Billy in his stall because it was raining—and he was dead in his stall."

"I suppose Dad called the rendering works?" She could see that big, once-red truck with a power wheel attached to a metal cable with a hook on the end to pull dead farm animals—cows, horses, large hogs, up into the truck, then off to the glue factory to be made into soap and minerals, and, she supposed, real glue. You could see the truck driving along the road, with maybe a horse's hoof sticking up in the air, the horse stiff with death, bloated, too, if the weather was warm. She couldn't bear to think of Billy like that. She bit her lip harder.

"No, Johnny, he didn't. Your father buried Billy."

Johnny put her arms around her mother and cried. Digging a hole for a horse was more than a day's hard labor.

"Mother, Dad meant his promise to Frichjof, didn't he? Dad's a good guy. I hope he's around when Maud gets old."

She ate a raisin cookie, and she went upstairs to change her school clothes. Manley had already changed and was out with his pigs. She went to find him.

"What are you looking so sad about?" he asked, and she told him, and he said she ought to be glad, she'd never liked Billy that much, had she? And she said he'd been the first horse she ridden, and even if she didn't love him, she admired him and his old stubborn ways, and then she asked him to go with her to the cottonwood grove, did he know their dad had *buried* him, showing how much he loved Billy. Manley corrected her, saying it was a debt of honor, not love, that they were different. But he would go.

They walked through the late Indian-summer day, past the ripening and pungent grapes in the fruit orchard, leaves on the vines curling as they turned sere in late Indian summer: the nights chill, lingering warm days that didn't want to let go of summer.

Above their heads the cottonwoods whispered in a slight breeze. Andrea knew that they had been witness today to old Billy's death, but that they would keep their secret. His grave was not hard to find, still damp with fresh earth. She suspected that her mother had not told her the whole truth, that somewhere in Billy's veins was the substance that had put him to sleep forever. Dad's friend and vet Chet Maxwell, had come in the morning to do the job, and Dad would have gone outside…No, Mother had it wrong. She had made a mistake in telling Johnny that old Billy had died in the barn. He would already have *been* in the pasture when Chet came, near this grave. And after Chet had patted him and reminded Billy of how many times he had looked after him, he would have eased the needle into Billy's neck and waited for a minute. Then he would have leaned against Billy, to ease his fall. Dad would have waited for him in the house. They would have drunk a cup of coffee together afterward, and talked about the horses, or dogs, or cattle Chet had saved and the ones he hadn't, particular ones, using their names. No mention would have been made of old Billy.

She looked at Manley, both of them amazed at the size of a hole their Dad had dug. "Johnny, I never thought Dad would have done this, did you?" Manley had tears in his eyes; he looked away as he wiped them, quickly, with the back of his hand.

"I love this grove," he said, telling her that it was his favorite place on the whole farm, because it wasn't *farmed,* their dad didn't cut down those worthless trees—did she know that cottonwoods were about as useless as tits on a bull? But he loved the way the leaves whispered in a sad way that was comforting at the same time, that was why he sometimes came there when he was sad. And she asked him what he was sad about, and he said he didn't know for sure, wasn't she sometimes?

At that moment, she wanted to be with Manley always, just there, standing in the cottonwood grove, each with a lump in their throats the size of a walnut for no reason at all. For Billy, of course, but she knew that he wasn't the reason. They turned and walked back to their farm chores. Manley put his arm on his sister's shoulder. Neither of them spoke.

Johnny wondered, then, if Manley suspected what she *knew*. If he did, he didn't speak of it, and she wouldn't say it. Of course old Billy had been fine in the morning, as her mother said. Except for his age. But now she would be free to raise a colt—doing it before would have been Billy's death warrant, because she had promised her dad not to insist—she didn't know why he was so against it, but she learned to go one step at a time with her dad if she wanted something, and not to challenge his reasons. Later, her mother told her that it hadn't to do with Billy at all, that her dad had lost too many foals to want to tempt fate again.

"Dad, I want to raise a colt," Johnny said in early May, after Maud's first winter at the Endresens. "For 4-H, Dad," she added quickly, meaning not just for herself. She was standing on the sun porch where Viktor was reading the paper after Saturday lunch. The warm May sun was already hot through the glass, fields were green with young clover beginning to flower, and Viktor was finishing the spring plowing. By mid-May he would begin corn planting.

"Thought you got tired of getting up to take care of Ludwig. Think what it would be with a foal, and then a weanling. They got to have exercise, not like a calf."

"I get up to take care of Maud, don't I, like Manley does with his Berkshires?" But Viktor was concentrating on the *TR*, as the *Marshalltown Times Republican* was known, reading an item in area news that Klara had pointed out to him. "Mr. and Mrs. Viktor Endresen, of Rural Route 2 in Tilman, Iowa, announce the engagement of their son, Bernard, to Dorothy Macmillan, of Newburg. A June wedding is planned."

Viktor was thinking back over the conversation of only a few days ago. "You're too young, Bernie," he had said when Bernie told his parents he was getting engaged; a shock of unruly dark hair had obscured one eye. He'd been nervous and jumpy, as Bernie could be.

"How old do you think you were, Viktor?" Klara had asked. She was less interested in Bernie's getting married than she was in Bernie getting what he wanted.

"But I had a farm, and I knew how to work. Bernie hasn't even finished college, and what he's going to do after? Me, I went to work when I was a kid. Don't even know how old I was, come to think of it. I didn't have much play."

"She's a sensible girl, Viktor. She'll be a good wife," Klara had argued.

"She's only nineteen. Say, how come you're so interested in Bernie's getting married all of a sudden?"

Bernie interrupted, "Dad, I'm the one wanting to get married." Bernie had shifted uneasily on his feet in the kitchen, listening to his parents talk about him. "You're only young once, you know," Bernie had said.

"As though that's any news. But it doesn't last very long," Viktor had answered. "I s'pose you're going to need money, too."

"Dottie will work. She's a good secretary."

"But why so all-fired quick? Can't you wait till you finish school?"

"Everybody gets married in June, don't they?"

"When I was young, it was March. Before spring plowing and planting."

"Dad, times have changed," Bernie had said. *Did sons ever say anything else*, Viktor wondered.

"Kids have changed, if you want my opinion."

"Maybe they don't want the changes they get, Viktor," Klara had added. But she was smiling, knowing that Viktor, in his indirect way, had said yes. Grudgingly, but he'd said yes.

"Yeah, I'll probably be in the army before you know it," Bernie said. "But don't think I want to get married just to get out of it."

"We're not even in the war yet, and what's more, we're not going to be. Everybody says so," Klara said.

"I wouldn't be so sure. Are we going to let Europe go down the drain? Mother, even Norway is occupied. Hitler is a madman!"

Viktor rocked on his feet, looking uneasy. Europe was a long ways away, but Bernie was right, the news was bad. At least the United States wasn't in it. At least not yet.

"Dad, did you hear my question?" Johnny asked her dad.

"Not now. Later, we'll see," Viktor said to Johnny, still standing there, waiting. But Viktor was thinking of how easily Klara had extracted a yes from him when he'd never really meant it. And Johnny believed he'd said yes to her because he didn't say no.

* * *

Johnny and Martha were sitting together in the local Protestant church in early June before the wedding began, Martha, sixteen, in a blue dotted Swiss dress which fell softly around her and suited her young woman's figure. Johnny, aged twelve, was uncomfortable in white organdy with a white satin ribbon belt, *stuff babies wore*, she told Martha, who was pretty and sophisticated-looking. The short sleeves were scratchy on Johnny's arms, and she hoped that when the wedding was over and she stood up, her slip would not be see-through.

The altar was banked with multicolored bearded Irises from the bride's mother's garden; peonies and sprays of bridal wreath with tiny polka-dotted petals filled vases on the two steps leading to the pulpit. Women guests wore light summer dresses, mostly flowered prints, hats of navy straw, white straw, many with nets over their faces down to the chin, with polka-dotted random balls caught in the net, or with artificial flowers. Cousins and the bride's brothers ushered them in, with their husbands in serious colors. The bride's mother wore a powder-blue lace dress; Klara's was navy silk; both mothers were teary-eyed and solemn, as mothers always were.

To Johnny and Manley, the wedding ceremony was like any other, with its *Do you solemnly swears*, the *I dos*, and then rings, and then a kiss and the church soloist singing, "I Love You Truly," in a high squeaky voice, and then a reception in the church basement. Cucumber and chicken sandwiches, not big enough for a mouthful, on white store-bought bread with the crusts cut off, were piled up on platters, and served with coffee and fruit punch, while guests stood around chatting, waiting for the cutting of the wedding cake. Afterward, the bride threw her bouquet directly to her girlfriend, and everybody threw rice, and then the bride and groom, Bernie and Dottie, were gone. Off to live in a student apartment in Ames, where Bernie was finishing his degree in horticulture. He had finally left the pigs to Manley.

The five Endresens drove home, and Klara's silence seemed to spread uneasily over the family group. Klara was thinking about Bernie's having a wife, how it would be different between them, remembering *A son is a son till he gets a wife*. Manley was thinking of the August county fair and how many prizes he would win with his Berkshires. Martha was thinking of the secret rites of marriage that Dottie, just two years older than she, would be about to experience. Viktor was just driving home, and Johnny was thinking of changing her horrid child's dress into jeans as soon as she got home.

There was that feeling on a Sunday afternoon with the day mostly spent, how there would be an emptiness in the family that would take some rearrangement and concentration. But for the rest of the day, Johnny would saddle up Maud and ride down to the pasture. Manley would go and watch his pigs grow, and Martha would make sure that Johnny hung up her dress in the closet and put away her shoes in the room they shared. Viktor would have a nap before chore time, and their mother would worry about Bernie and Dottie. Everyone was sure of that.

Late that night, Johnny heard her parents' voices below her, coming up through the floor register, and knew it was, as usual, about Bernie. But he didn't matter anymore because he was married, so she dropped off to sleep. Her parents knew different.

"But Viktor, don't you think that was right?"

"Right? Damn-fool boy shouldn't be behaving like that. What's the matter with young people today?"

"But it *did* happen. You can't undo what is done. And who knows, maybe she did it deliberately."

"Klara, you don't want to blame your son, Bernie, do you? You always find some excuse for him, even making a girl responsible for something he did. It takes two."

"Viktor, do you mean to tell me that a woman, even me before we were married, couldn't have enticed you beyond your endurance?"

"Klara, you would be the last person capable of it." He chuckled, remembering how Klara had never wanted *it* to begin with.

"Well, leave *me* out of it, then. Another woman, maybe?"

"Klara, I never hung around whorehouses. I was as innocent as you. We never would have thought of trying."

"But Viktor, women are responsible. They shouldn't let themselves get into situations where men can't help themselves, because they lead men on. Then they pay the price as fallen women."

"Now listen here, Klara," Viktor sat up in bed, "I won't have you calling Bernie's wife a fallen woman. He has married her, you know."

"Yes, but Viktor, it is my fault." Klara began to cry. She went to the window and looked out the summer night sky.

"Why would you say a thing like that?" Viktor could see her outlined against the screen, her hair long since grown and braided again.

"Because Bernie came to me and…and said that, that they *had*. He was afraid that maybe she could be pregnant. Then what would he do? If he waited, and she was, everyone would know. So…" Klara watched her husband's face, lighted faintly by the June night sky that seemed to fill the room. She stood, back to the window.

"So? Then what! Klara, tell me!"

"He said they couldn't help themselves."

"What do you mean, couldn't help themselves? My son couldn't help himself, maybe ruin a woman, ruin himself, *because they couldn't help themselves*? Klara, what kind of a son have you raised? No son of mine would do that."

"Viktor, don't say that to me. He is our son. He came to me and asked my advice. And I said they had to marry, that he had to reap the consequences!"

"Oh my God, Klara. Can't you ever stop thinking of truth and consequences? If he wanted to marry her, for God's sake, why would you put it on such a basis, even suggest punishment? Didn't you ever ask him if he wanted to marry her, if he loved her?"

"No. I didn't. Anyway, that's not the issue."

"And *what* do you think the issue is?"

"Viktor, I was afraid you'd be too angry with Bernie—there's something between you two…"

"Nothing more than a doting mother who's spoiled him to death."

"Viktor," Klara said his name with a wail, "how can you say that?"

"Klara, what is the issue to you? Answer me that!"

"The issue is, did I fail him? Viktor?" Viktor was looking into the dark. "Viktor, answer me!"

"I'm glad he married her, and I hope he loves her. Forget about failing him or not failing him—you failed him long ago, making him your baby. Now it's about time he accepted responsibility, and for such a thing. I guess I wouldn't have been surprised if you'd told him not to see a woman like that again. But one thing, if my son couldn't help himself, what's it going to be like for their children, our grandchildren, if their parents *can't help themselves?*" Viktor lay down again and turned his back to his wife in their brass bed. She lay down again, staring at the window. Soon Viktor was snoring.

* * *

The palomino stallion stood quietly in a paddock, at Mr. Benton's farm, looking at them, his coat golden in the sun. Every now and then, he would shake his head up and down and paw the ground. Johnny stepped back from the fence. Manley laughed. Mr. Benton said "He's got a good disposition. That's important." Like some farmers, Mr. Benton kept a pedigreed mare or stallion for his own pleasure, to satisfy his love for the horses he'd once had, replaced now by tractors. Such farmers did not necessarily ride but would offer their stallion's services for breeding: stallions at stud were more trouble than mares.

"Manley, imagine mixing pearly white and gold. What would you get?" Manley only put black together with black—all his Berkshires were black.

"Well, I guess you'd get a jewel of some kind. I know: some precious mettle." Manley was as impressed with his cleverness as Johnny.

"Mr. Benton, I'll bring my mare then, when it's time," Johnny said, looking away.

Some weeks hence, when Maud began to whinny and run around with her tail in the air, Johnny checked her vagina for its telltale ooze. Then she called Mr. Benton and told her father.

"You are *what*?" he roared. "What in *hell* have you been doing? What have you done?" Viktor never said hell, ever.

"Dad, I asked you. And you said…you didn't say no."

He didn't listen. "You are going to do no such thing!"

Johnny knew what *such a thing* was. Such a thing was something she wasn't supposed to know about, or if she knew, she was to keep the knowledge of it to herself. He knew she knew that mares, in order to foal, had to be bred by stallions, that sows were bred by boars, cows by bulls, ewes by bucks, bitches by dogs. And that he himself performed this act upon her mother—the unspoken thing, that even she was born because of such an act of coupling. Once, in anger, her father had kicked their white collie, Queenie, because she had run off in heat and was going to have puppies because of it. "Bitch!" he'd shouted at her, kicking her. "Bitch!" Queenie had looked at him with unbelieving eyes and lowered her once proud head. Ever since that time, Queenie wouldn't come to him when he called, or, *if* she came, she crawled. Johnny looked away every time, not to see Queenie crawl like that.

Viktor couldn't even tell Mr. Benton that his daughter was *not* going to be involved in any such thing, so that, in the end, Johnny rode Maud to his farm to leave her for a few days, riding a loaned mare home. Maud careened around the corner of Mr. Benton's gatepost. Johnny heard the stallion's powerful whinny from deep within his body, between the calves of her legs, she felt the mare's body quiver. The stallion pawed the stable floor, though he could not see her. Mr. Benson secured Maud's bridle—he held her close to her nose—and handed Johnny the reins of a pinto mare. She had no choice but to leave, and there was nowhere to go but home. She felt cheated. She pressed her aching thighs down into the mare's withers, harder and harder. But alarm wilted whatever she felt. She slowed her loaned horse and sat up straight on her buttocks, grateful for the muteness of the mare.

Her mother said that thoughts themselves could be sins. Some of the words in the tree of sins in Sunday school were avarice, gluttony, lust. Dancing flowed into the branch called lust. Johnny pronounced it as she rode the spotted mare over the roadside grasses, passing the neat farms, and their occupants, all of whom she knew from the threshing run. They would call to her and wave, ask her about Maud and why she rode a spotted horse. She didn't know what to answer.

"Don't count your chickens before they hatch," Martha warned.

Maud was in foal, and Johnny was counting her chickens every day. Martha could steal her iron tablets, Manley could call her Andrea and keep her locked away from his thoughts, Dad could get angry with her for being so imperturbable, and Mother could wonder why she was. In school, she wasn't even impatient with Raymond Heissberg, who always stumbled over the simplest words as he read aloud in class, making class tedious and the girls snicker. But the foal didn't stop her from feeling sorry for Vivian Jones, who had come, always, to school in a thin cotton dress under a dirty sweater handed down from a brother, and who carried one jelly sandwich for lunch and no thermos, and whose face looked white and pasty, like store-bought bread.

Johnny put her finger on the date of that summer day when she rode Maud to Mr. Benson's house, looking out the window at the same time into the black branches of the winter trees, which on that day had been so deeply green, with sunlight flickering through leaves like goldfish in a mossy pond. Now it was dark before she went to school, dark when she came home.

Then it was June! Peepers and frogs hummed in the soft June air, whippoorwills whistled in the darkness, bob whites echoed the arriving dawn, and redwing blackbirds swooped with joy along the creek beds, the red of their wings flashing like semaphores.

"Dad, I think it will be soon, don't you?"

"Johnny, I don't know. I just can't say. But she will foal, that's for sure."

"Dad, don't you think we should call Dr. Maxwell when she does?"

"Not unless there's trouble."

"But then...then it will be too late."

"Johnny, listen. Problems are unusual. If she has any, we've got time. Tell you something: you check her every night before you go to bed. Mares usually foal at night."

That night she bumped into Viktor, coming from Maud's stall as she was going in. They laughed. And then the night came: Maud was restless, circling, pawing. She lay down with a thud. It was midnight, and Johnny had to wake Viktor—he got up at four o'clock in the summer—but he came outside in a minute. "You're right," he said in quick summation of Maud's behavior.

They sat down together in the deep yellow straw to wait. "Don't touch her, Johnny," her dad said, curbing her hand that reached out to touch, to rub. She'd seen pigs born, even a lamb, but they weren't anything compared to a horse. A horse was so big by comparison, that birth was big, maybe closer to people. She wondered if Viktor would send her away. He dozed instead, but she was electric-awake, watching the mare, now standing. Something was protruding from the back of her. "Dad. Dad! Wake up! She's in trouble."

"It's the head. That's the way it's supposed to be." The mare circled and lay down again, thud. And then, nothing. Minutes were hours to Johnny, and after a few of them, a steaming mass burst forth—it didn't look like anything but a moving sack in the darkness. Maud stood up, her muzzle touched the glob she had delivered, her tongue licked and licked, and her mouth massaged and nuzzled life into a lumpen thing. Tiny stilts unfolded like a butterfly opening its wet wings, just out of the chrysalis, even though the elastic shining membranes were still connected to its mother. Viktor stepped forward with his pocket knife and severed the silvery red-tinged connection to separate them forever, and the foal was born. Viktor wrapped the umbilical cord around his hand, pulling on the afterbirth, which was not ready to come. He pulled and waited, and the mare licked and breathed and pushed her foal, now four spindly legs, a little head, and two fuzzy ears that unfolded like a flower in a glass of water. The spindles spread out and tried to lift the small body. Not even dry, the spindles bent again and again, then straightened. Grasshopper legs, spider legs, bent and sprawling, pushing, collapsing, always bent, trying to straighten.

Johnny wanted to help and moved to lift the small body under the belly, raise him up into the world. "Don't touch him!" Viktor said. "There are things you don't do," and he nodded to the mare. "It's hers." Johnny reached out with such empty hands. "Johnny, don't you understand—some things she has to do, like bind him to her, so he'll always follow her. It's nature's way." Viktor separated the mare from her foal, and now the mare was binding them back together, with her body, with her bigness, her presence. Viktor pulled again on the afterbirth, and it released. "All's well. She did good, Johnny."

"Dad, I can't even tell what color it is, or what sex."

"It's a colt. Color don't matter. It'll change."

He was trying to stand. Three legs up, then he fell and tried again. Again. Johnny's hands reached out, but she didn't touch. He stood, teetering on rubbery legs, spread out, bracing that grasshopper body on stilts. Then fell. Again, front legs up, up, then hind legs, tucked under him, bracing, trying to rise, the mare nuzzling, almost pushing him over. He stood! And took a step toward something his tiny muzzle knew must be there. A teetering, wobbly step, and then another, his mouth reaching, finding the mare's chest, her front legs. Johnny wanted to turn him in the right direction; she put her hands behind her back. Along the mare's belly, his nose searched blindly for *something he knew not of but knew*. And found.

Dad always said all is well if he stands and suckles, and then she heard, "Time to leave, Johnny, I get up at four." They stepped out into a starry moonless night. Out from the depths of the Milky Way, a star streaked across the sky and was lost, blurring across Johnny's blurred eyes. An owl hooted...Viktor would be getting up in two hours.

Johnny lay in the dark warmth of the world and thought of the little lamb with the head broken off in the Quaker graveyard. Martha didn't see her wet face.

In the morning she went to the barn, not believing what she had seen in the night. There was Maud eating hay, beside her a foal, wobbly, but standing. He was pale, almost white. She saw a white star on his forehead. He would be a Palomino, like his sire, a white star on his head. She brought Mother and Martha and Manley to see him, and they all stood like the Magi. She let him out in the grassy meadow. The colt blinked in the warm sunshine, a small shadow next to his mother's big shade. The world was green and soft underfoot and blue and warm above, and a large moving presence was his alone. He suckled, bracing himself on four posts, tail working as hard as his mouth.

Johnny was kind and patient and volunteered for more housework than usual. She couldn't use up her burst of energy: she helped Manley notch his pigs ears, something she hated to do, like punching holes in leather except the leather was flesh and the tiny silk moleskins bled, and piglets squealed. Mother hummed. Dad's smile was as big as a crescent moon.

On the fifth morning, Johnny caught the foal napping. She knelt to feel his firm, muscled body, his velvety coat, and soft black muzzle; she curled her fingers around tiny hooves, sharp and precise, outlined the star on his head. Maud stood near by, touched him with her nose, whinnied. He didn't get up. She started to lift him. He was limp. She ran to the near cornfield where Viktor scythed weeds under fence rows.

"I tell you, Johnny, that colt stood and suckled!" He rubbed knobby, calloused hands over the foal while she wondered how hands with such hard skin could have any feeling in them, not knowing his hands were part of his brain, that the touch of his fingers found fever, injuries, anything amiss. "He's swollen in the abdomen, Johnny. Call Dr. Maxwell."

"But what's wrong. Dad, he won't..." But she couldn't finish her sentence.

"I don't know, Johnny. I don't know." Nor did Dr. Maxwell, who gave him castor oil, and he opened his mouth wide in distaste. The foal's whiskers were sticky with it. But he didn't get up and by afternoon, he had not suckled. The mare stood with a swollen udder. Dr. Maxwell stood him up, and he staggered, head hanging down. He fell.

Shadows lengthened, and Johnny sat, holding the foal's head in her lap, the mare nearby, touching him with her nose, nickering. Manley came and, together, they stood the foal up again, thinking, perhaps, that the mare would lick life back into him, or the hand of God would touch him as he once touched Adam. For a second they let go of him, meaning to. He fell, back to the ground. He didn't move. Manley knelt over him, put his ear to the foal's chest, his cheek to the foal's nostril. He gripped Johnny. "Johnny," he said. "He's dead."

She sat on the grave Manley had dug in the cottonwood grove, near old Billy. She squashed the flowers Manley had planted. "It's better to raise pigs, Johnny. They're not so beautiful, but if they die, there's always another one." He had tears in his eyes.

He led her back to the house, upstairs to her room. He brought her the two-faced doll and showed her the crying side, but she didn't look. Johnny wanted to be frail and fade from grief.

Her mother came upstairs where she sat on her bed, staring at the white horse on the cover of *Joan of Arc*. "Don't take it so hard, Johnny," her mother said, standing over her daughter's sobbing figure. "You mustn't. It's just a colt!"

"And a baby is *just* a baby!" she shouted. "Kristina Andrea was *just* a baby, and it was *just* a grandmother like Grandma Andrea, and it was *just* a grandfather like Salve—*just* your Papa! And your other dead baby, *just* a baby, too."

Klara put her arms around Johnny's heaving shoulders. "And God knew all along! He knew he'd made my colt with a wrong intestine. He knew it would burst, and—and…He meant to!" If she had looked up, Johnny would have seen tears other than her own. "I don't understand why everything dies. Look at you, Mother—everybody died. Everyone you loved. I know you don't think my colt was anything, and he wasn't, compared to babies. But he was mine!"

"Johnny, maybe you loved him too much. Maybe—"

"Don't tell me that! You're trying to say I *ought* to be punished, for loving something. What's *wrong* with loving?"

"Nothing's *wrong* with it." Klara stroked her daughter's bent head. "Only you mustn't forget to love God. Maybe love Him more."

"How can you love something you don't know, you can't even see." Johnny raised her head, more in anger than grief. "I just can't pick God out of the sky, or see Him up there, wherever He's supposed to be. Besides, even if He is, He's nothing but mean and nasty!"

"Johnny, it's easy to believe in things you can see, like your colt. But it's harder to believe in things you can't see."

"Then tell Him to show me! Tell Him to speak to me! But He can't. He's not there!"

"Johnny, you mustn't speak like that. You mustn't."

But Johnny fled from advice and comfort. She went downstairs, intending to go to the barn, but her mother took her hand and led her to the living room.

"Sit down, Johnny. Listen to me." She picked up the brass candlestick, explaining how it had been here longer than they both had, that it had witnessed tears and anger, but love and faith as well, that if it could speak, it would tell her tales of how, despite everything, life required belief, faith. Years thence, Johnny would remember her colt as a gift from God that she had had for a short time, but a gift, nevertheless, that made her grow.

Johnny looked at the candlestick and said how it was ugly, how it represented nothing but a dead grandmother as far as she was concerned, and now it would be a dead colt, too. "Now I'll hate it, Mother. Why don't you just let me alone?"

She went to the barn to be reminded of her loss. She disliked Maud because the mare looked calmly out of the top of the barn door into the empty barnyard, whinnying now and then, complacently chewing hay.

Johnny began to distance herself from Maud and to close doors on what she could not accept.

In December, Japan attacked Pearl Harbor.

CHAPTER FIFTEEN

After the colt died, Andrea decided she wanted to get as far away from home when she went to college as she could get. She chose New York City for the way the whole world seemed encapsulated in its streets, its cultures, its possibilities. When she went off to school, the city didn't disappoint.

Andrea's first trip home from New York was for Christmas. Going home was something she dreaded, except for Manley, but it was also something she wanted to do, in the faint hopes that all would be mended. Mother would be happy, Manley, too, and Bernie would have stopped drinking. Faint hopes!

After her long ride from New York City to Chicago, it was another four hours to Grinnell when the Rocket, a fast train, pulled gracefully into the Grinnell depot. She stood with her small bag in the exit passage, looking for Manley, and saw him before he saw her, and shouted his name, trying to imagine if she would choose him from a crowd as someone she wanted to know. She decided she couldn't disassociate him from being her brother—Manley was the left hand to her right. Their shared childhood had made it so.

"How's the big country boy?" she said, hugging him, bantering as they usually did. They skirted serious things at first, making fun of how indirectly things got said in their family, as though honesty was too unkind. Sometimes it was.

"How's the big-city girl!" he asked, as she hugged him, then held him at arm's length for a moment. Manley looked like their father—same hairline, deep-blue eyes, straight lashes. But his nose was broader than his, and his lips were full like their mother's, his gentleness was hers. Today, he seemed distracted.

"OK. I guess." Manley didn't seem too sure.

"I guess I'm OK, too. Can't you see? How's everybody at home?"

Andrea suspected the usual problems with Bernie and Mother.

Manley was living at home now, farming with Viktor and raising his Berkshires. It was always his plan to buy the land next door and take over Viktor's when he wanted to retire. The two adjacent farms would give him enough land to have a one-family operation and to concentrate on raising Berkshire hogs. Manley got out of the army late, in 1948, because he had been initially classified 4-F because of a spot on his lungs. At the same time his classmates were fighting in Europe and Asia, he felt desolate and cowardly; he had petitioned and repetitioned for reexamination, but by the time his lung spots were determined to be scar tissue from childhood pneumonia, the war was nearly over. Manley had felt like a deserter.

"You'll see, Andrea." Manley took her little bag, saying, "Come on. Let's go."

"Do you mean something's wrong?" she asked, following him through a crowd of students from Grinnell, girls wearing bobby socks and saddle shoes, plaid skirts and cardigans under their camel coats, the boys in jackets and ties, overcoats. Uniforms, she thought. The one-story station had a massive, slightly sloping roof with a large overhang to cover the platform and the outside entry. Inside, oak benches, heavy like the inside ribs of the roof, stood sentinel, churchlike. But they hurried through it to Manley's blue Ford parked in front.

"No more than usual," Manley said, opening the car door for her.

Andrea realized, as she thought of Manley in the army, that she'd never discussed it with him—other events took precedence, so she asked him how it had been in the army.

He'd got in too late, he said. Manfred Stonewall was killed, he reminded her, along with Keith Meier, who had been in his class. His voice trailed off. He never mentioned Bernie: he had been in Shanghai, a naval officer, leaving Dottie and three kids at home.

"Yeah, I know," Andrea answered. "Glider paratroops, both of them, weren't they? But Manley, how is it working out, being at home? Farming with Dad, I mean."

Manley was a born farmer. He loved the hard work, being his own boss. He loved careful breeding of the Berkshires, a breed to which

Bernie had introduced him. Manley had taken the breeding seriously and had become well known among national and international breeders before he went to the army, taking grand champions at the most prestigious livestock show—the International in Chicago. She remembered his sitting on the fence on a green summer afternoon after he'd fed his pigs—he knew each one—saying, "Andrea, I just like to sit here and watch them grow." Then he'd laugh, as though he didn't want Andrea to take him seriously. She would do the same about horses, watching them eat, move, stand.

Manley had had to disperse his herd when he went to the army for three years. Their dad didn't believe in purebreds. "Don't want hogs I have to baby," Viktor had said. "I want hogs that can take care of themselves."

Manley shifted the gears, and off they went through the flat town with its Gothic houses and college buildings, some of brick or stone, a more substantial town than most because of the college.

"Can we talk later?" Manley glanced sideways out of both windows, then looked back at the highway, stepping on the gas. "All of Me" played on Manley's radio, sung by Doris Day. "By the way, did you hear the big news?" Manley asked.

"No. What?"

Manley was smiling, as he said, "Guess who got married."

"You'll have to tell me," she said, relieved to think of something else.

"Shirley Temple. Just yesterday. I thought she was still Little Miss Muffet. She's twenty-two. Makes me feel old." Their grandmother Andrea had taken them to see a Shirley Temple movie, *The Poor Little Rich Girl*, on a snowy winter Saturday when a blizzard came up, and they'd been stuck on the way home.

"And Faulkner won the Nobel Prize!" she added to the news, thinking that Shirley Temple was a year older than she. She regarded Manley's profile, his hairline receding slightly—their father had been bald early.

"And Ingrid Bergman has blotted her copybook, in this affair with Rosselini," Manley added.

Andrea said nothing, wondering if he was serious, thinking of what Ingrid had said. "People saw me in Joan of Arc and declared me a saint. I'm not a saint."

After Andrea asked about the pigs, and Manley referred to "what's left of them," they went on to talk about the big snow of '36 when they had been home from school for six weeks. Sinatra sang "I'll Never Smile Again" with Tommy Dorsey's big band, and Manley said the song was appropriate for him right then. They passed the corner where they, together, had ridden their bicycles back and forth in front of men working on the road for the WPA, displaying black-lettered cardboard signs they'd made and wired to the handlebars and rear fenders: "WPA: We Play Around." "WPA: We're Probably Asleep." She asked Manley if he remembered.

"Sure," he said. "We were pretty dumb kids, weren't we? They could have knocked the stuffing out of us."

And then they were home. Manley was abrupt with the car, pulling faster than he needed into the driveway where Bernie's pickup blocked the way to the garage. The house, like most farmhouses built around 1890, was white clapboard with an open porch supported and decorated by small columns, now glassed in. Once it had a hand pump over a lead sink in the middle of the kitchen, but her mother had it remodeled in the early forties, putting in a then-modern kitchen, bathroom, new windows, and floors. The house was defined by the dark junipers in front of it; the barn and the outbuildings were white as well, all but the roofs were swallowed in whiteness, but the snow reflected pink from the setting sun. This house, once so big and so familiar, now seemed a place Andrea dreaded entering because of how complicated everything had become.

"Go on in, Andrea. I've got to go to the barn," Manley said. She felt his tension rise. Memory produced the sound of bells on Christmas morning, when their dad circled the house with his horses' sleigh bells around his neck; the whinny of her mare, Maud. Her throat hurt, and she didn't want to enter this sacred place at all.

She entered the back door of the washroom with its gray-painted cement floor sloping downward to a drain, laundry machines, a hotel-size stainless Amana freezer, the sink and mirror where her father shaved. Her parents' arms were outstretched to her, their voices called *Johnny*.

She was *home*, with its familiar sounds: the way the door creaked, the razor strop with its Sunday morning song as it sharpened her father's straight-edge razor, her father's chuckle. Her mother's love radiated over it all. They all talked at once, about snow, traffic, the cold winter. When Bernie appeared from the direction of the living room, there was a sudden silence.

"Well, I see you got home for Christmas!" he said, his eyes seemed glassy, and his voice was louder than she had remembered.

"I haven't missed one yet, Bernie. I hear you are almost living nearby. How nice for Mother. And Dad," she added.

"Haven't got in any trouble, have you, there in the big city?" Bernie's implications were coarser than Bernie had ever talked, at least that she'd ever heard. His face was slightly puffy, he'd gained some weight. Did she imagine it, thinking of his slim quickness, his natural elegance that he always seemed to want to hide. He once held a violin, playing in the school orchestra, his face pure concentration. She, nine years younger, had been convinced that he had entered a world where she could only stand from afar and worship him, waving to him occasionally, hoping he saw her.

"Bernie has finally got his chance at a greenhouse," Mother said proudly.

Viktor shifted his feet, not looking at anyone. "Johnny, you'll have to see my colt," he said. "Before you take your coat off!" He wanted to go with her now so that Bernie would leave.

"Go ahead. Just walk out, Andrea. But don't worry about me, I'm goin' anyway," Bernie said, putting on his jacket. Klara hovered over him, helping him. Viktor had put on his red blanket-lined denim jacket and cap with the ear flaps. The three of them went out together. She followed her dad, waving goodbye to Bernie, thinking that her sins could slip by unnoticed because of Bernie's. She wondered which one Mother would consider the worst, drinking, or—what would she call *it*?

Viktor had Maud bred when she went off to college. After losing the first foal, Andrea had never wanted to breed her again. After the second, Viktor's foal, she sold Maud. If she hadn't, the mare would have stayed in the barn and pasture, her coat a product of weather, her mane unkempt, her feet unshod. And so she would grow old. Andrea didn't want to see her mare like that.

Viktor opened the barn door. Inside was the palomino colt, dark gold dapples on his flanks, knee-deep in yellow straw, just the way she'd kept Maud. "Dad," she said huskily, "he's beautiful." She stroked his sleek, brushed coat, caressed his ears, nose. He nickered.

"Watch him," Viktor said. "He knows where I keep sugar. Here, you beauty." The colt nuzzled his jacket pocket with his strong rasping lip—it had a curl of hair on it—and Viktor brought out a sugar lump. Viktor's silences spoke, like many farmers'. But he broke that silence, his eyes moist, his voice husky as well, "Johnny, a man can love a horse."

"He's a little heavier than Maud, Dad. Darker in color. Dappled, too," she said, her eyes misty, too.

"Because he's a colt, not a filly," her dad said, his voice cleared. She knew he wouldn't talk about Bernie; his silence spoke very clearly. Once he had a hired man who said that the children's cough medicine smelled like brandy. The next day, Viktor fired him, believing that any man who knew the smell of it must have had a reason.

It was beginning to snow as they left the barn, big soft flakes like torn cotton balls were silhouetted by the light from the kitchen window where her mother could be seen, rushing from oven to sink, to refrigerator, to the dining room.

Inside, the oval oak table her mother had refinished was set with red candles and white linen, a bowl of evergreen with tiny red ornaments. The table had belonged to her dad's mother, Andrea. One of the candleholders was the old brass one that her mother's mother, Kristina, brought with her to America. Klara had found a second one, new, not very similar, to go with it. "Mother, you don't have to go to all this trouble. We could eat in the kitchen."

"When should I use the dining room, if not now?" she said, hugging Andrea. There were just the four of them, Manley and her and their mother and dad, the way it was after Martha left, first to work and then to marry. Andrea was the youngest, and Manley two years older.

They ate roast chicken and cherry pie. Andrea chatted about New York, trying to sound like she'd never left Iowa, hoping that she seemed no different as she told her dad how he wouldn't like New York at all, that there was too much traffic, too many skyscrapers. That there was no grass, that in some places not even the sky was visible.

"Maybe it's a place I ought to try," Manley said suddenly.

"But why, Manley? What do you mean?" she asked, looking across the candlelight at his flushed face.

He pushed his chair back as he said, "Ask Dad."

Their dad's eyes flashed. "Ask Klara," he said. Nobody looked at Klara.

"Everybody blames me for their problems. I don't understand it," she said.

"What you mean is, you won't admit you caused them!" Manley said, straightening in his pushed-back chair.

Andrea had never known Manley to condemn Klara for anything.

"Tell Andrea, Mother, what's going on. Tell her what my problem is. And while you're about it, tell her about Dad's problem and Bernie's too. Don't forget his!"

"And how about Martha's and mine," Andrea said, trying to defuse the conversation as she watched the candle burn in Kristina's candleholder. Her mother stared at Manley, her face startled and innocent.

"OK, then," Manley went on, "I'll tell her." He said how everyone in the family always knew he wanted to buy the O'Connell farm, how he'd come back from the army only to find that Mother had forced Dad to buy Bernie a greenhouse for $50,000, a rotten, bankrupt greenhouse, and that, because of it, Dad couldn't help him buy the farm; it was all Klara's fault. "Bernie was always her pet, you know," Manley said, turning to Andrea and adding, "You know he drinks, don't you?" His voice had risen steadily. His eyes flashed, the way

Dad's could when he was angry. He hit the table with his fist, and the flame jumped up from the candle. "A run-down, rotten greenhouse that will stay run-down and rotten because Bernie's nothing but a drunken bum!" Manley's normally gentle eyes burned bitter.

"Manley, don't speak to your mother like that!" Viktor stood up, eyes flashing.

"Dad, just admit it. You didn't want to do it, did you? You think Bernie's a bum! Admit it! How you mortgaged the farm, for *him*. How you stand to lose even this!" Manley swung his arm in a wide circle to indicate the whole farm.

Viktor sat down. "Andrea, Manley has some truth—"

But Klara interrupted him. "Viktor, you don't believe that Bernie won't make a go of it, do you? Say you don't! Say it!" Klara reached to her husband, shaking his arm.

"You mean—you mortgaged the farm?" Andrea asked, unbelieving, remembering the original mortgage that had hung over their father's head for years throughout the Depression, when she was too small to understand it. Sell corn, pay off part of it, remortgage to buy seed corn, to buy feeder cattle. For years, it was like that. And then the day came it was paid off, finally. Their mother had bought lutefisk and made lefse in honor of Viktor's mother, Andrea, who'd bought the farm in the first place, and of her father, Salve, who'd contributed a team of horses when they married. How could Dad remortgage?

"Answer her, Dad!" Manley said in a low voice. "Answer her."

She heard her father's low, breathless, "Yes."

"Mother, is it true?" Andrea knew it was, but she had to ask. "When did this happen?"

"Yes, Viktor mortgaged the farm. But he's done that before," her mother said.

"But he did it for himself, Mother. Not for Bernie," Manley's voice was still raised. Turning to his sister, his hopeful ally, he continued, "You saw Bernie, Andrea. He's not going to make a go of it. Mother's over there half the time, helping him. She's over there potting plants, cleaning up the mess the place was left in by Schmidt, who owned it before. Most of the windows are broken out."

"Nobody in this family wants to help Bernie. Bernie needs it more than Manley..." Klara had tears in her eyes.

Manley leaned forward. The candlelight leaped in his eyes. "Because I don't drink, Mother? I don't need it, because I don't drink?"

"Mother, did you decide who needs it most?" Andrea asked. "Didn't Dad have a vote at all? What about me? Can I vote? What if I say I vote for Manley?" She couldn't stop herself.

"Then I say Bernie needs me more than ever!" her mother said. Manley stood up and pushed his chair back abruptly, slamming the door to the upstairs. She and her father sat at the table looking at their cherry pie circled by a gold Greek key border on Lennox china.

"Dad, I'm going upstairs, too. I'm sorry, Dad." She put her hand on his then followed Manley. But she went to her room instead—Manley's door was shut. The room was cold, the upstairs hardly heated. She sat on the bed, noticing the clean cedar odor from the closet her mother had had lined with cedar during the house remodeling. Familiar objects from her childhood surrounded her: except for dust on the books it seemed as though a child still lived there. There was the small, orange, polka-dot book, black-bound: *One Hundred Best Poems for Boys and Girls*. And next to it, Mark Twain's illustrated *Joan of Arc*, with Joan on the cover, in armor, mounted on a white war horse. Joan, a virgin, had gone forth and saved France. Ingrid Bergman had played Joan, and she was now a fallen woman. She crossed to the bureau and picked up her doll—a laughing and crying doll, one face on either side of the sawdust-and-glue head, painted and glazed. Under the calico-printed dress her aunt Marna had made, she felt the cloth body stuffed with cotton batting. Impulsively, she went to Manley's door and knocked, carrying the doll.

"What do you want?"

"To come in, Manley." She paused to listen.

"OK, come in. Don't know why you'd want to." Manley was seated in his desk chair, holding his woven khaki Eagle Scout belt. Stenciled on it was the symbol of each merit badge he'd passed to become an Eagle. She'd always hoped he'd give it to her because she was proud of it and now, it was too small for him. He saw the doll. She held up the crying face to Manley so that she saw the laughing one. Then she reversed it. Manley didn't smile.

"I'm the crying one, Andrea."

"I'm both," she said, putting her hand on Manley's shoulder. Without looking up, still fingering the belt, Manley said very quietly, "Guess we're both hanging on to the tag-ends of our childhood. I couldn't wait to grow up. Now I'd go back, if I could be somebody else."

"What do you mean?"

"Why do we have to have parents and grandparents and houses and rules to program us into something we don't want to be, Andrea. Why?"

"Who would you be, then?"

"I'd like to be born without anyone to shape me into someone I don't want to be, someone I don't even have any choice about being. Andrea, everything we want is because we've been taught to want it. We don't make any choices of our own, and we don't even know the difference."

Even though she'd chosen to go away, she knew that Manley was right, that she would always drag around with her the ingrained standards she'd accumulated here, the guilt, the "striving to be perfect," her mother called it, in a world that didn't expect it or want it. She sat down on his bed, studying his face. "We're a long ways away from this belt, Manley," she said, referring to those years when he stenciled it, one badge at a time as he won them.

"You know, I'd just like to erase me. Start over." He paused and then looked at her intensely, reaching for her arms. "Do you like who you are?" he asked.

"I like you as a brother," she said, trying to defuse Manley's argument.

"Wouldn't you sometimes like to be born somebody else? Why do I even want a farm, this one and O'Connell's, if I hadn't been brought up *here*, to want it?"

"I guess that's right, that's why you care about it."

"That's what I'm saying. Don't you understand? I think I'd like to be born a monkey." Manley released her arms and motioned for her to sit down, on his bed, facing him in his chair.

"Me, too, if you were my brother." She didn't know how to answer Manley, nor did she want to go away and remember him like this. She didn't want to think about what he was saying.

"Andrea, how did you get away? What made you leave?"

She could not tell him that she'd had to leave, that she couldn't be a farmer and she wouldn't be a farmer's wife, and that she didn't want to watch what he saw: Bernie. She didn't tell him that she couldn't escape this place any more than he could, she would always carry it around with her, an albatross, a bag of old clothes, burdens. She got up.

"Night, Manley," she said, leaving before he saw her cry. He didn't get up. She closed his door.

After that evening, no real family conversations took place when Andrea was home—not even at Christmas dinner. There was enough crop-livestock conversation with Martha and her farmer husband, Howard, to occupy everyone engaged in farming, which everyone was, more or less. Bernie listened to them and was calm, and his wife, Dottie, was busy with their three young children. Her mother hovered over them, her grandchildren.

Christmas dinners never have conversations to be remembered, Andrea decided, listening to all of them talk about the weather, who got married, what the neighbors got for their corn, how many acres another one planted, how many hogs they raised. No one asked her anything. She was relieved. And hurt.

Before Martha and Howard went home, Martha took her hands in hers. "Andrea, I was so afraid you wouldn't come for Christmas," she said. "And yet, the sad part of your coming is that I always know you're going to leave." Andrea returned her sister's squeeze. They had never known each other, all the years they'd grown up together, had they? Not like she knew Manley. *Don't do that. Do this. Help in the house. Stop running outside all the time*, Martha had said. And then, the warning: *You'll make Mother sick.* Martha, four years older, had always been the caretaker, giving her sister time to rebel.

"Come see me tomorrow, will you?" she asked. And Andrea said yes.

Martha's house had been her in-laws' house—Howard's parents had moved to a nearby newly remodeled farmhouse, owned by Howard's family. That was the custom, that when a son married and took over the farm, he took over the family house as well, and there would be a little more redecorating and remodeling. Each wife in charge of the house must make it hers by these changes. Martha's were to redo the kitchen with new maple cabinets, a new stove, a change of paint. The rest of the house would have to wait until they had more money, until the babies came, until they grew. And the mother-in-law would watch and say, *It was good enough for me.* But in its lifetime, the house would change with each generation. Martha would have a gradual series of renovations, enlarging the kitchen, paneling a study with knotty pine she had seen pictured in *Better Homes and Gardens*, wall-to-wall carpeting covering the old pine floors, enclosing the porch with glass. And then, her as-yet-unborn son would move into it with his wife, and the changes would begin again.

Howard's barns were red, and much closer to the house than her father's were. The barnyard was muddy instead of green, and instead of a white board fence there was woven wire. Martha would hate that, Andrea knew. Gradually, she would have it closer to her liking by removing the fence entirely, by extending the lawn. Martha had only been married a year, and Andrea wondered if she weren't lonely, and wondered if Martha wondered if her sister wasn't homesick. But they didn't mention those things. How little they talked of what was closest to them—how Andrea couldn't wait to leave home, how Martha had gone to college but couldn't bear to be away. So she came home, and worked in the nearby town as a nurse's aide—abandoning the nurse's training she'd had her heart set on. She'd rented a room with a family she liked and came home weekends to help her mother. Then she met Howard. Now here she was, in her own home, a farmer's wife. Not far from her parents. It's what she always wanted.

"What will you do after this year, Andrea?" she asked, cutting a piece of angel food in her immaculate kitchen, serving it on her best china plate with a sterling fork, pouring coffee into thin cups.

"I don't know. I'd like to go to Europe."

"Whatever for? It's real bad over there, I hear. The war ruined everything."

"I'd just like to travel."

"Don't you think you should come back home? You could teach at the high school." Martha couldn't imagine why anyone would want to stay away from home, and Andrea couldn't imagine why Martha could be content with being here. Andrea would get up and leave and wish Martha well and mean it. As she was doing now, happy that Martha—someone—found what she wanted. Or thought she did, which amounted to the same thing.

But Andrea couldn't wait to leave this farmhouse heavy with families and the promise of babies and crops and winter and spring over and over again. She couldn't wait to leave Klara and Viktor and Bernie and his greenhouse. But she didn't want to leave Manley behind. She rose from the comfort of her sister's house, where the only thing that would change would be the years, and she embraced Martha who kissed her, her eyes filled with tears. Andrea went out through the kitchen door to her dad's black Ford—he always had Fords, and they were always black. Tomorrow, she would leave the comfort of repeating histories and known tomorrows, leave the secure niche she could make here, from which no one could ever dislodge her if she chose, not even hail or fire. Nothing could change the shape of the land and how it was sowed and harvested, how piglets and lambs and calves came every year, and how that renewal was enough, and should be enough, how staying beckoned her, how staying would resolve everything. Staying would, in itself, forgive her. But tomorrow, she would go back to New York.

The next morning the whole farmstead was covered with new snow, the angles of the roofs looked draped with sugar frosting. The sun was out, and the world glittered with diamond snowflakes like a Christmas Advent calendar with its little doors to open each day to new surprises. She tried to think of the days like that, but all she could see were doors closing on Manley, one by one, and her mother watching them, aching and torn with love. But *she* was leaving: it was her father and Manley who must stand by and watch things fall apart; maybe he would lose his farm, and then, when, *if* Manley found a farm to rent, it would be just Viktor and Klara. But they would never be free of Bernie, emotionally or financially.

When she brought her bag down to leave, she hesitated on the stairs, then went back to her room and picked up the doll. She looked at the crying face, and opening her bag, stuffed it in a corner.

Manley's car bumped along the road to the Grinnell train depot with silent occupants. Andrea wanted the car to fly and take her away, quickly, from where love was buffeted by drought and flood and, at the same time, she wanted Manley to turn the car around and take her home. She wanted never to have left, and she wanted never to have come back. She remembered Manley's words: *What did you find out there?* and she couldn't answer him. She wanted never to want anything anymore but what Martha had, to serve others without thoughts of herself. And she wanted to take Manley with her, faraway, and never come back, to hold his hand while they blew bird whistles from Sears, walking through endless orchards and pastures, a cottonwood grove. She looked at his face: stern, lips clenched against crying, eyes staring, and knew hers was the same. *To live was to suffer.* It was Ina who took the gifts of life and turned them into penance. Andrea felt her fists clench in her gloves. The car skidded just a bit in the snow, while Frank Sinatra again sang, "I'll Never Smile Again" on the radio. She pressed Manley's arm as he drove and asked him not to get out at the station.

The first lap back to New York was a train to Chicago, from where she would take a red-eye special night flight. She would have to wait six hours, alone, when she got to O'Hare. In Chicago, the train platform was bitter cold, the wind howling as she could remember it only in the Midwest. She wished she and Manley were together here, in Chicago, and together, they could think of something that would tear out grief by its roots, wipe out one desperate thing by another.

CHAPTER SIXTEEN

"Dear Mother," Andrea wrote in her tan room on her Smith Corona portable in early May, writing that she was going to Norway after she graduated—she'd won a summer scholarship from the University of Oslo to study Norwegian. Being a descendent of Norwegian emigrants helped, and she hoped her dad wouldn't be upset. He should know the scholarship would pay for ship's passage and all expenses. She asked if her mother would come to New York for her graduation, maybe with Aunt Marna or Aunt Iva. She would be their personal guide to the city. She emphasized how much it would mean to her if they came, that she was sorry *she* couldn't come home—having neither the time nor the money. Nor the heart for it, she meant.

If her mother came, Andrea would learn how things stood with Manley and Bernie, things that could not be written. Manley never wrote to her anyway, and Martha's letters referred to things "as usual" with their brothers. Her mother wrote that Bernie was doing well with the greenhouse, of how much he knew about plants and soils, of his *gifted hands*. And what of Manley?

If her father had written letters, he'd have told her the truth.

In her abbreviated style, Aunt Iva wrote, "I'm just thrilled you asked me to come to New York. I talked your mother into it. Viktor says the ladies should go. Nice brother he is. Can't wait."

Her mother wrote in her curving hand with the long looped *y*: "Johnny, I wish you'd come home instead. The roses are blooming, and the air is white with bridal wreath, spring lambs are running in the maple grove. Remember when Dad said if you could hold a lamb long enough, he wouldn't cut its tail off? But I'll come with Iva, to keep her company. I'm not sure what to wear." Andrea remembered a preschool spring when she'd clutched a wriggly lamb with a brown face and tail, trying to save its tail, but either it was too strong, or she was too small to keep it safe.

Aunt Iva and her mother arrived at La Guardia by plane on a steamy day in early June. Neither one had ever been any farther from home than Chicago or even seen an airplane, except in the sky. They stood on the tarmac, arm in arm, dressed for Sunday church in hats and gloves, their handbags clutched in front of them, scanning the waiting crowd. Andrea waved. Aunt Iva broke into a broad grin; her mother's face was uncertain. She hurried to them, hugging them both at once.

"We're sure glad to see you, Johnny," her mother said, kissing her daughter, relaxing, now she felt safe. "We were worried about what to do if we missed you."

She wore a navy-and-white rayon print dress Andrea had seen last June and carried a navy spring coat. Her new hat was white straw with wings of white feathers curving upward like a bird in flight. A small yellow daisy sat where the beak might have been. Aunt Iva, tall and bony, towered over Mother's slight figure, her face round as a moon, her lips narrow, her hair in a gray knot, eyes circled by round metal glasses. She was childless and lacked the round midriff her mother had, who'd borne six children. Aunt Iva's hat was black straw shaped like a layer cake—the kind of hat seen on the heads of women in churches on a summer Sunday all across America in 1950, where her lavender linen dress would also be at home. Her handbag was tapestried, and she carried a cream-colored umbrella, its handle a celluloid fox head with glass eyes. Neither wore any jewelry, except for wedding rings.

Andrea took each one by the arm to guide them into the terminal, collecting their identical gray Samsonite luggage, one bag each, which she carried. Her aunt and mother held onto her arms, wanting a point of contact between themselves and the world they'd left. From the bus they went to the Barbizon Plaza, where they checked in, traveled twenty flights on the elevator in seconds, then went for tea at the Plaza. They entered and scanned its palm-frocked interior, while the head waiter scanned them for his tip. "It's like the Palmer House," her mother said, but she'd never been there either.

"Much grander, Klara, don't you think?" Aunt Iva said as they were shown a table, her face cheerfully amazed. Andrea remembered how she usually gossiped, about her neighbor's lights burning all night long, or someone's new car they couldn't afford, and how she complained about the price of butter and the cost of coal and ill-mannered high-school kids who passed her house daily in the town of Gilman. But she loved all of New York.

Except for the play, *Mister Roberts*. *Peter Pan* with Julie Harris was sold out and Andrea wanted them to see a Broadway play. The sailors' language of sex and the street shocked both Klara and Iva. They exited stony faced and grim. "I hope you've not been influenced by such things in New York," her mother said. Andrea was sorry for taking them, not having known the play.

After Andrea steered them through the maze of the subway to the Planetarium, they took Fifth Avenue buses to the Metropolitan Museum, and walked through vast memorabilia of other worlds and other times. Her mother and aunt gazed with disbelief at worlds and times they knew nothing about, keeping their eyes on Andrea. Her mother was overwhelmed by gold and silver *graven images*—she called them—in their glass cases, things she'd read about in the Bible, from Babylonia and Old Testament places where kings drank wine from golden goblets and whored with temptresses. Andrea knew her mother thought that the world had become civilized since then, that now was better than then. Until she took them to see the religious paintings, her mother had only glanced disdainfully at everything.

"Johnny, look! There is the painting I have at home!" It was the original of Raphael's Madonna and Child her mother had. "But there are more!" She looked at the half dozen or so more Madonnas by Raphael. "Andrea, I didn't know that he painted so many." Her voice lowered: the surfeit spoiled her copy.

"He painted a great deal, Mother. And many Madonnas."

"I didn't know that," Klara said, her interest lost.

They took the Circle Line around Manhattan and a ferry to the Statue of Liberty; its tiny island was littered with tin cans and bottles, discarded paper; inside the paint was peeling from the crumbling walls. "We can take the elevator up, all the way to her head," Andrea told them. "Come on!"

"Oh yes! Let's!" Aunt Iva said.

"Johnny, please let's not go. It doesn't look safe," her mother said. "I'm happy enough to see it from here. You know, I wish that Papa and Mor had seen that, in 1885, when Mother came to America as a bride. But they landed in Quebec."

"My mother arrived in 1869," Aunt Iva said, telling them what they all knew, "when she was nine years old. Andrea, you are so lucky to go to Norway. I wish I was going, too." Then she added, "I'm glad you have Mother's name."

Her mother looked away to the vast channel of water leading to the ocean. On the other side of it lay Norway. Andrea imagined her mother wondering, as she looked at the water surrounding the tiny island, that if she touched it, cupped it in her hands, would it carry her hand's touch back to Norway, back up the stream she'd heard about, to Røyseland? Then would Kristina know, somehow, through the vast mysteries of the deep, how much she was remembered by a daughter who never knew her?

"I wish I'd known my mother, Johnny." Klara squeezed her arm.

"Me, too, Mother. But I'll see where she lived. I wish you were going, Mother, instead of me." She touched her mother's face, tracing tears that had made a little pathway through her face powder. Andrea swallowed hard, torn between loves that were opposed, knowing her mother would never approve of Max, even if she liked him, and she *would* like him if she met him. He was just the kind of man she would like. But he was an artist, who made, her mother might think, graven images.

"Where next?" Aunt Iva asked, impatient with sentiment. Sitting on the jumpy subway between Mother and Aunt Iva, Andrea saw in passing the subway station where she had vomited all over a Wanamaker fingertip white coat and her absent roommate's dress on the floor of the station after attending a Village party with a date she didn't care about. So she drank the poison of her grandfather Endresen and Bernie. At that moment, the glass eyes of Aunt Iva's fox-headed umbrella stared at her. Her mother leaned to her and said, "Johnny, I've never told you this, but you remind people of Kristina."

"But how would you know? You never knew her." Andrea was upset by the comparison to her grandmother, whose flawless character was legendary. Tales of her skill, her love, her selflessness were heard at all family gatherings from the time she was too little to know who it was. Kristina was fixed in her mind as an unattainable ideal, a woman who could do anything, card and spin wool from sheep she'd raised, sew, bake, can, cook, bear children, one after the other—there was no way to prevent their coming—a woman who waited seven years for a man she promised to marry who'd gone to America to find his fortune.

But her mother said Marna had known Kristina, and Ina Christiansen, and Karl, and each had said separately to her that Andrea *looked like* Kristina. But it was more than that, it was her voice, some mannerisms. Just now, Andrea didn't want to hear it.

Commencement took place on the baking steps of Columbia's cement campus, facing Low Library. A sea of caps and gowns covered the area, the mortarboard tassels hanging limp without a stir of air. The great number of graduates lessened the importance of the event to Klara, who said little about the occasion or the degree. But Aunt Iva announced, "I'm going to tell everyone how I came to New York and saw my niece get an important degree!"

Then it was time for them to leave, and time for Andrea to pack her bags for Norway. She took her mother and Aunt Iva by subway to the bus that would take them to La Guardia to catch a plane to Chicago, then the Rocket train to Grinnell where Viktor would meet them. Klara would be happy to escape a wicked city world, to return to Viktor and her house and garden, the roses with their first full June blooming, the humming of bees in the blossoms of the raspberries, the squeal of new baby pigs and the whinny of Viktor's colt. Andrea told her mother that she didn't seem very kindly toward Manley, and her mother's answer told her why: Manley was reading a book, *The God That Failed*, and suggested that his mother read it, and she'd said she didn't want to read a book like that, that he shouldn't be reading it either. Andrea tried to say that it was about communism, but her mother said the very title was an attack on God.

The two women sat nervously, apprehensive of the stranger next to them, the unknown languages spoken. Every person near them was a potential pickpocket; the two women's handbags were clasped tightly to their stomachs. They arrived at Grand Central subway station, and Andrea found a place for them to sit, saying, "Wait. I'll be right back." She wanted to get them something special to take home from New York, some token of their trip to a city they enjoyed but didn't like and would never see again. Encouraged by Aunt Iva, she had dragged her mother through one discomfort after another, through the humiliation of *Mister Roberts*. Andrea wanted to make up for it, for her going to Norway in two days' time, for not going home before, for her insisting on doing the things she wanted to do, for her "headstrong driven nature," as her mother often said.

She saw her mother's frozen eyes searching the landscape for her daughter as she returned; her mother couldn't understand why she'd left them in such a threatening place when they had so little time left together. She arrived with two boxes from the florists under the maze of the subway at Forty-Second Street, each with an orchid, whose spidery pale lavender petals would be worn once, and once only, and that would be in the Gilman church on Sunday. They would carry them carefully from the bus to the plane to the train, and hold them on their laps in the car.

"My niece in New York City gave this to me," Aunt Iva would explain to every stewardess and pilot and trainman between New York and Grinnell, Iowa, her tapestried handbag across her forearm where the fox head was held with its braided loop. Her mother would say nothing. The tears welling in her eyes would tell of her parting from her Johnny, and the literal and figurative ocean that would drift between them; and then the seas would part, leaving them both on dry, bottomless, uncrossable land, forever separate, yearning for the sea to close and a ship to sail. And even if it did, the seas were already parted, and neither of them really knew why.

As Andrea waved to them, she felt thin harp-like strings bind painfully around her heart. Then she didn't see her mother and Aunt Iva anymore, as the bus turned a corner and was gone. But she knew that Aunt Iva's face was red with excitement—she was going back to Iowa with vast experiences stored up to relate for the rest of her life, and the one orchid of her life, which would finally be pressed into the family Bible, an orchid not given to her by the love of her youth, but by a niece, out of a desire to offer pleasure by one extravagant gesture. But her mother's sober face had said to her daughter, *You handed me an orchid, when I wanted a moment of your heart.*

CHAPTER SEVENTEEN

Andrea had met Michael in London, after her summer in Norway and travels in England.

She didn't want to stay among strange familiarities that half greeted her around every bend in Norway, and after four months in England, where she felt as though she was forever in the act of half handshakes when only she extended her hand.

She met Michael after Holland, where she traveled with Maggie, by bicycle, from Denmark. Maggie, from California, had gone to the University of Oslo, where Andrea had met her. The two of them had been part of the early postwar exodus of American students to Europe. Many made their way into American-occupied Austria, looking for needed jobs with the military occupation. Many stayed.

She met Michael after France, where she'd seen Fontainbleau and Chartres, and had tried not to look through Ina's unforgiving eyes. For her, the Quaker meetinghouse on the prairie became the standard by which the world was judged: it turned cathedrals into graven images, the Renaissance into moral decline. Such treasures on earth were wrong. Ina would have seen the craftsmen and artists who built Chartres as the devil's slaves. For the citizens who lived within sight of its spires, whose landscape became the cathedral, Andrea wondered if it had merely replaced the grass and the trees, or if it offered more than the natural landscape of trees, flowers, of the sky, by offering temples of God-inspired men.

She'd had no reason to remain in France; she spoke no French. So she and Maggie had gone to London. They stood together in front of the Elgin marbles at the British Museum—she'd never heard of the Elgin marbles or knew that they'd been seized and transported from sun-flooded Greece to smog-blackened London. The veins throbbed taut on the horses' bellies, sinews were laced with nerves on their legs. There was the quivering crescent eye of HE, Rusty Malcom's black Percheron stallion, straining with all the coiled intensity of a thousand muscles and nerves pounding in unison. And the cool white marble of Maud. Andrea hated the fact that everything was colored by home: a mare, a stallion, loss.

"Maggie, they're, so—so beautiful. I had a white mare once, like that." She pointed to the half frieze of horses.

"One thing about these"—she smiled—"is that they never sculpted mares. Only stallions. Never castrated them either."

"How do you know that?" Andrea asked.

"Observing. Just notice any sculpted horse or equestrian statues—they're always stallions. It was humiliating for men to castrate a male horse." She said it as a simple fact, not as an acknowledgment of male dominance. Maggie was grounded in facts.

She and Maggie had traveled together or met every week or so, somewhere in London, or Paris, since they left Norway. To Andrea, Maggie was security. For Maggie, Andrea was companionship. Maggie was perpetually entertaining and entertained by the world. She carried all of her clothes in a small knapsack: the once-white nylon shirt going gray with toilet soap, rinsed in cold water, two no-color skirts, a cardigan and light coat. She wore saddle shoes aged with a grimy patina and added a hand-knitted cardigan from Norway to her possessions, as did everyone who traveled there. Men in her life were friends; because they were not lovers, they could be themselves. She was their sister, aunt, friend. Women were her friends because she was no threat, and she was not gay. She kept secrets. She was tall, with tight blonde curly hair and blue eyes, her nose too long for anyone's face, her mouth too wide.

Andrea wanted men to be friends without being lovers. She thought men could be neutral. Was it because of Manley that she preferred men? Even after *the boy in Iowa?* as Max had called Ron. Ron had first led her to the promise of paradise and then left her standing at closed gates. She had become the sinner without committing the sin: *It is the fact that you would with me that makes me know that you would with others.* Those words had burned into her flesh ever since: men's questioning glances made her feel like a fallen woman because of the guilt she already wore.

In early October 1950, Andrea walked out of the American Express on Haymarket in London. She looked back, by chance, or because she felt someone's eyes on her: a man, head turned to watch her, his hand on the arm of an older woman. Their eyes met. She looked away, he smiled, turning back to the woman, nodding to her, talking with her. It was a smile Manley could have given. Open. Without guile. Blue eyes, light brown hair, darkened a little with hair dressing. She saw one unruly strand over his eye. She went on to her small hotel on Russell Square, holding letters from her mother and from Martha.

Two days later, she saw him again, inside the American Express standing in the cashier's line. She was cashing a money order from her mother, borrowed only, she promised, until she found a job. She had been looking in London, but she could not get a work permit.

"Hello," he said. "I saw you two days ago."

"I saw you," she said.

"I was with my mother," he said.

"I was with my father," she said, smiling.

"You were alone."

"So I was." She was immediately sorry she'd mocked him. He didn't pick up girls; she didn't get picked up.

The third time she met him—everybody seemed to meet at the American Express in Haymarket—he introduced himself. "Michael Williams," he said. "I'm visiting London with my mother," adding, as a reason, "She was recently widowed. My father…"

Andrea had wanted to meet him after the first encounter. She introduced herself.

"You must be from Norway, or Sweden," he said.

"Iowa," she said.

"Oh," he said, as she collected her cash. "Look, we may never meet here again. I mean, it's chancy. Would you like to have some tea? Just near here, we could, if, if you would consider."

They drained the pot and ate little sandwiches. She learned that Michael Williams was an American consular officer in Salzburg, that he'd fought in the war, that he was from Boston, that he'd gone to

West Point instead of college because of the war, that his mother really *was* with him in London, that he hadn't seen her for a long time, that she was lonely, that he was her only son, though there was a daughter, married, living in New York.

"But you are doing all the interrogating," he said. "I've never been asked so many questions or told so much, all because I was trying to explain that the woman I was with really *is* my mother, and I knew you didn't believe me."

Although he was tall, they sat at nearly the same height. She had a long waist, so she must have short legs, and he must have long ones. She was comparing her body to his, her hands nearly as big as his, his nose straight and small. His smile that first day had stayed with her. She could trust that face.

Within three days' time Andrea had decided to go to Salzburg and look for a job with the American military. Michael had promised that jobs were plentiful, especially teaching jobs because of all the dependent children, that she would be provided with a place to live, that Salzburg was war torn but interesting, that there was good skiing, hiking. But it was Michael himself who made her want to go.

He was like a taller Manley, with a straighter nose, shy and open at the same time, cheerful the way Manley had always been growing up. She did not have to justify her past, or what she was doing alone in Europe. He did not undress her with his eyes, nor did his eyes question hers to learn if she *would*. She didn't have to marry him, or make love to him, but she would have the choice.

On the fifteenth of October, Andrea went out to a pub for supper with Maggie to say good-bye and tell her how she was virtually assured of a job in Salzburg, that maybe Maggie should consider it, too, if she wanted to stay in Europe. They'd been such good friends—like men friends, she said, believing whatever men did was so much more important than what *they* did—but she didn't use the word *women,* because no one did. She said *girls,* though even then it sounded demeaning, like *boy,* someone of no consequence. There was no word to use that was right. Maggie had asked her what had changed her mind all of a sudden—she'd come back from Scotland that afternoon, and Andrea told her how she'd met this man. Maggie asked where, and she told her, and Maggie asked her how long ago, and she told her, and Maggie just said, *Whew!* She hoped to find a teaching job, promising to pay Maggie back the money she'd borrowed; they would always keep in close touch, they'd spent so many good times together. Then Andrea pushed a sixpence coin to Maggie, and Maggie pushed back a cigarette. Andrea didn't smoke, she believed, but knew if she bought a pack she'd smoke them one after the other, so she paid for them one at a time, instead of bumming. She went on to tell Maggie that this one was different. Maggie didn't believe or disbelieve. She wasn't upset that Andrea was leaving, she just wanted to know if Andrea really knew what she was doing. Then the bartender said, *Time, please it's time,* and Maggie finished her beer and Andrea her cider, and they got up and went back in the rain to the Premier Hotel in Russell Square.

Andrea lay awake thinking Maggie thought she was a bit rash, but then, she'd never met Michael. It came to her that hidden in some corner of her mind was the idea of marriage as an ultimate goal. In the back of Maggie's mind, it was not that she subconsciously was thinking of the marriageability of Michael; Maggie knew it and she, Andrea, was being obtuse about it, because it was something she'd tried to reject but couldn't because that's the way she was brought up, despite her education and travel. Despite everything! Manley had tried to say this to her, understanding the bondage of their childhoods.

She was ready to leave London, with its rain and wind sweeping up the soggy leaves in Russell Square, the sawdust breakfast sausages in the hotel, and the legs of a marble horse that reminded her of her horse Maud. Michael said there would soon be snow in the Alps. She'd never seen the Alps. He said there were good hard rolls for Salzburg breakfasts instead of toast standing in cooling racks. She'd write to her mother after she got there. After she found a job. She wouldn't tell her that she was traveling there, by boat, then by train, with a man named Michael Williams, even if he was with his mother.

From the next day onward, it was Michael. She liked his work, which concerned the world. He told her that Alger Hiss had been sentenced to five years, that the Israelis had gone against their UN charter to make Jerusalem their capital, explaining what those decisions meant to the world—the witch hunt in the US, the Jewish state, after the Nazis. She told him that Edna St. Vincent Millay died, and how pleased she was that Faulkner had won the Nobel Prize, that she'd written her master's essay on him. She wanted to get Michael's response to Ingrid Bergman and Rosselini but didn't want to ask. And when they said good night, he'd hum a few bars of "Good Night, Irene," substituting her name. She hadn't liked the song until then.

Andrea realized later that she had already committed herself when she agreed to go to Salzburg. She committed herself on the long train ride as Michael ministered to his difficult and possessive mother, who considered Andrea little more than someone he picked up who needed a job, and being the gentleman that he was, he was going to help her find it. He treated both of them with equal respect, and although Andrea sensed his mother's rejection of her, she understood the rejection: an only son's commitment of time to his widowed mother lessened by an intruder, an intruder she felt was less interested in a job than in the possession of her son.

Their backgrounds were different, their families and their education—his parents and grandparents were university educated, hers were not. Michael had fought a war when she was finishing grammar school, she had a liberal arts education, he a military one. Despite such differences, their needs were the same. Michael was a boy brought up to be a gentleman, to pretend bravery if he didn't feel it, to act rather than feel. Andrea filled his underlying loneliness created by such separation of duty from self. Michael made Andrea feel put back together again, blameless. On these grounds, they met. Michael was Manley who had managed to escape the worst restraints of home, yet still honor it.

They stopped in Munich for two days. The shock of Munich's destruction was numbing to her. Munich was still full of bombed-out shells in 1951, and flimsily-built structures for temporary shops. "You'll get used to it, Andrea," Michael encouraged her. "Then you'll see the new construction instead of what's been destroyed."

He drove her around in the first few days, pointing out the half-destroyed building at Marienplatz where Hitler had given some of his great speeches to rally the German people. He told her about Salzburg's defeat and destruction, about his work—the flood of displaced persons—whole countries full of stateless people huddled in camps that the consular section was trying to deal with: emigration to the United States, Canada, Australia, if they didn't have TB or other contagious diseases. Malnutrition was acceptable. He spoke of the Red Cross's efforts to locate missing families in Eastern European countries, of a few Jews who had managed, miraculously, to survive, who looked for last traces of family members, meaning which camp they had died in. Did she know about the death camps, Michael asked her, as she realized that at the same time she was distraught over the death of a colt, whole families were dying in gas chambers, and bodies were dug out of rubble. The creation of art began to seem superfluous to her.

He found her an inexpensive Salzburg hotel and drove her to the personnel office the next day. There were, as Michael had promised, teaching jobs available. She could begin in a week—sixth grade or tenth, what was her choice? So in a week's time, it was as though she were in an American classroom, teaching bored tenth graders reluctant to read any more than they had to, none of whom had any more knowledge about Salzburg than she had, but who weren't going to get more. There was no shopping in Salzburg shops, no fraternization, the military word for *no GIs sleeping around with Salzburg shatzies*. GIs were kings and princes to them; they had access to cigarettes worth a fortune on the black market and to GI currency, called *script* dollars. United States green was not used.

Andrea disliked the teaching as much as she had in Iowa during one semester between undergraduate and graduate school. Except for Michael, she would have gone anywhere else. To Switzerland—she feared she would have liked Switzerland more than Salzburg.

In April, Andrea and Michael went skiing in Kitzbüehel, Austria, during Andrea's spring break from school. They had been skiing all winter, but they had slept in separate rooms. They had not made love, even in his apartment, though his mother had gone home by Christmas. He had never asked her to make love or share rooms.

Spring had come to the Alps, even though the winter's snow accumulation was still several feet deep. Meters, she should say. It was at least a meter, but in sunny places, protected from wind by overhanging pines, grass was showing in patches. In the daytime the snow was wet, and at night it froze to ice. Morning skiing was hard and fast for Andrea, just learning. That day, they had made one run down from the Hahnenkamm, had eaten *palatshinken* for lunch, sitting on a weathered terrace of an old chalet. The hot, cut-up pancakes with jam and powdered sugar. A squeeze of lemon seemed just right for the lazy time of day, along with hot black coffee. They sat across from each other, eyes closed, faces turned to the sun. Andrea felt Michael's hand on her hand.

"Andrea, you may think I am slow." She opened her eyes to his. "In truth," he went on, "I haven't wanted to rush you. But by now, you must know how I feel. I...I hope you feel the same."

Andrea knew how carefully he had rehearsed what he had just said. She looked into his eyes, in the way of an answer. He removed his hand from hers and clasped his together, leaning on his elbows. Then Michael talked of all the things he'd been thinking for the past six months, how every night he dreamed of her so intensely that he felt he was nearly trespassing on her privacy, that he'd known the first time he saw her in Haymarket that she was the one for him, that he didn't want her to think he had taken advantage of her when he suggested she come to Salzburg, that if she hadn't, he had thought seriously of transferring to London, until he remembered that she was just a tourist there, as he'd been.

She looked away, down the gradually sloping mountain, easy to ski and inviting to her, the sun hot upon her face, her arms, her body, the line of deep green fir trees on either side of the ski run, the chalets on the other side of the valley, now in shade, then into Michael's sea-blue eyes, and nothing ever seemed so right to her as that moment. She looked back at Michael, took both his hands in hers. She could not stop her tears as she said, "Michael Williams, are you proposing to me, when you haven't even made love to me yet?"

They rose to put on their skis. Andrea fell down on the second turn, Michael stopped to help her up, taking off his skis to do so, covering her mouth with his as she lay there, covering her body with his arms, his hands on her face, her hair, her neck. Skiers passed by, wondering how a couple could make love when one of them wore skis.

She told him how they'd lie there and eventually freeze if they didn't ski down the mountain before sunset, and he said he'd more likely burn a hole in the snow and down to the grass, singeing it as he went down, with her, that he needed the snow so he wouldn't burn himself up, and her with it. Then he put on his skis, and they tried to ski the rest of the way holding two hands together, the other each carrying two ski poles, but the rest of the way was gradual, and they did not fall down.

He called her Andrea. She liked that. No nicknames. Not yet. It was later that he called her *Mrs.* and *Little One.* He was not experienced, he was not enamored of love itself: he was enamored of her, so his body was innocent. It was pure. Pure enough to take her back to her own innocence. That is where she wanted to go. She felt his body's entire cool length against hers. Like marble, she thought, like Maud, and she outlined and caressed his face, traced his ears, touched his shoulders and every rise of a rib, his taut abdomen, his penis, erect for her. For the first time, she wanted to kiss his maleness with her mouth but did not. They made love repeatedly in the single bed which squeaked into the darkness. They didn't know what time it was, but both at once said they were hungry.

"Andrea," Michael said, leaning on his elbows, looking into her face, touching her breasts, "you are so beautiful, and you are mine. You *will* marry me, won't you?"

She raised her head to kiss his lips, to say that she could not answer right now, at least, perhaps not tonight, saying maybe tomorrow, and she smiled so serenely that he had no doubt of her intentions. Only she of her own.

They dressed and found the hotel restaurant still open. Michael ordered champagne. Andrea said she was sorry, but she really didn't like it. Michael told her the taste was acquired, that eventually she would acquire it. But she said she didn't like wine very much either, that in her family, spirits were not allowed, adding that tonight she would try a little champagne, that they should celebrate, although they already had, she said, hadn't they?

At dinner, she told him about her family, about Manley, especially, how much she loved him—she didn't say how much Michael reminded her of him. She told him about her horses, her studies, her need to leave home—*wanderlust,* she called it, although she knew it was more than that. She told him only good things about Bernie, creating him under her very eyes as the handsome and adored older brother he'd once been. She liked those memories of him, all of which were true, so why not use them? He would find out later, if and when…

She wove her stories of home, shaping them the way she wanted to, creating home as she would like it, ignoring what had made her leave, ignoring the undiscardable sense of guilt that she carried around, how it just sat there, pointing its finger. She didn't tell him about Ina.

He told her about his family, editing as well, she learned much later. He spoke more of his grandfather than his father, and Andrea thought the grief of his death was too recent for him to speak of it, and thought the grandfather was still alive, until she learned that Michael had never known him, that he had died before Michael was born, the same year his parents married and moved into his grandfather's house, the one where he was born. But mostly, they both told the truth. It was what they didn't tell each other that they learned later.

After dinner, they walked the streets of Kitzbüehel, stopped in at Tony Praxmaier's bar where they saw *Schuhplattler* folk dances, where men in leather knickerbockers, wearing hats with quills of chamois hairs like a shaving brush, hopped and slapped their shoes loudly in what Andrea called a mating dance. She drank tea and Michael had a wine, but the music and voices were too loud for new lovers.

They walked back to their hotel, toward the Hahnenkamm, the

snow melted in the town, the wet puddles freezing by now, and Michael spoke eagerly of when they would marry, and where—in Salzburg, he said—and where they would travel in their lives together, already mapping out what, where, when. She would like Washington DC, he said, where they would live when not on foreign assignment. She was enchanted to have someone plan her life, her travels. Children, he said, too. She nodded.

She believed that he would spend the night with her, but he left her at her door, saying that he would come get her for breakfast. He did not want to take advantage of her, he said, just because…He kissed her lightly and left her. She was disappointed, but alone, she could think about marrying Michael, how she needed someone with the sun in him, even if it was cloudy. She needed that: she had too much winter in her, Iowa winters, Norwegian winters. She would marry Michael and have babies and be a good mother, and Michael would be there, always. He would never let her grieve or suffer simply because it was not part of his life. His commitment to life was like her father's: each day was new, connecting to the previous day and to the following days like a string of pearls, each one the same, but each one needing to be complete, and each day, a knot would be tied to secure it before the next was added, an addition each day of one more pearl. That is how her life would be with Michael. She needed that.

Marrying would be like putting Johnny away in a fluted box and placing it in the attic, to be among never-to-be-looked-at relics of the past. Marrying would be to grow up; Johnny was her childhood relic. Michael had helped her see that.

On Sunday evening back in Salzburg, letters from Martha and her mother were waiting for her, handed to her by her new roommate, Kay. "Mother won't say this," Martha wrote, "but she's worried to death about you, being in Europe when war is about to begin in Korea. I think you should come home." Her mother wrote that Andrea has been away for quite a while, and maybe she was thinking of coming home, but of course she would have to finish the school year. Had she made any applications for schools in Iowa, she wondered, and added that Manley had found a girl he liked. Nothing else. She didn't say who the girl was, if he were serious about the girl, or if her mother liked her. Andrea wondered if this were the way her mother would report to Manley what she would write about Michael. How *would* she write about Michael?

In October, Michael's mother returned to Salzburg to stay with him until their January wedding. By then, Michael had written to her father to ask for her hand. Andrea knew that it would be her mother who answered. She didn't tell Michael that her father couldn't compose letters, except for postcards on the rare occasions he went to Nebraska or Kansas to buy feeder calves. Then it was, "Having fine time, from Dad," in a wavering script one could see was not easy for the writer.

Her mother's answer to Michael came on a small white informal note, saying that if their daughter—she spoke for her husband and herself—felt that she wanted to marry him, they trusted her judgment and would welcome him into the family. That was essentially it. Her mother had no artifice; it was a letter of pure honesty.

Michael's mother was offended that her son, who had dated debutantes, rated no higher praise than this, no greater enthusiasm, in fact, no enthusiasm at all! What more could her mother have said about a man she'd never met, a man her Johnny was going to marry? She had to trust her daughter, that is all she had to go on.

Andrea went home to Iowa for Christmas. She went to see her friends at the hilltop college to get their reassurance and blessing. She visited Aunt Iva and Marna and all the aunts and uncles and their families, who congratulated her more than they queried her about Michael. Some of them thought the State Department was a branch of the military, that she was marrying a general, or a colonel at the least, when she said officer in the foreign service.

Bernie asked her if she knew the facts of life, but he had tears in his eyes to see his little sister go off to marry a man no one knew, and despite his crudeness, she knew it was an expression of love— he hadn't known what else to say. Martha was pleased to have her sister settle down and seemed to accept Michael without question, but she told Andrea that their mother would never say how upset she was. Andrea said she didn't see it, that her mother was wise and understanding and did not scold her for marrying away from home. Her dad seemed most worried, pacing up and down now and then, with his restless, flashing eyes. She hadn't gone out to see the colt, Spice—it was too cold, and she had too much to do. She told Manley one of the reasons she loved Michael was because he reminded her of him, that they were quite alike, true, someone you could always count on. She asked him about his girl, but he brushed the subject off. They never really had time to talk: upstairs was too cold, and someone was always downstairs with them, her mother, or father, or Aunt Iva, or cousins, or Martha.

She borrowed Martha's wedding dress, plain, heavy satin, and Aunt Marna took it in at the waist and shortened it in the front, easing it into the train. It was a beautiful dress, simple and elegant, Andrea thought, who had helped choose it for Martha. One afternoon with her mother, she bought white satin shoes and two pink net bridesmaids' dresses at Younkers, one for Kay, her new roommate, and one for Maggie, who promised to come. Large sizes. When they got home, her mother went to the attic and brought down to the living room an old battered leather suitcase. It creaked as she opened it, and folds of aged tissue paper crinkled as she unwrapped its contents. She held out a pair of satin slippers with little bows with sequins. The dress was net lace over silk, yellowed, the lace torn.

"Mother," Andrea said, both of them kneeling, leaning over the dress, the shoes, "couldn't you come, please, to Salzburg?" She was afraid she'd cry, so she looked away, fighting tears.

"Johnny, I don't like to travel like you do. I didn't even like New York. What shall I do in winter in a strange city when you go off on a wedding trip? Viktor would never go, you know."

Through tears, Andrea understood the entire impossibility of it all: of course her mother wouldn't want to come—it would be worse than New York, a foreign language, winter. Michael wanted champagne for his wedding, and her mother wouldn't understand or approve. Michael's mother would be less than friendly—Andrea hadn't told her mother about Mrs. Williams, who disapproved of her because she knew nothing about Andrea's family, and there was probably nothing to know, but that Michael was his own man and cognizant of her prejudices.

"Don't mind Mother," he'd said to her once. "She doesn't represent me. Remember that I've been away from home since I was twelve. Mother had a hard life, and I'm trying to make a little of the rest of it happier." She honored him for that.

"Mother, did you have a big wedding?"

"It was only my dad, your Uncle Karl, Aunt Marna, and their mates. Quakers never had what you call weddings: they had marriages that took place in the meeting for business. We were married in the courthouse because your father wasn't Quaker." She hesitated and looked into the distance, toward the long windows that looked out to the evergreens.

"Mother, you've hardly said anything to me. Mother?"

"Andrea, I brought you up to trust you. I have to do that now."

Andrea looked across the wedding dress at her mother. Her mother trusted her and could not say how she suffered the fact that she would not be present at Johnny's wedding, and to a man she had never met. So that is all Andrea and her mother said to each other on the eve of Andrea's marriage. Andrea could ask no more.

Maggie came all the way from California to her wedding, saying she wanted to ski anyway. Her Salzburg friend and roommate, Kay, was her maid of honor, as unlike Maggie as north from south. She was serious and insecure, and she measured the world daily on her philosophical scale, as Andrea did. While Michael and his friends had a traditional bachelor's party the night before their wedding, Andrea took Maggie and Kay out to dinner at a Salzburg restaurant. They ate *natursnitzel* and drank a half liter of Rhine wine. Andrea told them both that she was nervous about the next day, but they said they were both there to hold her up and get her to the church on time. She joked and said, but what if I change my mind? and they said they'd have to know why and then weigh the reasons. They were there, after all, as *her* friends, not the groom's, and Andrea said that she was sorry she wasn't home, and how would their own mothers feel if they did what she was doing—marrying away from home, but they didn't think too much of that, saying it really depended upon family tradition, how independent one was, that if one wasn't, it would be different. That Andrea was independent, they knew. She loved them—they were her sisters, she said.

Then Andrea got teary, which Maggie never did and didn't even like, but Andrea said it was the wine. They went home to the apartment Kay shared with her, where Andrea slept on a couch, curled up under a big fat comforter more like a large pillow, and Maggie would sleep in a sleeping bag she was never without. As they undressed for bed, Kay said she understood how Andrea felt, but the whole point was, did she love Michael, and she said she did. And Andrea said then that she was not entirely sure she was doing the right thing, and Kay said that absolute certainty about anything would make one omnipotent and she doubted that omnipotence existed, that living in spite of uncertainty was human fate. Then Kay embraced her and said how truly she would miss her as a roommate and turned out the light.

The next day was cold and sunny, and Maggie and Kay, looking a little silly in pink net dresses, got her to the church at the exact time. When Andrea saw Michael standing at the altar, waiting for her to come down the aisle on the arm of a mutual and good friend, her heart filled with joy, and with pride in him. But as she walked down the aisle to the wedding march in the Lutheran church, she looked sideways at the faces, all of them familiar and few of them dear to her, feeling the lump in her throat grow so large that at that moment she could not have said *I do*. She saw herself, willful and headstrong, and her mother's somber face and heard the words, *Be careful what you set your heart upon, Johnny...*

Had she set it on Michael?

At the reception in the officers' club, which was the modern and elegant Kunsthaus, they waltzed and drank champagne and ate smoked salmon with small gray globs of caviar. Then Maggie and Kay helped her change into a tawny-orange wool dress and cloche and a gray wide-sleeved tuxedo coat. She descended the wide staircase to meet Michael, his hand reaching out for her, smiling to her. *On behalf of my wife and myself,* he said, thanking the guests for helping him celebrate his marriage to the lovely Andrea, who found the sudden use of *my wife* quite startling.

A year later, Rosalind was born.

When she was a year and a half old, they were posted to Washington. Her family would meet Michael and her child.

Their first visit to Iowa together had failed at the beginning. Michael was formal and restrained, manners her father could not understand. Her mother had been polite and welcoming to a man who was her daughter's husband and the father of her grandchild, the way she'd been in the letter she wrote to Michael, but she waited for him to offer affection. She did not stand on ceremony, she did not praise a man she had never met, who was going to marry her beloved Johnny.

Michael could not see that they waited for him to make the first move. He simply hadn't known, nor was he used to affection in families. And the weather had been hot and humid, after years of cool Salzburg. They'd had to keep the windows closed against flies—the screens had been removed for house-painting. Dinner was too early for Michael, it was too plain. Family members sat wrapped in silence, except for *please pass the potatoes* and *won't you have some more meat.* Rosalind, eighteen months old, had saved them all. She'd loved the farm animals and allowed her grandfather to carry her to see Spice and her grandmother to feed her and hold her. She was the same age as the second of Martha's children, a girl, and of Bernie's fourth child, Vicki, named after her grandfather. Her mother planned a big Roseland picnic, to which all the Endresens came as well, with their picnic baskets, and dozens of Kristina and Salve's grandchildren and great-grandchildren, who'd taken turns to walk with Rosalind, pull her in the wagon, carry her, as though she were different from them, born so faraway.

Michael could not unbend, and Andrea could not help him. When Manley arrived with his bride and child, Nan, one month younger than Rosalind, things became unstuck. Manley had welcomed Michael as though he'd always known him. Michael had relaxed, and the world turned around. Irene laughed a lot and said little. Andrea wondered if she knew how close sister and brother had been, she and Manley, because she guarded her husband so closely that any attempts to speak to him in confidence was to trespass on Irene. Her mother's silences about Irene spoke. Martha was hostile: airs, she told Andrea. But like her mother, Andrea was kind to Irene.

CHAPTER EIGHTEEN

Klara looked almost girlish, moving lightly in her flowered summer dress, humming a little, animated. "Finished?" she asked Roz, who wore shorts and a blouse. Kari and Sarah were still in blue-check bathrobes, jam on their faces. They all jumped up from their seats in the breakfast nook where the sun slanted across the table. Klara took them by the hands, and they went outside.

"What is it, Dad? Do you know about Mother's surprise?" Andrea and her father stayed at the table. Andrea was still surprised to see him in the wheelchair, after the bout with arteriosclerosis meant he needed both legs amputated to prevent a blood clot from passing to his heart. Viktor gave her his egg to dispose of—she put it under toast crusts, with her own, and crossed in stealth to the garbage, burying the eggs under a butter wrapper. Klara hadn't noticed their untouched breakfast plates.

Calling her Johnny, Viktor said that he didn't know what Klara was talking about, that she should go and see, just in case. His words were heavy, his face drawn. He called Klara Mother. Usually he'd called her that in front of the family, when she was present. Andrea got up quickly and went out the washroom door, really the back door, now used exclusively, thinking about the "just in case." She had wanted to go with them but didn't want to leave her father.

The humidity had cleared; the day was clear, still fresh from morning. She looked across the undulating sweep of the corn rows, the cornflower-blue sky with a few cotton puffs floating, and felt comforted. She heard the murmur of her children's voices and saw her mother and her daughters squatting near the chrysanthemum bed on the edge of the Norway spruce grove.

She thought of Michael, now in Warsaw. She longed for him. Would he be discussing Gary Powers and the spy plane right at this moment, or wondering where his family would live? She wanted to ask him what she should do. He would say she knew best, how could *he* say what to do for *her* family.

"Easy" she heard Klara say to her daughters. "You can each carry one. Be gentle."

"We have duck eggs, and they're about to hatch," Kari whispered, as though loud voices might prevent their hatching.

"Grandma says the mother left these in the nest," Sarah said, "and she knows how to hatch them." She cupped an egg gently; it filled her small hands, a pale greenish-buff on the white of her hands. She carried it carefully, walking stiffly, her elbows propped against her rib cage. She nearly tripped on her bathrobe. Andrea took Kari's arm to steady her steps. In Kari's hands, the small egg looked bigger.

"Sarah, be careful," Rosalind warned.

Their grandmother led the procession to the kitchen, passing by her husband, who'd moved his wheelchair into the washroom. Klara placed a waffled dishcloth in a white cereal bowl that she held down for each granddaughter to place her egg in. She sprinkled the cracked eggs' drying membranes with warm water, folded the cloth around them, then gave it to Rosalind to place in the oven, and all the while she was explaining to Viktor that the wild mallard hen that had a nest in the chrysanthemum bed had taken her hatched ducklings and left behind four cracked eggs.

"Mommie, they're alive," Rosalind cried, holding the basket up to her mother. Andrea could see little beaks pecking at the shell. "Will they really hatch?"

"Wait and see!" Andrea smiled, and ran her hands down the heads of her daughters, half-encouraged, half-fearful.

The empty day was filled, so far. She smiled at her daughters, who would spend it by the oven—her mother had turned it on to low warm—until the eggs hatched, if they did. Her mother turned to her, "You must go to see Bernie today and take the children. Remember?"

"We can't go, Grandma. We must help the ducks hatch," Rosalind announced as the three small sisters stood trying to peer through the crack in the oven door.

Andrea's mother promised Rosalind to watch them, saying how many ducklings and chickens she'd hatched. Even goslings. Andrea remembered the entire process, beginning with the prize Houdan rooster that cost ten dollars and came in a crate brought by the mailman. A little scale had weighed each egg as it was candled—light shone through the translucent membranes to determine if it were fertile. Fertile eggs were placed on pull-out wire mesh trays in an oven heated with kerosene burners in the cellar, requiring constant attention: filling, cleaning, watching the temperature, her dad wondering why they had to buy a ten-dollar rooster when any rooster would do, her mother saying, as she turned each egg, that the meat was whiter and more tender, and the chickens were smaller so they ate less food and were not so bony as Rhode Island Reds, which everybody had. Besides, Houdans were beautiful: bouffant feather headdresses, all black and white, red combs framing their beaks, although her mother didn't *say* that. When the chickens hatched, they were spotted black-and-yellow puffballs. Bernie had once cuddled so many of them when Viktor was busy with the kerosene heater, he'd squeezed a dozen to death. Her mother told her that, smiling, thinking of Bernie's little tender heart going out to them.

Now Andrea looked at her daughters, Rosalind now standing, facing her, protesting, asking if she really had to go somewhere she'd never been, adding that Sarah didn't want to go either, knowing Sarah's wishes were important to their mother these days. They hadn't asked Kari, but they never did. Roz said that the ducks would hatch when they were gone, and they'd miss all the fun, that they wanted to *see* them hatch, to be *here* when they did, because Grandma said that they'd attach themselves to whoever *was* here.

"We won't go." Rosalind took her well-known intractable stance, chin out, feet planted. She took Sarah by the hand. Kari stood next to Sarah, backs to the oven door.

"Mother, I'll go alone. Can the girls stay with you?" Andrea didn't know what kind of condition Bernie would be in. She turned to her dad. "Say, shouldn't I be feeding Spice?"

"He's been fed. Charlie Benson's boy comes."

Hearing the sound of tires on gravel, Andrea looked out to see Martha arrive, alone. Leaving the scene around the oven door, she went out to greet her. "Where are Lena and Jo?"

"Bible school. It's only for two weeks in June. But I have to pick them up by noon." She continued to sit in the car. Andrea leaned over to see her face, standing on the opposite side with her elbows on the open window. Martha's brown hair was windblown, fluffed up to frame her face, a way she ought to wear it instead of the usual way each strand was wrestled in place. Today, she looked like Bernie—in his better days he was the handsomest of them all. "How's Mother?" she asked, after hesitation.

Andrea wondered what to say. But Martha made it easy.

"Andrea, I've been thinking. I'm sure Mother expects you to see Bernie today, doesn't she?"

"Yes, how did you know?"

"I knew she would. Surprised she didn't want you to go last night." Andrea glanced hastily at the house, saw her dad in his chair through the washroom door, Mother undoubtedly hovering over the oven with the girls, as excited as they.

"Well," Martha continued. "This is what I was thinking. Howard thinks it's a good idea, too. Worth a try, at least."

Andrea thought of Howard sitting in his black naugahyde recliner with his newspaper, possibly trying to read the hog futures in the room with the TV going full blast, and Martha talking to him about Klara. Did she ever talk about anything else? Did Howard object to her coming here, day after day, cleaning, watching, wondering, upset with worry?

"Mother has had such a hard time of it, taking care of everyone, blaming herself for Bernie's drinking. I thought if you, you *and* Bernie, could get her to make weekly visits to a psychiatrist—not that I believe in them, but that it might help. Help Dad, anyway. I'm afraid she's going to have a nervous breakdown."

Andrea jabbed her elbows into the car window and hit her crazy bone. The shock ran up her arm. She straightened, rubbed it, grimacing. Martha's face was calm, her voice quiet. She really wanted to convince Klara. She needed Andrea to agree.

"It would help everybody, probably Mother, too. At least, it wouldn't hurt her."

"How would I get her to go?"

"You might talk Bernie into taking her to see Dr. John. He *ought* to help, he *is* our family doctor." Martha emphasized the responsibility family doctors had that Andrea wasn't sure existed, but they hadn't had a family doctor when Sarah had been ill.

"Why Bernie?" Andrea asked. She leaned on the car again. They both hoped it might seem to their mother, if she were watching, that they were probably talking about the weather, or crops, or gardens.

Martha inclined her head toward Andrea's face. "Don't you yet realize that she only listens to him?"

Andrea straightened to ease her back and looked directly at Martha. "But what kind of…condition is he in? Would he do it?"

"He'd like to help, I think. Doesn't know how. If we had a plan, suggested it to him, I think he'd go along with it."

Andrea, still standing, glanced over the car toward the barn, seeing the colt's head looking out of his stall, wondering if the horse saw their mother. She wanted to turn around and look at the house to see if she were watching them. "Do you see Mother?"

Martha glanced very quickly toward the house, without turning her head, then shook it negatively.

Elbows on the car again, Andrea continued, "And how do you propose to deal with Dr. John?" not believing that Martha had worked this all out. She kept looking at Spice.

"*You* call him. Explain to him. Tell him he should suggest that she go to a weekly clinic. No hospitalization. Then you and Bernie could take Mother to see him, together."

"Did Howard think of this?" she asked, not believing that Martha would have this all worked out.

"He helped." Martha opened the car door, getting out, continuing to talk. "Mother sees us talking." Martha went on to say that she must make up her mind, that there wasn't time to lose, that Andrea would have to go see Bernie, today. "Would you?" she asked.

That is what it came down to. Would Andrea do it now? They both started toward the house, and Andrea hadn't even told Martha about the ducks, or about last night's appearance of their mother, who would, by now, wonder what her daughters had been talking about for so long. Viktor would know. The two of them walked together, arm in arm. Andrea decided she wouldn't tell Martha about last night. She forgot that she was already on her way to see Bernie. Now that Martha was here, she'd feel better leaving the girls.

She drove the five miles to Bernie's greenhouse, bought with so much sacrifice by her father for a son he knew wouldn't make a success of it. *Mother made me*, Viktor had said, simply, ten years ago. It meant that Manley couldn't buy the O'Connell farm adjacent to Viktor's. It meant that Manley had to farm for someone else, all because of Bernie. Many farmers spent their lives on somebody else's farm, never able to save enough to buy their own. Manley had grown up independent. Now he'd become a tenant farmer. She couldn't blame him for being bitter. The car lurched forward. She had a problem with the manual gas feed.

During the last half mile, the road sliced into earth like a wound—a small pocket of land turned red, the clay opened like an abscess in the midst of rich black loam. It was here, on land too poor for farming, that Schmidt had built his greenhouse and had failed in the venture. She remembered passing it as a child—much of the glass broken, rusty farm machinery lying about, abandoned, a dissolved enterprise—weeds having the run of the place. She remembered Schmidt's slovenly wife in a cotton print, winter and summer, living in an unfinished house with the many children, snotty-nosed and untended, like the farm, like the greenhouse. *Look at that machinery! You can't farm that way*, her dad always said, passing by. *You gotta keep the weeds down, to be a farmer,* he'd add. *Or run a greenhouse.* In those days, Bernie would have agreed. No wonder Schmidt sold out.

The appearance wasn't a lot better now. How her dad hated to come here, to see a rotting greenhouse and his blurry-eyed son. She, too, hated to think it was her brother who operated this run-down place, who lived in a half-built asbestos-shingled house. It was

Manley she wanted to see, who lived too faraway to drop in. He'd promised to arrive tomorrow.

She drove down the red-scarred driveway, rutted except where there was scattered gravel. Dottie came to the door. Except for her teeth, she was lovely: pale skin, dark hair, perfect jaw and nose, green eyes. She had married such a promising, handsome boy exactly eighteen years ago this June. Andrea remembered Bernie in his white jacket, his dark hair and smooth skin, his shy, boyish smile; and Dottie in gleaming satin, like a princess. Her own stiff white organdy dress had irritated her sunburn and her budding breasts.

"Andrea! How good to see you." Dottie emphasized good—she meant it. She was good-natured and kind. Andrea liked her but felt ill at ease and guilty, thinking of the way her brother, Dottie's husband, had turned out. "Bernie, he's a little late this morning. I'll get him. Coffee?"

"Thanks." Dottie handed her sister-in-law coffee in a green mug from a set of earthenware Andrea remembered that her mother had had, then she disappeared into the bedroom, off the living-dining room where Andrea sat in a green tweed chair staring out a picture window whose *picture* was the nearby road. In the forties, every house in the countryside had to have a picture window, most of which looked out on the road, as though what each wanted most to see was the cars passing by, who went where, how fast they drove, if and when neighbors bought new cars or tractors. Under this window was a brown sofa, with tapestried ferns. Children's rubber boots and jackets were hanging in the kitchen but the children were in Bible camp by a swampy lake where mosquitos were as big as grasshoppers, she remembered, a two-week event sponsored by the church. Bible study classes occupied the morning, sports the afternoon.

Bernie came out of the bedroom in his stocking feet, face swollen with sleep and lengthy use of alcohol, hair grizzled and mussed. His belly was showing as it never had, his eyes were bloodshot. His once good looks were blurred. He walked unsteadily to the sofa and sat down. "Haven't seen you in a while," he said.

"No," she said. That he had been up for a while, she could tell. There was probably a half-empty bottle somewhere in his room.

"Coffee, Bernie?" Dottie asked.

"How about a beer?" Bernie waved her away, and Dottie winced.

Be kind to Bernie, Mother had said. *He needs your love….What that boy needs*, Dad would say, *is a kick in the pants! He's been spoiled all his life.*

She had never known an alcoholic. Willpower was supposed to be the treatment. Dottie gave him coffee. Her eyes pleaded with him to drink it. He pushed it away, spilling it on the already-stained beige broadloom, saying, "I told I you don't want that slop!" Dottie watched the spilled coffee disappear into the rug then turned to take the cup back to the adjacent kitchen. She didn't come back.

"Bernie, have you been around Mother and Dad very much, recently? Do you know how bad things are with them?"

"Have you? Fine daughter you are! I s'pose you've come to dictate to me! My fault and all that shit, my dear sister!" Nobody Andrea knew used the word *shit*.

"Dad and I've talked." She watched Bernie, his face backlighted from the picture window so that he was more of a silhouette than a face. His beer belly was visible under his stained, unbuttoned shirt, his eyes were glassy, impatient. Andrea remembered her unquestioned love and admiration of him when she was small, his patience with her as he taught her the Latin names of trees from a box of labeled twigs from his horticulture class at Iowa State; her only reason to learn them was to be noticed by Bernie. *That boy will go far*, everyone said about that handsome, restless, ambitious boy. Long, long ago he'd taken the world by the tail. Andrea had wanted to follow in his footsteps. Watching him now, her eyes teared over.

"Why don't you just leave me alone, all of you! I never wanted anything Mother or Dad wanted for me. Once I believed some of the stuff she told me, like *Be careful what you set your heart upon*…all that crap. Listen, sister, I set my heart upon some goddamned thing that doesn't make any difference now anyway. If I'd *got* it, I mean, because I wouldn't want it now."

He stood and started to wave his arms around the room. He said that he had something to say, now that he was letting it all hang out: the problem with Mother is, was, which ever it was...And then he laughed. The problem, he continued, is that she always wanted her kids to be purrfect like she wanted to be purrfect, and he wondered how she felt about it now, having such a *purrfect* son. A *noble* son! How she always liked noble people, the word, *noble*! That she hadn't known there wasn't one in all of Marshall Country. Or the state of Iowa, for that matter. Maybe the whole damned country. That even George Washington had a woman. "Noble? Hogshit, is what I say. Hogshit."

Bernie had it mixed up, Andrea thought. Mother believed that one was born perfect—as the Quakers believed—that it was the world that stained and corrupted, *where moth doth consume*. It was he, then, who allowed himself to be corrupted, to fall away from perfection.

Bernie staggered back laughing, then he stepped forward and shook his finger at the world. "I am the purrfect father, husband—ask Dottie!"

Andrea was too stunned to cry. Her mission was pointless.

Bernie returned to the sofa and sat down. In a lowered voice he said, "So what did you and Dad talk about? 'Bout me, I suppose. 'That Bernie, he's a good-for-nothin.'" Then he repeated what all of them had grown up hearing their dad say: "You'll never amount to anything if you can't get up in the morning," except Bernie said amount to *nothin'*.

"No, Dad didn't say that."

"What'd he say, then?" Bernie's voice was gruff, forced up from his diaphragm instead of coming naturally. He looked not at, but through her.

"He said—we said—he thought I ought to talk to Dr. John. Tell him how hard Mother has been having it at home."

"Well, how is it?"

Was there any point in talking with Bernie? The less she said and heard the better, because their mother would pressure her to repeat every word of their conversation. Bernie too, might tell their mother what Andrea told him, *if* she could bring herself to go through with Martha's plan.

"It's a shock to see her."

"I don't see much wrong with her. It's you and Dad. And Martha—she keeps agitating and stirrin' things up."

"Look, Bernie, I don't live here. I don't have to *do* anything. As a matter of fact, if you shaped up, I think *everything* else would!" She stood up, walked to the kitchen, and looked in for no real reason. Then she stared out the picture window at the raw red road, feeling such a great and binding sorrow that she wanted to put her arms around Bernie and Dottie, both at once, telling them how beautiful they had been on their wedding day, how things could be better, how they must try. But she said that she must try to help Martha, who did nothing but try to keep their parents' lives together in the best way she could: cooking, cleaning, caring. She was sorry for the words as soon as she said them.

"Blame me! Everyone blames me. Martha, for being alive. Manley, for stealing his farm. Dad, for this wreck." He gestured to indicate the greenhouse, house, everything he had. "Except Mother. Hey, wait a minute, what did you say about Dr. John?"

"We—Dad thinks we should go see Dr. John, explain Mother's agitation, self-blame—you know about that, don't you? She thinks it's her fault that you drink."

"Well, maybe it is!" Bernie shouted at her, standing up again, waving his arms. She heard the kitchen door slam—Dottie must have listened to them, standing alone in the kitchen, until she didn't want to hear more. Andrea imagined her thinking of her wedding day, how full of hopes she had been, the future unrolling like the white unblemished pathway that had covered the church's red carpet.

Andrea said he couldn't blame others for his own problems, and Bernie asked her who *she* was to talk, and what did *she* know about him. She noticed how his eyes flashed like Viktor's when he was angry, adding that she wasn't trying to be accusing but just trying to talk to him about their mother. So Bernie calmed down and asked her what she wanted him to do.

She began her elaborate lie, weaving it from the green tweed background of the chair she sat in, how they wanted to have their mother talk to Dr. John Parrish, who would advise her to go for weekly visits to a psychiatrist, after they explained things to him, of course. And because Mother respected doctors, especially Dr. John, the son of their family doctor, friend, counselor, she would take his advice.

"What's it got to do with me?"

"We thought if you were behind it—you know, she trusts you—that you could get her to go, you could take her."

"What kind of a goddamned traitor do you think I am?" he shouted, red-faced, flushed, scorning deceit. "You want me to tell Mother that her family has decided that a goddamned psychiatrist would be better for her than Jesus Christ himself? "

No wonder Mother loved him best. "I know, Bernie," she said. "It's for Dad, though, you know."

"Well, I ain't going to call Dr. John. Maybe I'll go along, but I ain't calling him."

So Andrea agreed to call him—quickly, before Bernie changed his mind—pleased that Bernie would go along. She called on Bernie's phone. Dr. John agreed, said he understood the situation, that the suggestion for seeing a psychiatrist—he would say *counselor*—would come from him, after talking with Klara. Andrea hoped he wouldn't forget.

"That's right," she said. "It isn't such a bad idea, is it? It can't hurt anything." She wanted reinforcement. Dr. John answered that it might be helpful. Certainly no harm in it. "As long as Mother doesn't know her family is suggesting it, right?" she emphasized.

"Right," he said. They'd left it at that.

Andrea left Bernie's house without seeing Dottie again, but she was somewhat hopeful about Martha's plan. Bernie went to his greenhouse. In July, he hadn't a lot to do, he'd said, because all the plants—tomato, cucumbers, broccoli, green beans, his main crops—had been delivered to retailers, and it was too early for mums, poinsettias, his Christmas plants. She would like to see him there in his element, knowledgeable of garden and household plants' growth, their requirements and diseases, the way she'd like best to remember him, his face intent, alert, bending over leaves so small they were nearly invisible to her, with his hands of love and tenderness.

The air was clear and fresh on the drive home, the heaviness of yesterday a vanished weight. Few of the farms she knew and passed had livestock anymore, and barns meant for dairy cattle—built before hay balers with vast cathedral spaces for mountains of loose hay—stood as empty as Viktor's trouser legs. Even bales didn't need barns anymore, and barns didn't substitute very well as shelter for hogs. Farming was changing, but she didn't understand it. There was a general uneasiness among the farmers, except for Howard, who had inherited a lot of land—more than a thousand acres. Other farmers had a quarter section, or less.

At home the ducklings' arrival was heaven-sent. Hatched into bronze fluff-balls, they had imprinted themselves upon the children, chiefly Rosalind. It seemed extraordinary that, as soon as they hatched, wild ducks and geese accepted the first creature present as their *mother*. Andrea thought of a ewe refusing to accept its own lamb, which would die without a surrogate mother—another ewe had to be tricked into acceptance, or there must be a warm box by the kitchen stove, a bottle and nipple, and someone to feed it every few hours, as she and Manley had done. She remembered her father skinning stillborn lambs and putting the skin on an orphaned or rejected lamb to present to a ewe as her own...If her mother hadn't found the mallard eggs, the ducklings would have died, half-hatched, dried, and stuck to the shell. Did the hen know that four more may have been too many and would threaten them all, or were the ducklings part of the Grand Design to give her mother something to fill her lost purpose: mothering. Was Bernie an extension of her need, too—that nurturing fed oneself? The whole interdependency and responsibility of the relationship seemed awesome.

Her mother had made a little pen of chicken wire and lathe stakes, so it could be moved anywhere on the lawn. She wasn't tired, nor did she seem to remember the events of last night. The girls sat with the four mustard-colored plush ducklings crawling over them, pecking the little girls' soft hands with their baby beaks, the girls sitting quietly, as they had been taught by Grandmother: the beginning of a long commitment for daughters, she thought.

"I am their mother," Rosalind said proudly. "Look how they follow me."

The children were occupied all day with the ducklings. They pretended to be the ducks and piled their bodies together in an entwinement of limbs, pretending to sleep as the ducks slept, heads a semblance of being tucked under their arms, murmurs of duckling contentment. Food, sleep, sun. What more was there? Her dad was outside in his chair, watching them, watching the horizon, as he always had. Andrea felt both happy and uneasy: Dr. John Parrish would see her mother tomorrow. Bernie would go with her. Martha was very happy with what she had done, so they didn't quarrel.

"Don't come tomorrow," Andrea told her. "I'll take care of things." She kissed Martha. They felt like sisters. Thanks to the ducks and Manley's arrival, the day went well.

He arrived almost unheard, his pickup sliding itself into the driveway, unlike Bernie's screech of brakes. "Manley!" She rushed into his arms, leaping up from the ducklings' pen as he got out of the pickup, apologizing for his work clothes, smiling, awkward.

"Hiya, kid. How's the mom?" he said, seeing Andrea's daughters absorbed in the ducks. From the grove of black walnut trees and cottonwoods in the small permanent pasture beyond the apples and raspberry bushes, seed puffs of silky cotton balls floated, and the tall Norway spruce whispered breathlessly in a faint breeze, their tall tops moving almost imperceptibly against the blue air of the sky.

"How's Pop?" she asked him, now that he, too, was the parent of three children.

"I've got boys," he said. "Better...even if I once thought *you* were as good as one." He hesitated and then looked down at her, still in his arms. He dropped his arms. "But then, you were Johnny." His smile faded. "Long ago," he added.

Andrea looked for changes in Manley: his hairline had receded more than ever, he was thinner, he had a two-to-three-day beard, tawny, like stubble in a wheat field. One thing different about

Manley from most farmers was that he didn't have a white forehead from living in a striped denim cap with a visor. He took pains not to, because he'd always laughed at such farmers. *Look at the half-moon head*, he'd say, adding, *What do you suppose he does for a living?* Nor would he ever wear bib overalls. Denim pants for Manley, with a leather belt and low-topped work shoes. *What you trying to be, a feed salesman or a car dealer?* Bernie would ask.

"I hope you're staying for dinner, Manley. Supper, I mean. And for the night?"

"Naw, can't. Got to get this feed back to the hawgs. They're crying big hog tears, waitin' for supper." Manley used to ridicule the language he now used.

"Not even for supper! You can't stay for supper?" She saw that he didn't want to, and looking at him, and then at her daughters, she saw the years that had flowed between them like rain, drowning some, carrying others to a far shore, dumping them on unfamiliar sandbanks. She was on such a sandbank that shifted constantly. Her first love had said, when she spoke of wanting to live in Europe, or New York: *Go back to your boy in Iowa. Don't you know, no matter where you go, you will only be home in Iowa? When you're not there, you won't really exist anymore.*

Was that what was wrong with Manley, that the very soil he touched didn't speak to him? Even though it was only sixty miles away, it was different. Wasn't home movable for so few miles! She thought of her pending move to Poland. What then, for her and for her children?

Under the Norway spruce near the ducklings' chicken-wire pen, which Andrea's daughters were inside as often as the ducklings were, was the old chair swing she and Manley used to climb up with an umbrella for a parachute. Their father had replaced the rotted wooden boards on the metal frame and repainted it white. If there weren't the ducklings, her daughters would be in the chair swing.

"I just came to see you, Johnny," Manley said. "Let's go sit in the chair swing. Want to climb up?" He was more wistful than laughing.

They sat down, pushing their feet against the floor boards, waiting to hear the familiar rasp of the metal frame as it reached the end of one direction and returned to the other. "Hey, where's the squeak? Dad must of oiled it good." Andrea looked at him quizzically.

"I'm one of the boys now, don't you know? You can't go around saying 'he doesn't' and be a farmer. Farmers don't have no airs." She looked into his face as his smile faded. He looked into the distance. "Andrea, things have changed," he said.

He went on to tell her how he worked for a good farmer, a brother-in-law of Cousin Johanna, that he got to raise all the pigs he wanted, but how he had to farm six hundred acres of flat, black land on the halves, that he got only half of the products of his labor. His kids were fine. "Nan's as smart as a whip," he said, "about Rosalind's age." It was the only time Andrea saw his eyes light up. He never mentioned Irene, his wife. Martha had told Andrea stories she hadn't wanted to hear, how Irene browbeat him all the time about money, or the lack of it, telling him how he'd got a raw deal from his father, how the family farm should have been his long ago.

"Now what about you? Is Michael over there saving us from the reds? He turned to his sister, who had wanted to ask why he hadn't brought the kids. But she knew why: he had to visit hog breeders, discuss exchanges, sales, purchases, and, possibly, he wanted to get away from home, if not from his kids.

"Is that all I'm going to hear about you?" She realized that they'd stopped swinging, noting the absent squeak.

"The rest you don't want to hear," he said, putting his hand on her arms. "Honest."

"Manley, we always told each other the truth. Has that changed?"

"Everything's changed."

"But Manley, you can't just sit back and let this *everything* happen to you. You may be better off, I say, than being here. You don't know what goes on."

Manley looked straight ahead now, at the lanky cottonwoods appearing through the darker patches of spruce. "You went away, Andrea. I stayed. I wish I hadn't." His hands gripped hers. "I wish I'd never heard of a farm, of Iowa. I wish I'd never heard of land and learned to love it. Dad's especially. It's been in the family so long, Andrea. What did you find out there that meant anything to you?" He stopped, and looked into the distance again, adding that he'd found his ideal job, made for him, if only…

Andrea asked him, "If only what?"

Manley, still looking into the distance, said that he'd just seen the movie *Ben Hur*. Had she? He'd like to go and be the groom to those white horses. Did she remember the white horses, the *quadriga*?

She couldn't even answer. She shook her head.

He looked in her face. "I thought maybe you'd found something. Maybe that's what's wrong with me, because I never found anything but grief by staying here, but it grabbed on to me and followed me, wherever I went. Didn't it do that for you? Why do you come back here? That's what I don't understand."

"Because I don't know any better, I guess. Because, Manley, you know why! Because it's home. Because of you," she added, her voice breaking.

"Don't," he said. "Please don't, Andrea. I can't bear…Tell you what! I'll give you my Eagle Scout belt, if you will be a good girl and not cry and let me go. OK?" He wiped his eyes with the back of his sleeve.

"OK!" she said. "Right now?"

"Right now!" And she and Manley went upstairs to his boyhood room—he knew where in the closet to find what once were treasures. He fondled it, looking at nearly every badge he'd won and had stenciled on his belt. Then he handed it to her, asking, "Where is the laughing/crying doll?"

She told him that she'd taken it with her long ago, one Christmas when she'd been home. He kissed her hurriedly and left after greeting his parents, saying that he didn't have time to stop. "Next time," he promised. His words drifted up the stairs where Andrea remained looking out of the window, fingering the belt.

Bernie came the next day on schedule, stopping with a screech of brakes, dust flying from the gravel. Andrea and Viktor saw him from the small glassed-in porch next to the living room where Viktor liked to lie on the couch while her mother napped in her bed. They heard Bernie enter the washroom, the screen door slamming. They didn't get up. He came through the kitchen and banged a cupboard door closed. He lurched into the sun porch where they were. The odor of whiskey preceded him, and the smell of beer had saturated his clothes, his hair, his breath. All attempts to disguise it were only wintergreen mints on top of whiskey. Andrea couldn't even smell the varnish anymore—it had always faintly permeated the porch. Viktor contracted his nostrils slightly as he half reclined on the couch, without words, without greeting, looking away.

"Nice to be greeted so warmly, Dad," Bernie said. Viktor looked out the windows across the adjacent living room, at the evergreens, perhaps, how they swept to the ground, maybe thinking of how long ago they'd been planted. "Don't know what I'm supposed to be doin' here," he said to his mother who entered, pinning her hair up as she walked. "Andrea said I'd better talk to you. Said that…" and his *th* was thick as molasses in January—Bernie always used to say that about someone slow, or drunk.

Klara looked at Andrea sharply. "Mother, do you want me to go with you?" Bernie asked, standing in stained, unpressed trousers. He crossed to the platform rocker, adjacent in the living room, sitting down in the chair Klara had rescued from her father's garage and refinished, and recovered with floral upholstery. Andrea heard its mild, rhythmic squeak as Bernie began to rock. She and her mother remained standing, facing each other, but now they watched Bernie.

"Go where? I'm not going anywhere," Klara said, emphatically. Then she turned her gravest of faces to Andrea, asking in a quiet but condemning voice, "Andrea, what've you been talking to Bernie about?" Her hands became agitated as she clasped and reclasped them, looking at and frowning at her daughter who stood in the doorway, between the porch and the living room.

"Mother, Bernie and I, Bernie thought it would be a good idea—Dad, too—for you to see Dr. John. I agreed, and so…so Bernie called him, yesterday. That's all. Bernie said he wanted to talk to Dr. John, too."

She couldn't stop the untruths she was telling, fearful of looking at anyone straight in the face—she told what she wanted to be true. She wanted Bernie to have done it, fearful he would betray her. She continued, not wanting to give Bernie a chance to deny it. "Will you, Mother, just for us? For Bernie?" For Andrea, so that she could escape to Washington, to Poland. For Martha, because she couldn't. For Dad, because he lay there, looking at his safety pins. For Bernie, because he was too weak to rise to the occasion, which was mostly his fault anyway.

"Come on and go, Mother. What have ya got to lose?" Bernie said, looking down. Andrea wanted to hug him! Her eyes filled with tears. Did Dad know Bernie had behaved like a prince, accepting her lies? Bernie's chair squeaked gently.

"Do you think so, Bernie?" Klara asked, turning to him with the compliance of a sweet child. And Bernie nodded.

A half hour later, Klara had changed into her going-out clothes, worn to church, to the doctor's, to go shopping. In July, this was a rayon navy-and-white print dress, white handbag, and navy straw hat. Bernie had stayed in the living room while their mother changed. Andrea stood, astride the two rooms, her dad reclining on the couch in one, and Bernie rocking in the living room. When they talked, it was about the weather: that it was nice, that it wasn't hot, that last July it was, until Klara came in, dressed, and stood next to Bernie.

Klara watched the three of them, while she reached for her hat, taking the elastic from under her mass of hair, removing it. "I'm not going anywhere with anyone. I know what you're planning, Viktor. Don't think I don't know!" She turned toward Bernie, "What are you planning, Bernie? Why are you here?"

Bernie shifted in his chair. What he said and what he did was crucial. He will tell, Andrea thought—he's too drunk not to. He looked away from her, from his mother, who went to the couch on the porch where her husband lay.

"Viktor! Viktor!" she cried, "Don't let Andrea take me. Viktor, please! We've been married, haven't we, for forty-five years?" She clung to his gone legs, imploring him, in the name of their dead babies, in the name of her father, Salve, and her mother, Kristina, to keep her at home. Her tears fell on his empty trousers.

Bernie rose from his chair and from his stupor, going to his mother, whispering to her. He smoothed her hair, his hands cupped her face, "Mother, I wouldn't lie to you, would I?" His face was red, his breath short. As he stroked her hair, their mother calmed. Bernie extended his hand to her, and she rose, replaced her hat, and then went outside and into the backseat of the car with him to wait for Andrea.

Andrea wanted to stop the entire charade, but how could she, now that Bernie was keeping his bargain? Who was holding it up and who was letting it down? She didn't know what color the sky was anymore—she could have believed it was a place to fall off from at the end of the flat world where she saw a white farmhouse, a man in a wheelchair, a drunken man leading a woman in a summer hat, and three little girls absorbed in four ducklings.

As she entered Dr. John's office, Andrea thought of the sicknesses and injuries her family had had and of the confidence they'd had in simple medicine. The same disinfectant odors were present, the white metal boxes for instruments, the closet that was probably still inhabited by the skeleton. Dr. John Parrish did not smile, ever. But that he would remember their plan, she was certain. *I'll merely suggest that she make weekly visits to a psychiatrist, is that what you want?* he'd asked.

He looked straight at Klara. "How are you feeling, Mrs. Endresen? Anything the matter?"

Andrea wished Manley were there, and Martha, and her father in his wheelchair. She wished they could all be together in this scene that seemed so useless, that tried to unfix and reorder love and blame and hope. They'd all rejected this kind of treatment long ago, treatment that probably even Dr. John, in all his years of medicine, had no hope for or confidence in. Even though a psychiatrist was a doctor, such a man would know nothing of her mother. Andrea did not really know why they were here, when all of them were reluctant to come and held no hope for success. Like drowning persons clinging to a half-submerged and soggy beam, they were here.

Their mother fixed her eyes on no one, on nothing in the room, and said, as if thinking about it, "I think I'm all right. Sometimes I'm nervous. Andrea thinks I am, I think."

Dr. John leaned forward in his seat behind his desk and looked her mother in the face. "Andrea says you need psychiatric care, maybe hospitalization," he said.

Her mother stared into Andrea's stricken face as if she were watching a stranger count the silver pieces and then seeing the face blur into her daughter's. Andrea clutched her neck and looked at Bernie, who stared at Dr. John. Bernie sat stunned and unbelieving, as if wondering if he'd heard the words he thought he'd heard. Andrea saw Bernie try to understand *who* was most cruel, if he, too, had been tricked, as he watched his sister plummet from grace. Then he looked at his mother with a tenderness and such deep sorrow, Andrea could see how much he loved her and why she loved him. She saw, too, that she was no longer one of them…

Her mother rose at the same time Bernie did, arms open to each other. They walked out the door, Bernie leaning over his mother, his arms around her, leading her. She sat, staring at Dr. John. She looked at his balding head and angular face, his wire-framed glasses framing pale-blue eyes, icy eyes, she thought. Then she was certain that she saw a bonnet tied under a chin, a long gray dress; she saw a finger unfold from a shawl and point at her; she heard a voice say, *I only speak the truth: you would have me tell lies. This will teach you a lesson.*

She ran from the room, not knowing what room it was. She got behind the wheel of her father's car—she knew it was his because of a hand gas feed. A man and a woman were in the backseat. They did not speak. She drove, but the car seemed to know where to go. It hadn't been many places: back and forth to Grinnell, to a doctor's office and a hospital. That's what Grinnell had always meant to the Endresens. That and trains that arrived and departed for her. Before airplanes took over.

The tires sang on the blacktop, and as she drove, she knew that she would remember this day forever: how many steps from the doctor's office to the car, the particular noise of the car door when it opened, and the sound of the key in the ignition, the low hum of the Ford motor when it started. She would remember the bleached spot on her periwinkle-blue knit shirt where she'd spilled a drop of Clorox, a shirt that she would never want to wear again, but not because of the bleached spot; she would always hear the quiet sounds of wordless breathing coming to her from the backseat and remember how her whole body ached for Michael to wrap her up in his arms and take her away. She half believed, in desperate circumstances, that people could communicate by intense concentration, that by *willing* a person's presence, that person would stop whatever he was doing and send thought waves to the other. But she couldn't concentrate enough.

She knew what would happen now. They would get home, and Bernie would open the car door for Klara, as Viktor would watch from his wheelchair behind the screen door, his fingers drumming on the chrome chair arm. Bernie would lead her to the house, Viktor would push open the door, his face and body tension asking what had happened; he would never ask with words. Bernie and Klara would walk in, Klara would go to her bedroom without speaking to take off her hat. She would return to the kitchen, where Bernie would already be sitting in the breakfast nook, Viktor's wheelchair turned to the kitchen. They would talk about the weather. Klara would offer Bernie coffee.

By that time, Andrea would have put the car in the garage and closed the overhead door; reached up to grasp the handle of the overhead door to start its descent and then stepped outside to ease it closed. Her children would be so occupied with the ducklings in the shade of the spruce grove, that only then would they see her and call her, and she would go to them. Then came the part she wanted to avoid: she would kneel, gather up Sarah in her arms, and burst into tears. Kari's brow would wrinkle as she watched her mother cry: Roz would try to protect her and pretend there was nothing wrong. Finally she, Andrea, would stop abruptly, dry her tears, and say nothing to her daughters who circled around her, patting her, soothing her, as she did so often to them. Bernie would leave, starting up his truck more quietly than usual. He would not say good-bye. Then, together with her daughters, she would go inside. Nothing more would be said about the day's events by anyone. She would have to visit Martha to tell her what had happened, although she would never be able to tell what had happened to herself.

An abyss had just opened in the black earth that a family must stare into forever after: Viktor, bowed in his wheelchair, watching Klara wring her grieving hands; Bernie, remembering with renewed pain his mother's betrayal by a daughter, echoing his own betrayal; Martha, resenting her sister's failed attempt as she picked up her burden again; Manley watching them all snarled together in familial love and anger of which he was a part; Klara herself, with another wound to suffer, another child she'd failed because the child had failed her, her Johnny, who would soon be saying good-bye again, bearing a sorrow she would never lose.

How could Andrea have known that was the last time she would see her mother? She had gone back to Poland with her three daughters, who had wanted to take the baby ducks. Maybe they would have brightened the gray Communist country that was so grim. Their apartment was grim, the food was grim, faint sunshine was the loss of the lightness and brightness of Iowa.

She could not explain to Michael what had happened in Iowa, that she had tried to help Martha in a plot set up by her, involving Bernie. It wasn't Martha's fault. She did need help. Andrea could understand her burden, her despair. But she herself left Iowa in despair over what she had done. It was really Dr. John who had betrayed her. It would have been so simple for him to have followed her plan, Martha's plan. And the amazing fact was that Bernie went along with it. He really tried to help, and she had seen how deep was the bond between her mother and Bernie. A bond she didn't have, although she dearly, dearly loved her mother.

So back to Poland they went, having bought clothes for growing daughters and her herself, for her wardrobe. Poland had nothing to buy, absolutely nothing, except old cow filet passed off as a beef tenderloin, chickens in the market killed in front of your eyes.

Andrea and her family went back to the routines they had had in Poland. It was early September, and she had not written to her mother because she was too ashamed of what she had done, taking her to Dr. John, who betrayed her. She didn't know what to write. *Dearest Mother, I'm sorry for what I have done. I'm sorry I hurt you. I'm sorry sorry sorry about everything, about my trip to Iowa. But not about the ducks. Mother, I love you love you love you. I hope you know that.*

But she didn't write that. Nor did she write anything else. She was so shamed by what she had done.

Christmas came, and her mother sent gifts to the girls, quilted bathrobes of blue-and-white-checked flannel with lace collars. She had peeked before Christmas. Yet Andrea still had not written.

On Christmas Eve, after the girls had opened their present from Grandmother Klara and had a glass of cranberry juice—red wine they called it—and were tucked in bed, she and Michael went to the cathedral in the *Stare Miasto*, the old city, entirely destroyed by the Nazis and rebuilt. The cathedral was entirely renovated and was alive with Christmas and Easter celebrations. The crèches provided a sense of escape from the restrictions of the Communist government. All the vitality and religions fervor and artistry of the Poles was shown in their crèches of Christmas and Easter. On Christmas Eve, the cardinal of the cathedral would lay the Christ Child in the manger, where Mary waited for her son. The animals were nearly real, the straw, the manger were. It was so dramatic and meaningful that tears were evident in eyes of the congregation. Sore lumps were in Andrea's throat. This ceremony was an expression of hope to the Polish people, an end to Communism which so destroyed everything they wanted: hope, God, even decent food like meat and bread. Shoppers' lines were everywhere.

Their neighbors, Tom and Nancy Ross, were equally moved and speechless, with reverence, with awe. They parted silently and entered their adjacent doors without speaking.

Still, without saying anything, Michael and Andrea entered their quiet house only to hear the harsh ring of the telephone.

"A provocation," he volunteered. "Some girl at the Bristol Bar wants me to come and have a Christmas drink with her, a frequent occurrance in Poland. Here, Andrea you answer her."

Andrea took the telephone in her hand, delighted to do so. But instead of an enticing female voice, she heard static, a distant voice sounding like Martha's. "Andrea, Andrea. Is that you?" Andrea froze, trying to calculate the time in Iowa, plus seven hours to Poland. No, minus. No, plus. It must be one o'clock, plus seven. That would be eight o'clock. So it would be a Merry Christmas call. Martha was never cognizant of other time zones. One o'clock in the morning.

There was a lot of static. "Andrea, Andrea, Mother is in the hospital. She is a coma. She has pneumonia. She won't last the night. Andrea! Andrea! Can you hear me?"

Andrea slumped on the sofa. She had not written to her mother, not since their terrible last meeting. How cruel of her, how dreadfully selfish, how horrible a memory of her cruelty. *Never put off till tomorrow, Johnny, what things you can do today.*

Andrea slumped on the sofa, hearing her mother's voice as she fingered the candlestick base, wondering if salt from tears would strip the old brass of its patina. She knew that this day would never be erased by tomorrows, that each second would drip like a watched leaky faucet, each drop endless in its beginning, filling and dropping even as another began. And after today, there would be tomorrow. It loomed ahead of her like the Polish winter. Today would be a clock, broken and stopped on a fixed point.

She was aware of Michael, bringing tea. "Andrea, here, drink this. You're cold." She took the warming mug of tea in both hands, her tearstained and swollen face unable to look at Michael.

"Shall I stay with you, Andrea, or would you rather be left alone?" She reached up and squeezed his hand—she didn't know what he should do. How could she? "I'll listen for the girls to wake up, and I'll tell them you want to rest awhile. OK?" he said.

"You'll have to tell them why."

"What should I say?" Michael seemed uncertain.

"Tell them the truth."

"Will they understand, do you think, Andrea? No one in our

family *died* before." The word had been unpronounceable to her, and now Michael was using it, almost easily.

"I don't know...what—what they'll understand," she said.

"Andrea, why don't you go back to bed? That way I can bring the girls downstairs when they wake, and each can open a present. We'll be quiet."

She nodded and rose from the sofa. Michael took her by the arm, leading her upstairs, carrying her half-drunk tea, and eased her into bed. She knew that eventually Michael would tell her, "You just have to face up to it. It isn't the end of the world."

"Did Grandma go to a place in the sky?" Kari asked. Rosalind told her that Grandma now lived together with God and Jesus. Sarah said that her Barbie was crying for Grandma. Even after four days, Andrea's children played in hushed voices. Their neighbor, Nancy Ross, often took them to play at her house. She loaded up seven children in her small station wagon and took them sledding, to a puppet show, ice skating.

Andrea waited with dread for Martha's letter, which would tell her of her mother's funeral and be accompanied by photographs that Andrea would not be able to look at for a long time. Martha would write how she had chosen Mother's black dress with the blue and gold-beaded belt, *the one you always liked*, the one they'd chosen together for their mother's twenty-fifth wedding anniversary. Martha thought Andrea would approve that she'd had them put her glasses on her, that their mother didn't look *natural* without them, as though she should look alive. She wrote how helpful Manley was, how brave and silent Viktor was, as always, and, because Bernie wouldn't be mentioned, Andrea would know that he had disgraced them. In losing his mother, Bernie had lost his only friend and ally.

Finally, she'd have to look at the photos, taken for the absent family member, just the way her mother's first baby, Kristina Andrea, had been photographed in her tiny coffin for her ill and absent mother to see, *for Klara. Here is your baby,* Viktor had to say, handing her the photograph. Her mother would still have been in the hospital...Martha would write on the back of the photographs, *this is the way Mother looked on the day she was buried:* for Andrea, once called Johnny, always absent from home.

When Martha's letter *did* arrive, Andrea felt the hard edges of the photos through the envelope. Her fingers traced them over and over again, photos she didn't want to see, that would confirm what she didn't want to believe. She wanted to think that this past week had been a bad dream of unendurable length, just to teach her a lesson, and it would be a lesson well earned *and* learned. Except for this hard evidence felt in her fingers, it was only Martha's word that her mother was buried, closed up in a white satin-lined box—what else?—and Andrea was six thousand miles away and couldn't contest it.

Later, Andrea gave the photos to Nancy, without taking them out of the envelope. "Keep them for a few days, Nancy. You may look at them, if you want." Her face was swollen again after receiving them—she'd thought she was dealing with her grief toward her children; they should never see a mother cry. But her real grief was regret for what could never be altered—she had married a man her parents had never met, married him away from home, and had her first child away from home. She'd gone to Norway for six weeks in 1951 and only returned home after four years, with a husband and a child.

Her three children came in the door from Nancy's house and up to Andrea's room. They held something behind their backs. She called them to her, and they came with sober faces, looking up at her, wondering. She smoothed back Kari's hair, then Sarah's. She squeezed Rosalind's hands and leaned forward from where she lay on the bed, pressing them to her.

"Mommy, are you sick?" Kari asked, but Roz nudged her, saying, "Let Mother alone." Sarah patted her mother's cheek, saying that Grandma would come back. Roz grabbed Sarah's hand to lead her out of the room, but Andrea asked them all to stay, telling them how sorry she was to be in bed when they needed her. Kari asked if she'd still be sick on her birthday. She'd forgotten her birthday, two days after New Year's. Sarah shushed Kari and tiptoed out of the room, smiling secretly. She hoped Mommy would be well, Kari said.

But on her birthday, Andrea miscarried—she hadn't even been certain that she was pregnant. Nancy called Michael at the embassy. He wrapped her up in sheets and carried her to the blue Chevrolet to take her to the Klinika Kobiety—Nancy had arranged that, too, while three little girls stood awestruck and terrified, watching the redness soak through the whiteness of the sheets, Sarah screaming, *Grandma's dead! Now Mommy!*

Coming through the ether voyage back to light in a small green room of the Women's Clinic, Andrea felt Michael's hand upon hers. "Michael, we have lost your son, the one you always hoped for. Now you must be content with daughters." Michael said nothing. He was waiting, she knew, for her grief to mend.

Tom Ross came to see her, bearing a rose, apologizing for all that had happened to her and that he had never expressed regrets for her loss of her mother. He looked down at her, smoothed back her hair with his hand, then pressed her hands. He said he'd never got to know her very well, except through Nancy, but he just wanted to come himself.

She thought of him and Nancy together—Nancy spoke of their marriage as one-sided. Nancy said she should never have married, but convention would have it so. Now, they had four children. Andrea realized she knew nothing of Tom's side, who looked so lonely, so lost. Is that why he came? She had estranged herself from Michael since her mother's death, because he did not know how to respond to her loss. Was she to condemn him forever for it?

CHAPTER NINETEEN

The Williams family returned to Washington, DC, after three eventful years in Poland: Andrea's mother's death, three years of "making do" with what had been available to eat, and the consciousness that she and Michael were always being watched and recorded. They went back happily to their white-painted brick house next to Andrea's close friend, Elizabeth, back to their pink and white azaleas, pink dogwoods in spring, autumns of orange and red trees. Back to good schools, the National Gallery, the Air and Space Museum—and all the wonderful offerings in their capital city.

It was also easier to visit her family in Iowa, or what was left of them without their mother. So as soon as she resettled their house, the furniture back from storage, shipments from Poland unpacked, food in the fridge, Andrea went to Iowa alone.

Martha met her at the airport as she had done so many times. For Andrea, each visit made her parents' absence as visible as the general decay of farms. Before she returned to the States, Viktor had died from gangrene, an infection caused by the amputation of his legs. Martha was used to the empty places their parents had left at Sunday dinners, used to the black Ford that *didn't* turn in her driveway anymore, bringing a pint of shucked oysters from the Piggly Wiggly grocery from Marshalltown for Saturday night oyster stew.

Martha and her brothers, but mostly Martha, had arranged the known rites of death in the Midwest: the open casket for Viktor in the church, friends and relatives passing by to observe a painted face: *he looks so natural*, all would say, with his makeup, puffed-up cheeks, darkened eyebrows. The funeral parlor covered up his leg stumps and closed the lid of the coffin after all had passed by. And then to the graveyard. Andrea wanted to keep her memory of his incredibly sky-blue eyes, his big scarred hands that were so capable, now so still.

She and Martha now relaxed together; they were becoming what sisters could be to each other, even though their closeness was based on the mutuality of what they'd lost, not what they'd gained.

On the way to Martha's home, they made frequent detours, past farms Andrea had remembered years before. Martha knew them all: who had gone where, who had been foreclosed, what price they paid, what their kids had done in the world, who died, who was born. She postponed asking Martha about Manley and the family farm, knowing too much already. Then she'd get around to Bernie.

Andrea wanted to see Salve's house, where their mother was born and grew up. The approaching road was blacktopped, familiar landmarks were gone—the big oak at the mile corner, farm buildings, animals grazing in fields—and there were no fences. Martha slowed her Pontiac and stopped in front of the house Andrea did not recognize.

"We can stop, nobody's home. Both Tom and his wife work in town."

The barnyard was full of rusting farm machinery, some built to be pulled by horses, with hitches altered for tractor use: old hay rakes; a manure spreader; the sickle bar of a reaper, toothless, its sickle-guard fangs still in rows, leaning at an angle—a giant's comb. The outbuildings were falling down, some gone altogether. There was no way to know what once was there, except by memory. Both Andrea and Martha had plenty of that, remembering machine sheds, pig barns, poultry houses, where Salve's grandchildren had played hide-and-seek. The barn, built to stable a dozen horses, cow stanchions for twenty cows and hay enough for all of them in winter, stood forlorn, its sides caved in—only pigeons and the weather entered. The house was still occupied, although it didn't look it: once-torn screens on the porch were disintegrated into red-rust powder; abandoned on its rotting boards were a child's broken bicycle, rotting lawn chairs—all become a lacework of rust.

Martha pulled into the driveway and stopped. "Do you want to get out?"

"Isn't that snooping?"

"Nobody minds. I mean, it *is* the old home place. We all stop by, now and then."

So they walked on the unmowed lawn, skirted its tall weed patches and a sagging rubber tire that once held flowers. Andrea noted its rubbery odor, and the metallic scent of dry rust powder from the porch. Occasional patches of chalky white were visible on the bare, weathered clapboard. They peered inside an interior they'd known so well: new/old wall-to-wall carpeting was stained with years, the nap worn down to the carpet's back and turned to holes by the door. The many-times-remodeled kitchen was full of old gadgetry, little buttons that ground and mixed and heated, and through the open door of the nearby pantry, they saw rows of dusty green mason jars, all empty, the space occupied by a vintage chest-type freezer.

"I'll bet I know what's in it," Martha remarked. "Birdseye succotash and frost. Millie doesn't like to defrost freezers, and all they seem to eat is frozen vegetables." She added that at family reunions that was all Millie ever brought: frozen succotash in a casserole, daubed with margarine. Salve's great-grandchildren worked in factories in Marshalltown, making valves for motors, or they worked at the meat-packing plant, or as carpenters; their wives had become clerks, schoolteachers, secretaries.

"Martha, let's get out of here." Andrea didn't want to know any more. She looked at her sister, hands on her hips, as Martha explained what had happened since their childhood. Martha's hair was grayer than Andrea remembered.

"Yeah, I know, I've gone gray. I had it colored once—Howard wanted me to, but I just didn't feel good, being artificial."

Artifice was trickery: trickery was lies: truth must be unmasked, naked, or ignored. Andrea was home.

"The land belongs to a corporation," Martha continued, "if you want the complete story. That's why the fences are gone. It's been like this for a long time."

Salve's farmhouse had been like that even before Manley bought the mortgage of their family farm after Viktor died. Manley, after all those years, after the good times had passed, when livestock was leaving the farm, or had already left: *too little land, too late. Gave Bernie more than the girls ever got, or Manley, buying that greenhouse for him*, Viktor had said. Klara hadn't been there to hold out for Bernie. *You can't farm the way Manley does anymore.*

Andrea knew how corn pickers tore down fences and ground up everything in sight, how they came like locusts, like tanks, like war, flattening once-tended fences, ripping out trees, roaring across the land, consuming eight thousand bushels of corn a day, picking, shelling, and drying millions of orange kernels in their belly, spewing out chewed-up stalks in clouds mixed with dust and exhaust. With such machines, the land became naked as the early prairie, but *without* prairie grasses and the buffalo, without even the smoking trains that had crawled across it, blowing their long mournful cries across the echoing flatness. Andrea remembered those trains, but only Salve and Kristina had known the time before the early settlers planted trees on the lost prairie.

"Manley's got to change his ways!" Martha told how Viktor's cottonwoods would have to go, the walnut trees be cut down with the Norway spruce, the creek tiled and drained and filled in to grow more corn, to make terrain for the efficient giants. "Creeks and ditches cost time: time is money." Martha added how there was no need for hay or straw because there were no animals to eat it or bed in it. The empty barn should go, because it cost tax money, it occupied land that could be planted. "What it comes down to is the fact that Manley doesn't live in modern times."

Andrea knew what the barn was empty of: hay and whinnies, 4-H calves, lambs, barn cats' frequent litters, and empty as the farms were empty, too, of neighbors, sold out and gone, like O'Connell, buildings gone, houses vacated. Milk and eggs came from paper cartons, meat came flattened in paper trays, covered with plastic wrap. "Old MacDonald's Farm" could not be sung anymore. *Who even knew such a time?* Andrea wondered. The animals remaining were only Manley's pigs. But that, Manley hesitated to destroy, she knew.

Get smart, Irene told Manley. *Let's get out of here like everybody else does! You don't need to live here to grow corn and beans.* Once he said that Irene told him that, Martha said. But he didn't talk about it anymore.

It was true that many farmers had gone to factories, *or* they went to Florida, Martha said, *if* they'd been the lucky ones to buy land at market low, to buy machinery low—*if* they'd had the money, *if* they'd had good seasons, *if* they'd been smart, *if* they'd had luck or hope, *if* things broke right for them. But Manley'd bought at market high, and when he needed machinery, the prices had skyrocketed. He needed fertilizers, weed killers. Fertilizer, too, had risen in price and in need; it had replaced rotation. Andrea knew how Howard farmed. All nutrients now were poured back into the soil by commercial tons: nitrates, phosphorus, eaten up by corn and beans yielding over two hundred bushels an acre, almost four times what her father had harvested.

Andrea sat on the porch of Martha's house, looking out on the endless rows of corn and the tiny budding leaves of beans undulating off into the distance toward the big sky. She heard her father's voice. *Two years clover,* Viktor said, *and one of corn: rotation, and manure.* He had loaded and dumped heavy straw-filled cow manure over his fields. And when Viktor wasn't spreading manure, he was keeping up fences and keeping down weeds—burdock, thistles, milkweed— and trimming fence rows. Viktor had picked two wagonloads a day with Dan and Kate, one in the morning, one in the afternoon. In between loads, he ate pot roast and cherry pie, or roast pork and sour cream raisin pie. Viktor had picked 120 bushels in one day—almost two acres at a yield of sixty an acre—the corn husking champion of the state of Iowa. Every day, all fall he'd picked, until the snow came. Most farmers had picked less.

By all these statistics thrown at her by Howard and Martha, Andrea figured out that Manley's acreage wouldn't have occupied a corn picker for one day: eight thousand bushels! His used tractor wasn't paid for, his mortgage payments late, his hogs needed to be redesigned with newer bloodlines for leaner pork, *if* he'd had enough land, *if* the tractor was paid for, *if* Irene had supported him. Rather, she'd shouted, even in front of Martha: *I'm not goddamned hanging around! You keep your stinking farm, stinking hogs. I thought I married a farm and a man! Some substance..."* Martha heard it all. She'd watched Manley pale.

Martha drove Andrea to the farm—strange to hear Martha call it Manley's house—and left her for the day. Manley stood at the washroom door, waiting for her. She walked up the narrow sidewalk, stepped up on the square of cement outside the door that had been made for Viktor's wheelchair—she didn't look at the house, or the fences, the barn, the trees—she only looked at Manley. He held the door open, but not his arms. She embraced him anyway, feeling his body, thinner than she'd ever known him. "Hi," she said. Her arms withdrew by themselves, falling to her sides, like Manley's.

"Hi, too," he said. He didn't know what else to say.

He had a three-day beard, his hairline had crept back almost as much as their dad's, but Manley's was still light brown. He wore clean but faded blue-green trousers, a denim shirt, one sleeve torn.

"I wasn't looking forward to this," Manley said.

Andrea looked away. She searched her skirt pocket for a Kleenex. "Don't say that, Manley. Come on, let's go outside, to the swing, or just sit in Dad's chairs."

"Do you want coffee?"

"Is it made?" she asked, hating their politeness.

"Yes. You go out. I'll bring it."

For the first time, Andrea looked at the barn, its paint almost peeled off. She looked at the once-white corn and grain building, the fence between the barn and hog house, gone.

Manley came with coffee mugs and a folding aluminum chair for her. "Andrea, why should I keep the buildings up? I don't use them anymore...I know, the house needs painting. I'd like to paint the fence. I did fix it."

"No reason you should."

"I've tried to repair the fences..."

He'd tried to repair Dad's fences instead of taking them down? Andrea wondered. *What was he trying to do, make a cemetery garden plot for Dad's legs? Was he making a memorial to old Billy, by repairing fences?* He left the barn, he hadn't cut down the trees. Howard and Martha had convinced her of the uselessness of Manley's farming methods.

"Andrea, I love this land, every inch of it. I grew up here, and so did you. Now everything is changing. So many farmers have given up, or lost their farms to mortgage, or been bought out by bigger farmers who don't even farm. I guess I want to hang on to the past. I'm not made for corporations or big farmers without animals. Pigs and cattle are becoming factories now. No grazing, no freedom of outdoors, or grass under their feet. Seems like the world I love doesn't want me anymore, even though my pigs do."

"It doesn't seem like anyone needs barns anymore, Manley. Why should you fix them?"

"Don't sound like Irene!" he said. "'What are you, some kind of fool, or something?' That's what she said," he said, "before she took off in the family car. 'Just to go somewhere,' she said. Probably Colorado." Manley shrugged. "She likes Colorado."

Once he started talking, he told her how his second-hand tractor cost more than the O'Connell farm at the time Bernie bought the greenhouse. But the tractor was too old. "It's like trying to race the Spirit of St. Louis with a Spitfire," Manley said, "but I've got to do it. If I can just hang on till machinery goes down, till hogs go up." He told how corn cost him too much to grow to feed his hogs, how things had to change, how they always had: prices and times went up and down, down and up. *Up* was the thing, and what he had to do until then was to hang on. Manley's voice was exhausted and trailing, its energy and humor gone.

Andrea kept swallowing, glancing at Manley in their father's rusted chair that Viktor had always put in the garage for the winter. She glanced at one of the big maples just inside the board fence that had been struck by lightning, and remained a jagged trunk against the sky, a reminder of the fury of summer storms. Manley saw her look: "Yeah, that happened over a year ago." He nodded in the direction of the tree.

Johnny, I just like to see the pigs grow. If I stay long enough, I can see it, Manley's voice of long ago, so full of hope…*Johnny, the aparagus Bernie planted for me grows an inch an hour. You could sit and watch it. You could measure it, if you don't believe me. If you had time,* her mother's voice. Viktor's words: *Johnny, a man can love a horse…*

"The bank manager is getting impatient, Andrea. I know sentiment never paid the interest." Manley said he didn't even remember the guy's name anymore, that he didn't want to remember, that he never wanted, ever, to receive notification of the *thing* Dad had fought against all his life, the thing that hung over all of them like a sentence during the Depression years and long after: *mortgage*. One bad year: one season's loss of pigs from pneumonia, or scours, or a failed corn crop, or drought, or hail, or flood, or, locusts, like '32, meant *foreclosure*.

"You know, it seems like all our parents taught us was lies, or else the world has changed since then," Manley said, leaning forward to put his coffee cup on the ground. He didn't wait for Andrea to ask what he meant as he talked on; the process was a *given:* work equals success. That and honesty made a foolproof formula. Now only fools believed it. What was missing now was belief. The dream—the black soil Salve saw, gone. Could Salve imagine, did Andrea think, that his grandson would be sitting here, surveying a wasteland of his hopes? That those horizons, once unlimited, were gone promises, like the whole country. Look at Watergate. When it gets down to the president lying, cheating, what are you supposed to believe?

"Andrea, is it just me?" He grabbed onto her arm then slumped back in his chair. Andrea was too choked up to answer.

"Remember when I asked you what you'd found out there? Remember? Well, what did you find? The same as me? That our childhood was a dream, or we just weren't equipped to deal with…" He hesitated, and then added in a voice so low Andrea could hardly hear, "the rest."

They both heard the vast silence. They both looked at the fenceless rows of foot-high corn across the road that passed by the house. Row after row led their eyes off to the distant horizon, on land once belonging to their Uncle Orrin, Viktor's brother, land now corporate.

"Manley, you, this land…does it mean so little to you, now?"

"I have my dream—this land. But not for long. The bank looks me over every few weeks. Two days ago, the guy came out for the hundredth time, it seems."

Andrea could see how the bank agent saw Manley's fences still up, along with all the old farm buildings, the white board fence repaired but not yet painted, how he would have sighed and shaken his head as Manley said, "Times will change for me…"

But now he said, "Maybe Irene is right…"

Did he mean, *some kind of fool,* is that what he meant? Andrea wondered. She didn't ask. Instead she said, "Manley, you love this place, don't you?"

"You always did, too, Andrea."

"Yes, I do." Andrea's eyes swept its space, remembering everything she'd lost. "I'm glad you're here, even if…" She caught herself.

"I know what you're thinking. Maybe it *is* foolish." Manley was looking beyond where she could see, into a future made of the June air, full of gone sounds. "It's for my sons, Andrea. I want it for them, I want it so bad. I grew up here, it was his father's, and ours—Dad's. No one else has a right to it. I wish I could have seen what Salve and Kristina saw—limitless black earth, rolling and rolling away into the distance, coming from Norway, a land of stones. And now, here is their grandson, me, losing it, unable to pass it to my sons. But my sons must have a past so they can have a future!"

Eric worked in Marshalltown at Fisher's, making valves, and Dale was hitching around somewhere—Manley didn't know where he was—"He's just a kid, Andrea." Andrea wanted to ask about him. "What about Bernie?" she asked instead.

"I guess it's going to be hard to believe, but since Dad's death, we've become friends. We don't talk much. Just sit together." Manley told how much there was to think about that they didn't need to say, how Bernie felt guilty for the shape he was in with the farm, the mortgage, how they were brothers after all. "Doesn't mean he stopped drinking," he added.

Long ago, Manley had forgiven her for not writing to Mother—his forgiveness helped Andrea to heal herself; he had forgiven Bernie. It was only himself he could not forgive, for not paying off the mortgage, for not providing more *substance* for Irene, land for his sons.

"Manley, I…" but Andrea saw that Manley wasn't listening to the words she couldn't say anyway because her throat hurt too much, and her arms that wanted to speak for her clung woodenly to her sides.

Manley asked if she wanted to see his hogs, a dying breed, he called them, and she asked why, and he said that breeding hogs or cattle, not corporate, was a dead enterprise. He was carrying the banner, but the banner was flagging. He wondered if his dad would laugh at him now—he'd never liked Berkshires, if she remembered, but if he sold off his breeding stock, where would he be? But then, where was he anyway?

Andrea said she'd stay where she was, sit in the chair swing, maybe, but Manley said the boards were a little rotten, like everything else. She sat where she was while Manley disappeared, to take care of the hogs, she supposed. She didn't look at the buildings and the fence anymore, but stared at a bare spot where lawn had been. She tried hard to remember nothing at all from her childhood, but rather, places she'd lived, imagining what it would have been like if she'd been born in Norway. But she could not imagine what had not happened, so she stared again at the bare lawn at her feet, the crab grass, the thick bridal wreath now choking the house, blooms gone. It probably had bloomed—that was something you couldn't stop.

Manley returned to say he had an errand, and he'd drop her off at Martha's a little early, if she didn't mind. They spoke little on the way, of the weather, of former neighbors moved away, *if* Andrea asked him. At Martha's house, Manley didn't get out. "See ya," he said.

Andrea knew that Manley didn't even hear the words of the man who got out of a red Buick wagon on a mid-June morning, two days later: *Take this like a man. We've done all we can*...and handed him the formal papers of the *thing t*hat he'd grown up afraid of.

That same day, Bernie called Martha. Andrea answered the phone. Bernie asked for Martha. His voice sounded hoarse, Andrea thought. She stood watching Martha's face as she listened. Before she said anything, Martha started to cry. She leaned over the kitchen counter, the phone grasped in both hands.

"When?" She couldn't talk. "Where?" she rasped. "We'll come right away." Martha slid down into a chair, her face in her hands, sobbing. "It's Manley. He shot himself—"

"Is he—?"

"He's dead."

Bernie was sitting in Viktor's rusted chair, outside on the lawn, when Andrea and Martha got there. They approached him but held back to look at him, their faces white and tear-streaked. Bernie seemed cold sober. Martha sat in the folding chair Andrea had sat in—was it only one—no, two days ago? Andrea slumped down on the grass, her arms on Bernie's knees. Martha's arms were around them both.

He'd had an intuition, Bernie began, and so he'd come to the farm late morning, but he found no one. "Not a sound. The tractor was here. The pickup. Hogs had been fed." He told how he'd called Manley's name and was answered by echoes. "It was eerie," he said, "quiet as a church, and not even a pig grunt." That then he went to the gun closet, where Mother used to keep her fold-up ironing board. Bernie said he didn't know why he went there, he just did, and then he found the shotgun gone. He knew Manley never used it anymore. Then he got real nervous—that, and seeing the notice of foreclosure lying there on the kitchen table. He'd seen that next.

First place he went to, he said, was the barn, and he'd looked up into the empty mow. He didn't know why he thought of the hay trolley, when the gun was gone. So he ran, to the cottonwood grove, and even at a distance, he said, he saw Manley lying there.

"He couldn't have been there more than an hour, I don't think," he said. "Right through the heart! Both Manley and the farm gone," he said. "Somehow I always knew they'd stick together, or fall together, whichever way it was." Bernie raised his head and looked toward the evergreens. His eyes focused on nothing in particular. "I wouldn't have cared if it had been the greenhouse," he added.

Crows cawed over the tops of the cottonwoods, and its seed-puffs drifted down like snow. And they were now only three, and they were crying together in each other's arms, blowing their noses, daubing their eyes, not believing their losses, trying to remember the set routines of death.

Andrea located Michael at the State Department in an emergency call.

"What's up?" he asked.

She told him about Manley, stopping to compose herself now and then. She said he *had* to come, *with* the girls. She didn't care what they were doing or where they were, that he should find them and come immediately. Michael said he didn't know what *they* could do, but…

Andrea interrupted him to say that he, they, could *be here*, with her, that their presence would be enough. For herself, for Martha, for all of her sorrows that she could not bear alone. She needed *them*, she said. Manley's loss was like a swollen river, sweeping her down its stream. She wanted her family to understand that. She didn't want to have to say it. She needed them, not so that she would have to *contain* her grief; she needed them to share it with her.

Did Manley know, then, when he'd driven her back to Martha's house? They had hardly talked on the way. She had been too full of tears. Had he said good-bye as they'd sat looking at the corporate rows of corn and his sagging barn, and she had not known it? Had he tried to tell her that he could not have the old ways nor accept the new? What had she last said to him? Had she failed him, too, as she'd failed her mother? What good did her *presence* do? Maybe she was *destined* to be absent! Maybe it was better.

Andrea met Michael and the girls on the tarmac at the airport. She stood there, with her too-late thoughts, seeing solemn-faced daughters approach, their blond hair blowing in the wind; she saw Michael with the lock of hair always on his forehead, wondering if it was fair of her to have insisted that they come, after so long, to a funeral?

Michael embraced her, looking anxious.

"Hot, isn't it?" she said. "I hope you didn't mind coming, too much…"

"Mother," Sarah began, "we haven't been here for so long, I don't even remember what we ever saw from what you told us."

Sarah meant the good parts, she knew: horses, the piglets, Manley. What else? She walked, arm in arm with Michael, to the parking lot. For a moment, she forgot where she'd parked Martha's car.

Michael drove. Andrea directed him, left here, right there, straight ahead on the road so flat and blue that one saw little oasis-like pools of water receding in front of them. He waited for Andrea to talk.

Kari began. "Mum, you know, we've been talking a bit, and we'd all like to see the farm. We're not sure we remember." None of them mentioned Manley's death. They would wait for her to tell them about it.

"It was five years ago," Andrea said. "The summer we went to Norway."

"But we stayed with Aunt Martha. Did we see the farm?"

Yes, they had, she said. But things had changed by then.

"I remember Grandpa, and the ducks, and the colt—we fed him. And Maud, and Manley's pigs," Sarah said.

"You don't remember Maud, Sarah. None of us ever saw her. And Manley never had pigs when we were there," Roz said. She was right.

Andrea knew that most of what her daughters knew about the farm was from her own memory. And the farm they wanted to see wasn't even theirs anymore. She wondered if she could bear to take them.

"If you don't want to, Mum, it's OK."

Andrea didn't look at her daughters. She was thinking of how it was that she had deliberately kept them from this place, of why, even now, when she'd brought them here, she was trying to keep them from a past that was theirs, too. Kristina and Salve were their great-grandparents, and, along with her own parents, were almost unknown to them.

"I will take you. But please not today. Tomorrow. I promise." Then, facing the road, her eyes fixed on the far horizon, she told them about Manley, her last visit to him, their conversation. Through her tears and her grief she told them about their bird whistles, and about *two times XXXX* (she wouldn't name the word), the willow switch of her father. She told them about the calf she raised that Manley said was no good, about his Eagle Scout belt, how Manley wanted to keep the family farm for his sons, for all of them, and about how he'd lost it—what Howard and Martha had said about today's farming. She did not tell them about Bernie and how he acquired the greenhouse.

When she finished, she heard muffled sobs from the backseat. They drove the rest of the way in silence, but the soft June day beguiled them: the outlines of the deserted farmhouses were softened by the scent of peonies' falling petals, the blue-bearded Irises that bloomed, unmindful of the empty houses. Fields undulated into the distance with the rowed corn's expanse of promise, and occasional pink and green carpets of alfalfa blurred by, dotted with a very few black beef cattle like a remnant of the past, or belonging to corporate farmers, who just liked the sight of them against the green fields.

The rest of the day the girls spent with cousins whose strangeness to them was eased by the simple needs of Manley's children, Nan and Eric. They had loved their father, and they did not blame him. Death by one's own hand was not uncommon among farmers who lost their family farms. Who wanted to watch someone else plow his sacred acres? To trade his plow for an assembly line?

Lena and Jo were tall, dark-haired, and gracious to their blond cousins. Eric looked like Manley; Nan, hazel-eyed and dark, had Manley's smile. The seven talked of schools and popular songs. They went together to see *The Way We Were* when they had wanted to see *The Exorcist*—both Martha and Andrea said no.

Michael spent the days touring the farm with Howard.

No one but Andrea and Martha seemed to remember what day it was when the day of the funeral arrived, sunny and bright. By two o'clock, they were gathered in the Gilman church that the Endresens had all attended. A small electric organ played "Nearer My God to Thee" and "Jesus Calls Us, One by One." Relatives filed in: Aunt Marna and Aunt Inger, their sons and daughters, their children. Knud's and Karl's and Johann's children, and their children. Viktor's sisters: Aunt Iva and Aunt Berit, both childless. Eric was a pallbearer, and Bernie, and Howard. They hadn't located Dale or Irene. The church was filled, rooms back of the pews were opened, folding chairs gradually unfolded to fill it.

Martha had chosen the hymn "The Old Rugged Cross." Voices carried out of the open church door with the words, "that emblem of suffering and shame…I will cling to that old rugged cross, and exchange it someday for a crown…"

Andrea knew that Manley would have shrugged over the rites

for the dead, nor did he expect, or want, a crown. "Forgive us our weaknesses..." the minister said, not *our trespasses*. Here was the same hard forgiveness that the world had had for Bernie and he for himself. Manley, too, had had it for himself. Andrea looked at Bernie's red eyes, eyes that had added another recrimination to his long list. She saw Martha's bowed head and understood how Martha had borne the grief for them all and had made peace with it, a peace Andrea knew she herself did not possess.

Martha nudged her, and she stood, the organ whined, and they filed out of the pews to pass by the open casket. Andrea wanted to bolt, but Michael's hand steadied her to follow Martha. She thought of her daughters passing by Manley, dead and made-up—they had never even been to a funeral—but she could not help them. Her feet walked her past the coffin, but she didn't look at Manley. His face was in the archive of her heart.

Then family members stood by an open grave in the Stavanger Quaker cemetery in Legrand, Iowa, and watched a coffin lowered into the ground. No one threw dirt on Manley's coffin: Manley would have liked it if they had; he wouldn't have liked the grass carpet unrolled by the yard that covered each grain of raw earth. *Dust thou art...* Andrea heard herself say, thinking of Manley's element, knowing the earth was his friend. Sarah heard her and squeezed her hand.

One by one, the aunts and cousins filed by the grave and then left, until only Martha and Andrea and Bernie's families remained, and Manley's quiet son, Eric, and his daughter, Nan. On a sunny June day in a small cemetery, they stood in the midst of low gravestones surrounded by cornfields. Fallen petals of peonies lay like small, scattered carpets around dark clusters of forked leaves, their scent still in the air.

Andrea reached down, pulled back the plastic grass, and motioned to her girls to pick up a handful of earth. Michael followed them. Andrea took from her bag a small sack of dirt and scattered it on Manley's coffin. "This same earth, Manley, that you have loved, I send with you," she said. It fell on peonies that lay on the coffin— their mother had planted them long ago, they were nurtured by the same earth that had nurtured Manley, and all of them.

Michael and their daughters followed, dropping the soil of the Quaker graveyard on top of soil from Viktor's farm. Eric and Nan did the same. Martha put her arms around Nan and Eric and led them out of the graveyard. Nan sobbed. Bernie followed, head on his right hand.

Andrea turned to walk to other graves, beginning with her parents'. She knew exactly where each one was: Klara Roseland Endresen, next to Viktor Bernard Endresen, names engraved on the same headstone. Names and dates of birth and death, that was all. In another row, an earlier part of the cemetery, Kristina Karlsen Roseland and Salve Knudsen Roseland, on the same stone. Bertha Norland Roseland, a row away, alone. Reier Reiersen, Marthe, Andrea's mother. But not Grandmother Andrea: she was Lutheran. Andrea heard her parents' voices. She returned to her parents' stone: *Here I am Mother, I have come back. Forgive me.*

There is nothing to forgive. Forgive grief? Grief is love, Johnny.

Manley bound the Williams girls to their cousins: their mother's love for Manley bound tighter than blood, but blood was there, too, theirs as well. Manley's blood was Martha's and Andrea's and their shared childhood was even more than blood, and all their children were bound by that blood: Eric and Nan, and Jo and Lena and Howie. Now Manley's loss belonged to Roz and Sarah and Kari, and to her husband, Michael. They would share it with her, and her loss would be lightened.

Andrea turned her wet face to Sarah and Kari and to Rosalind, who pressed against her. Michael came and encircled them all with his arms, saying hoarsely, "Andrea, I'm sorry…"

They were all here: her mother and her father, and Salve and Kristina, the Old Country and the New, the meetinghouse and the farm and the white mare and the dead foal, and Manley and Bernie and Martha. And now, her children, and Michael. Some of them were alive, and some of them were deep in this soil, like Dad's legs in the cornfield.

She turned to Michael. "You were always part Manley," she said. "And n-now, you'll have to be a-all of him." The girls disengaged themselves, leaving their parents standing together, their mother closed in their father's arms.

Sarah stepped back to her mother, to whisper to her, "Mother, there was nothing else for Manley to do. The minister was wrong."

Andrea turned to put her hand on Sarah's face, a face brimming with love. "Mom, I'm sorry I've been so, so selfish, when you…" Sarah looked away.

"What? Sarah, say it, please," Andrea said.

"I see why you didn't bring us here often, Mother. You came home to loss—your mother, and then your dad, always someone. I…I remember Poland, you seemed gone from us. I thought you didn't care about us. Now Manley. You tried to keep us from all of *that*. I would have too, Mother, for my children…"

"Mom," Rosalind said, returning to her, "I want to see the other graves." Kari stood next to her and said, "Yes!" Sarah turned away.

Andrea led the way to another grave, remembering exactly where it was, a small gray slab with a reclining lamb on top, its head missing.

"This is my baby sister's grave."

Her daughters knelt to examine the small body of the lamb, trying to read the lichen-covered letters. Roz read, *"Kristina Andrea En-dre-seen, March 20 to May 20, 1916.* Mother, the head is gone."

"Ever since I was a child," Andrea said.

"Vandals even then, Mother. Even here?" Kari asked.

After coffee and cakes and sandwiches at Martha's house for the many relatives, men's conversation turned to planting, and weather, and rainfall. Women refilled cups of coffee and passed cakes. Cousins and aunts compared the faces of Roz and Kari and Sarah to Klara's face, or a nose, or eyes, to Kristina's, or to Johnny's, a smile to Viktor's smile. They never compared them to Michael. Only Andrea's genes counted here. Andrea's girls, they said. Martha's children. Manley's boys.

The next morning, Andrea agreed to visit the farm. Too late she felt it was a mistake. Five days ago she'd sat with Manley, on these chairs, now forlorn and empty on the lawn. Two days ago, it had been with Bernie and Martha—they had sat, she had knelt. She remembered the cawing of the crows, the floating cottonwood puffs. She walked to the rusted chair and sat in it, where Manley had sat, putting her face in her hands.

"Michael, there isn't anything here anymore. I can't..." Roz came up to her and leaned over her, embracing her mother. Kari and Sarah followed, Michael his arms around them all, tears in his eyes. She did not know how long it was that four pair of arms were around her. She looked through that protective cage of arms and saw, toward the chair swing, what once had been a bed of chrysanthemums. In that bed, her mother had found four left-behind eggs, with live ducks inside. *Why did the mommy duck leave them?* she heard Sarah's child's voice.

On this land, near the grove of cottonwoods, perhaps with the Norway spruce sighing, she was begat, born, nurtured, a place she'd kept a dark secret from her daughters. It was an aching absence, to have shut them out.

Andrea heard their voices echoing out of houses they'd lived in: *Mother, you had a real home,* Kari said. Roz had written to Andrea from where she had been studying in Norway, separated from them: *Where would you call home now, Mom, if you were me?* Andrea had made her daughters exiles when she'd tried to give them roots in the world, not in a place of grief. Andrea felt those many arms around her, her daughters' hands on her face, on her head: *We are here,* they said.

"Mother," Roz said, spokesperson again, her voice almost inaudible, "this is home, for all of us. Now, we'll always know that. Even when you go back to Washington, you'll be here, and we'll be here, together."

A particular thrust of her shoulders showed Andrea's resolution. "Let me show you everything," she said. She put her arms across Roz's shoulders, then across Sarah's, reaching Kari's arm across Sarah's shoulder. She walked to the lost bed of chrysanthemums, "This is where the duck eggs were found, and here's the old chair swing. Manley twisted his knee when we jumped off it with umbrellas..." Michael put his arm around Kari and walked behind.

"Let's see the barn, Mum, and Maud's stall," Kari said. They walked to the weathered barn, and Andrea reached her hand up to the latches of the doors that opened in halves, opening the top half. It creaked.

"This was Maud's stall, and where the colt stood, watching Grandpa."

"I remember, Mom, he used to just stand here and look out," Roz said.

Andrea tried to pull open the door's bottom half. Michael pulled it hard—how long since it had been opened? she wondered. It gave, and they stepped over the high threshold the white mare had refused that starry night, the same night Manley had stayed to encourage her. If anyone was loco, he'd said, maybe, it was herself and her own fear. She told them, again, about that starry night.

"Here is where Maud foaled," she said gesturing around the stall, where they stood on a plank floor caked with dust that stirred up in the dry and acrid air under their footsteps. Roz found a horseshoe. "May I have it, Mom? It's good luck, you know."

"And old Billy, Mother, where did Grandpa bury him?" Sarah wanted to know. Why did she want to know that?

"In the cottonwood grove," Andrea answered. Michael put his arm around her waist as they walked in that direction, urging her on. She didn't want to go there.

"I want to see, Mum." Kari would.

"There is nothing to see, just a grove of trees." But even as Andrea said it, her feet walked in that direction, with those of her three daughters and her husband.

Nobody owns that land any more than the air is owned, the earth itself, or childhood memories, any more than she owned her daughters, or herself. One foot moved ahead of the other, then the next, toward the cottonwood grove where her father buried Billy; she wanted them to go backward. They didn't know that this was where Manley died.

She held Michael's arm and thrust her chin forward, as though every day of her life she walked through a cottonwood grove on the edge of what once had been a prairie, to a place where ghosts rose. It had rained the night Manley died, a harsh, quick-falling rain she remembered. She saw the exact spot where Viktor took a day of his life to dig a hole, and under it old Billy's bones lay. Exactly there—that's what Bernie said—was where Manley fell, his blood spilling on the soil above, and then the rain had eased it downward, right into Old Billy's bones, and maybe into some of Viktor's. Manley would have liked that.

That's where he wanted to be, all along.

Røyseland

Victor Swift Farm, Greencastle Township,
Marshall County, Gilman, Iowa. 1939

ABOUT THE AUTHOR

Arlene Swift Jones (1928–2013) grew up on a farm in Iowa and became a much-travelled, prize-winning poet and memoirist, whose book, *God, Put Out One of My Eyes,* (Antrim House, 2010) describes her days as the wife of a CIA agent in Cyprus just before and during the bloody civil war between Cypriot Greeks and Turks in the 1960s. She is the author of two collections of poetry: *Deenewood, A Sequence,* winner of the Tales Prize from Turning Point Press in 2004, and *Pomegranate Wine,* published in 2005 and a finalist for four of the country's most prestigious literary contests. Her poetry has been anthologized and published in many journals, including *Prairie Schooner, Kansas Quarterly, Tar River Poetry,* and *Cimarron Review.* In 1989, at age seventy-one, she earned a master of fine arts in writing from Warren Wilson College in North Carolina. In addition to the awards she has won for her writing, she has received fellowships from the MacDowell Colony and the Ragdale Foundation.

AF Jones
Jones, Arlene Swift.
No stones in heaven /

31000000165354
2015-12-08 NPL

Athens County Public Libraries

DATE DUE

JAN 0 6 2016			
JAN 2 1 2016			
JAN 2 1 2016 / FEB 0 9 2016			
MAR 2 9 2016			

PRINTED IN U.S.A.